WITHDRAWN
NDSU

Selective Service and American Society

Selective Service and American Society

ROGER W. LITTLE, EDITOR

RUSSELL SAGE FOUNDATION
NEW YORK   1969

PUBLICATIONS OF RUSSELL SAGE FOUNDATION

Russell Sage Foundation was established in 1907 by Mrs. Russell Sage for the improvement of social and living conditions in the United States. In carrying out its purpose the Foundation conducts research under the direction of members of the staff or in close collaboration with other institutions, and supports programs designed to develop and demonstrate productive working relations between social scientists and other professional groups. As an integral part of its operations, the Foundation from time to time publishes books or pamphlets resulting from these activities. Publication under the imprint of the Foundation does not necessarily imply agreement by the Foundation, its Trustees, or its staff with the interpretations or conclusions of the authors.

© *1969 by Russell Sage Foundation*
Printed in the United States of America by
Connecticut Printers, Inc., Hartford, Connecticut

Library of Congress Catalog Card Number: 68-54411

Contents

Contributors, vii
Acknowledgments, ix
Introduction, xi

Procurement of manpower : an institutional analysis ROGER W. LITTLE	*1*
Historical background of Selective Service in the United States HARRY A. MARMION	*35*
A social profile of local draft board members : the case of Wisconsin JAMES W. DAVIS, JR., *and* KENNETH M. DOLBEARE	*53*
Decision-making in local boards : a case study GARY L. WAMSLEY	*83*
Juvenile delinquency and military service MERRILL ROFF	*109*
The Negro and the draft CHARLES C. MOSKOS, JR.	*139*
Military service and occupational mobility IRVIN G. KATENBRINK, JR.	*163*
Conclusion : implications for change ROGER W. LITTLE	*191*

Bibliography, 197
Index, 215

Contributors

ROGER W. LITTLE is Associate Professor of Sociology, the University of Illinois at Chicago Circle. He collaborated with Morris Janowitz in the preparation of SOCIOLOGY AND THE MILITARY ESTABLISHMENT. He was a Lieutenant Colonel while on active service.

HARRY A. MARMION, Staff Associate, Commission on Federal Relations, American Council on Education, has been especially concerned with the subject of student deferments. Mr. Marmion is a Major in the Marine Corps Reserve.

JAMES W. DAVIS, JR. *and* KENNETH M. DOLBEARE, Assistant Professors of Political Science, University of Wisconsin, were Consultants to the National Advisory Commission on Selective Service.

GARY L. WAMSLEY is Assistant Professor of Political Science, Vanderbilt University. His contribution is part of a large study prepared at the Graduate School of Public and International Affairs, University of Pittsburgh. He is a Captain in the Air Force Reserve.

MERRILL ROFF, Professor of Psychology, Institute of Child Development, University of Minnesota, has written several research reports on the experience of delinquents in the armed forces.

CHARLES C. MOSKOS, JR., is Associate Professor of Sociology, Northwestern University. He has been concerned with studies of the enlisted man in military organization. He was an enlisted man while on active service.

IRVIN G. KATENBRINK, JR., was formerly Instructor in Sociology, United States Military Academy, West Point, New York. He is a Regular Army officer who has served as a Battalion Advisor to the Army of South Vietnam.

ACKNOWLEDGMENTS

The conception of this collection of essays emerged from the excitement of the Summer of 1966. The turbulence of the draft reform movement was especially apparent at the University of Chicago. Morris Janowitz, as Chairman of the Inter-University Seminar on Armed Forces and Society, asked me to conduct a seminar on Selective Service during that Summer Term. Meanwhile, I was active on the planning committee of the University of Chicago Conference on the Draft. Despite the sudden profusion of essays about the draft issue, we noticed that many serious studies then in progress were being neglected. Again, it was Morris Janowitz who suggested that I solicit a set of essays on topics related to the central issue of military manpower procurement, essays which would have some enduring value. Whatever success we may have achieved is due to his inspiration and solicitude. The shortcomings, of course, can be attributed only to the editor.

Introduction

An institution as vital to a democratic society as one charged with the procurement of military manpower can ill afford to ignore the continuous barrage of criticism directed at Selective Service. Such criticism, even though at times poorly informed, threatens to undermine the legitimacy of the institution unless it is carefully examined and its relevance determined. The debate about Selective Service that became intensified in 1965 has served to remind us of how little is known about the operation of the system and its effects on the larger society. The public concern for Selective Service in the past is perhaps symbolized by the dingy, barren office space and furniture of many local boards. Neglect for many years—by scholars as well as legislators and the public at large—has been mistaken for acceptance.

This collection of research essays is organized around the analysis of the major institutions for obtaining military manpower. Our objective is an intensive analysis of selected but significant problematic aspects of military manpower procurement in a democratic society. The essays were written in the midst of the public debate about the draft in 1966. Since enactment of the Military Selective Service Act of 1967, some significant changes have occurred.[1] The full-time undergraduate student deferment category has become a statutory right rather than a local board option. The composition of local boards has been changed by limiting tenure to

---

[1] Public law 90–40, 90th Congress, S.1432, June 30, 1967 (81 Stat. 100), "An Act To Amend the Universal Military Training and Service Act, and for other purposes. ..."

25 years, by the inclusion of women, and by minority group representation. These changes, however, do not substantially affect the validity of the analysis expressed in the essays.

The division of the manpower pool with which critics are concerned presents three major categories: one-third required for military service, one-third rejected for failing to meet the minimum mental and physical standards of the armed forces, and one-third surplus to current military needs. The annual increment of 18-year-old youths was, in 1967, about 1.8 million, and will increase in size after a temporary decline during the next three years. The annual military replacement need—prior to Vietnam—was about 600,000 men. There were about 600,000 mental and physical rejections of both draftees and enlistees. The disposition of the remaining 600,000 is the major issue confronting Selective Service. To the extent that one-third of a nation is disqualified and another third excused from participation the burden of service would appear to be unequally distributed. Our concern is with the effect of that unequal distribution.

Three viewpoints have emerged as proposed solutions. The first is to abandon completely the existing system and to rely on economic incentives to attract an all-volunteer force. It is asserted that, given a wage competitive with civilian industry and at varying levels, an adequate armed force—short of total mobilization—can be obtained by voluntary recruitment alone. Conscription is viewed as repugnant to a democratic society while voluntarism is held to be one of its principal values. The loss in wages due to compulsory military service is represented as a tax, since the required services are obtained at less than a competitive wage only because of coercion. The "voluntary army" proposal ignores the concept of universality and seems to many to be an attractive and simple solution to a complex problem.

The second viewpoint incorporates the concept of universality and proposes to expand it by offering alternatives to military service. Recognizing that current and prospective manpower needs of the military organization are unlikely to utilize fully the accumulation of registrants, advocates of this approach seek to create additional outlets for the discharge of civic obligation in the form of service in the Peace Corps, Volunteers in Service to America (VISTA), the Teacher Corps, and other activities with voluntary associations. The virtue of the "national service" proposal is that it retains the concept of universal liability for military service and extends the concept to a range of civic activities sufficiently comprehensive to utilize all eligible youth. Difficult problems inhere in how such a plan can be related to military service, and whether it should be compulsory or voluntary.

A third proposal is to retain the existing Selective Service System—with modifications—but to base selections on a random selection of registrants or a "lottery." This proposal retains and extends the principle of universality and directly confronts the problem of surplus-third registrants. It is sufficiently flexible to be incorporated with the national service proposal. However, it fails to alleviate the problem of declining rates of participation.

Our analysis begins with the assumption that some system of conscription is still necessary to maintain effective force levels, either by direct induction or impelled enlistments. The question is how this can be done while eliminating or minimizing the objections that now threaten its acceptance as a legitimate procedure in a democratic society.

In the first essay, I have compared the recruiting services with the Selective Service System. They are organized in different ways to accomplish the same objectives. But the type of personnel obtained by voluntary enlistment is suggestive of the results of military manpower procurement without the principles of universality and coercion. Recruiting has been generally successful in meeting almost completely the military manpower needs of all services except the Army. However, to some extent their effectiveness has been enhanced by pressures exerted by the draft. In all the services, the principal value of voluntary recruiting has been to provide a pool of potential re-enlistees for the career cadre of military organizations. However, a deficit has remained, especially in the category of Army enlisted personnel, in the manpower resources needed to fill sudden expansion needs for large numbers of men trainable in elementary military skills for short periods of service. Increasingly, Selective Service has deviated from the principle of universality chiefly by more permissive application of deferment criteria; hence it tends to procure from the same pool as voluntary recruiting.

The historical solution to the problem of demands for greatly expanded military manpower needs is traced by Harry Marmion. The manpower situation in 1917 was in many respects similar to that of today : a relatively large supply and smaller demand for military personnel. Then, as proposed today, the solution was found in a lottery. Early legislation emphasized the separation of Selective Service from military influence, unlike current arrangements. The present policy of college deferments is described as emerging in the context of Universal Military Training, and in a general climate of concern for national technological supremacy. Although the policy of college deferments was established at the national level, the responsibilities for decisions were delegated to the local boards of the Selective Service System.

The local boards, as the basic procurement and decisional echelon of the Selective Service System, are the subject of the essay by James Davis and Kenneth Dolbeare. Their essay, although limited to the State of Wisconsin, constitutes the first survey of the methods of recruitment, population characteristics, and attitudes of local board members. They conclude that the local board, rather than constituting a "little group of neighbors" as officially portrayed by national headquarters, is usually representative of the community in a very limited sense. It is significant that even local boards feel that social class factors intrude in the selection process to the disadvantage of lower-class youth. The greatest area of consensus among local board members was in the attitude that membership in the Reserves and National Guard was a means of avoiding the draft.

The detailed behavior of a series of local boards in a metropolitan area is described and analyzed by Gary Wamsley. He noted the dilemma with which local board members were faced when required to make decisions without adequate criteria as to what constituted "activities in the national health, safety, and interest." Such ambiguous language provides the maximum latitude for local board decisions, but simultaneously permits greater variability from one board to another than would be the case if more precise guidance were provided. Without adequate criteria, local board members tended to make decisions in terms of local middle-class values, their impressions of the character of the registrant, and other considerations of limited relevance to "the national health, safety, and interest."

Leaving the general issues of the military manpower procurement and the operation of the Selective Service System, we turn now to three special issues that bear on the extent to which military service is truly universal : juvenile delinquents, Negroes, and unskilled lower-class youth.

Many youths are rejected for service because of a record of juvenile delinquency and an assumption that their delinquency will recur in the service. Their exclusion is a deviation from the principle of universal service as well as a serious waste of a potential source of military manpower. Merrill Roff discusses the military experience of two samples of juvenile delinquents. His data indicate that for minor offenders—who had been confined only in local detention facilities—military service appeared to have some reformative effect. Only 30 percent were judged as having "unsatisfactory service," while 40 percent were promoted. Roff's data suggest the need for more precise criteria for evaluating the significance of delinquency as an impediment to service, especially in large urban areas.

Using data from several sources, Charles Moskos demonstrates the anomalous position of the Negro with respect to military service. Although relatively fewer qualify for either induction or enlistment, relatively more ultimately serve than would be expected by their incidence in the population. Of those who serve, a disproportionate number—because of aptitude and skill deficiencies—are more likely to think of the draft as "fair" than are whites, and the rate of Negroes who re-enlist after their first term of service is almost twice that of whites. Moskos attributes the favorable disposition toward the draft and military service to the relatively superior "equity" that the Negro enjoys in military organization as compared to the larger society.

Similar evaluations of military service among white youths is reported by Irvin Katenbrink in a study of members of a Reserve unit in Newburgh, New York. Comparing them with an age cohort without military service in the same community, he found that men with military service were likely to report more substantial progress beyond their fathers' socioeconomic status than youths without military service. Within the military sample, consisting of ex-draftees and enlisted Reservists with only six months of active duty training, he found that draftees entered the service with distinctly lower socioeconomic status than enlisted reservists but achieved significantly greater improvement in status after service than did the Reservists. He attributes their progress to participation in the off-duty education program, as well as to a maturation factor that may operate as an occupational credential to employers. Katenbrink's data and conclusions are also significant in defining the motives for initial enlistments. It would appear that the major inducements for enlistment—technical occupational training or a high school diploma through the Armed Forces Institute—can be achieved in the first term. Once these goals have been achieved, however, motivation for service recedes and the tendency to decline re-enlistment increases.

Through each of these essays runs a theme that the changing needs of a democratic society require innovations in organizational forms, policies, and methods of obtaining military manpower. The search for a solution to the problems of the draft has provoked a crisis that is also an opportunity for advocates who have specific proposals for change. There is a danger, however, that this opportunity will be wasted in trivial modifications of methods or organizational structures, or that well-designed innovations will be neutralized by being superimposed on archaic foundations. Substantial, well-considered changes should be proposed if the opportunity is to be fully exploited. Such proposals should serve as challenges not only to the Selective Service System, but also to the armed services, to insure a more efficient utilization of the manpower delivered to them.

Selective Service and American Society

Procurement of manpower: an institutional analysis

ROGER W. LITTLE

MILITARY MANPOWER in the United States is procured by a dual system of voluntary recruitment and the operations of the Selective Service System. Any effort to understand how these systems actually operate and to formulate recommendations for change must take into consideration not only official policies but also the reality of the institutions that execute these policies. Selective Service, in short, cannot be understood without regard to the full range of other agencies involved in obtaining military manpower.

Institutions, policies, and organizational formats are usually products of a process of growth and accretion and are frequently found to be obsolete for contemporary purposes. Historical experience is not always an accurate guide for dealing with present realities, and indeed is often used to defend an obsolete system against the necessity for change. Thus the adverse reaction to the federal enrollment officers of the Civil War led to development of the local draft board concept, introduced more than fifty years later in the draft legislation of 1917 and continued unchanged to the present day. Originally it appeared to be relevant to a society with a very simple industrial structure and a relatively diffuse relationship between local communities and the federal government. In recent years, however, profound changes in American society, such as urbanization, mass communications and transportation, a heightened awareness of social inequities, and the pervasive and direct influence of the federal government on the local community, have greatly altered the relevance of such a concept as the local board.

This essay deals with the organizational structures and policies by which the armed forces obtained enlisted men from 1948 to 1966. The analysis proceeds by first establishing three ideal criteria of the efficiency and effectiveness of these organizations and methods in a democratic society. The two primary sources of military manpower—voluntary enlistees and draftees—are then evaluated in terms of these ideal criteria. Next we have analyzed their variable impact on the larger society. Finally, we have attempted to show how the professional military perspective is related to the task of obtaining manpower by either enlistment or the draft.

Our analysis focuses on enlisted personnel for active service because this group presents the persistent and core issue of procurement in the United States. However, both voluntary recruitment of enlisted personnel and Selective Service have important effects on other recruitment programs. For example, officer procurement is enhanced in two ways. Many youths enlist for the opportunity to become officers by outstanding performance as enlisted men. Selective Service promotes Reserve officer procurement by accepting participation in college ROTC as a deferment category. Similarly, the Reserve forces are manned predominantly by men who have elected an extended period of Reserve service as an alternative to two or more years of active service.

Elements of procurement policy

There are three essential elements in military manpower policy. The first consideration is the timing and magnitude of the demand and the criteria of selection. The second element is the size and quality of the manpower pool that is drawn upon. The third element consists of the combination of agencies and procedures established to procure the personnel. These procurement agencies must meet at least three criteria if they are to be effective organizations for implementing national military manpower policy.

The first criterion is one of adequacy to meet the dual manpower demands of military organization. One type of demand is that required for the on-going, continuous maintenance of a regular force at a magnitude that tends to remain stable. Another type of demand is for supplementary personnel for emergency periods of limited duration, a quantity that varies as widely as the conditions that generate the demand. The criterion of adequacy can be met only by two kinds of manpower inputs, each adapted to the type of demand that is to be fulfilled. Thus emergency manpower needs require that a maximum demand be anticipated, and that the pool of men be examined for trainability and classified for availability before the necessity for their induction occurs. In addition, the pool from which inductions or enlistments are to be made must be sufficiently large to insure that there will still be enough men left to fulfill the requirements after attrition due to failures to meet entry criteria.

The second criterion is one of universality, and requires that the demand be fulfilled by drawing equitably from a universe that is distributed broadly across the entire society. This criterion requires that the selection process conform to an ethic of social justice and insure that membership in a particular region, community, class, ethnic group, occupational category, or other significant grouping of the larger society will not unfairly bias the chances of being called into service. There is also a technical requirement for maintaining a large universe of selection. The larger the universe of potential recruits, the more likely is each procurement quota (in the aggregate) to obtain a fair sample of all the skills available in the larger society. Conversely, factors that operate to restrict the universe, to exclude special groups from the chances of selection, or to promote selection from other groupings of the society, tend correspondingly to limit the range of skills obtained as well as to deviate from the ethic of social justice. Thus, occupational and student deferments tend to restrict the procurement universe and exclude highly valued skills, while voluntary recruitment tends to obtain a relatively larger number of men with undeveloped skills.

A broad distribution in the selection process fosters the involvement of a corresponding range of segments of the larger society in the activities of military organization. To the extent that the military member maintains an active affiliation with his family and civilian community, family members may be more attentive to military issues because they have a personal stake in military operations.

The third criterion is that procurement should interfere as little as possible with the essential routine functions of the larger society. In practice, this criterion is difficult to satisfy. Procurement agencies must take into account the fact that persons eligible for service are not all equally critical to the continued efficiency of nonmilitary activities. The loss of some skilled persons from such activities may be greater in real cost than the contribution they would make as members of military organizations. In effect, voluntary recruitment avoids this dilemma by accepting persons who are as yet relatively "unplaced" in the social structure by reason of age, family status, or lack of skills. Selective Service attempts to meet the problem by the classification and deferment process. Some roles (such as father, student, or scarce scientific personnel) are defined as more important for the continued effectiveness of the larger society than military service.

Much criticism of the Selective Service System has been based on this apparent deviation from the criterion of universality. However, issues of social justice must be balanced against the reality that the service of some persons would entail relatively greater social costs than others. Thus, by the induction of a parent the society may incur costs in the long-range effects of the interruption of family life. The induction of a skilled worker may initiate a succession of substitutions or the necessity of training a replacement, thus contributing to the reduced efficiency of one or more industrial elements. However, the balance of requirements and social costs may dictate military duty on the part of persons with such exceptional skills as physicians and dentists whose services are especially critical to military organization. Their temporary absence from the larger society is held to be less critical to its survival than the necessity for their services in military organization.

Organizations for obtaining manpower

Two organizational forms have evolved for securing military manpower. The first, voluntary recruitment, is geared to the routine replacement of attrition in a stable force. The second, Selective Service, has developed as a means for obtaining supplementary personnel, especially in emergency periods when the demand exceeds the supply of volunteers. Both procedures have evolved in the context of American beliefs and practices, and are supported by a general acceptance of the value of military service as a form of training for citizenship. Thus one survey of public opinion on the draft in 1966 concluded:

> The picture, then, is one of general support for a system that is considered to have worked fairly well in the past. But, there are real reservations over the fairness of certain of the selectivity standards and the manner in which they are applied. The draft is accepted because its need is recognized. Only twelve per cent feel that the military should accomplish its manpower goals strictly through voluntary recruitment.[1]

Other institutions support these values. The National Cadet Corps (or "High School ROTC") annually enrolls about 91,000 youths and provides a brief introduction to military life at a very formative stage in development. In addition, the community service activities of veterans' organizations foster identification with military role models. More influential than all others, probably, is the military experience of the current parental generation. Even as recently as 1958, 70 percent of all twenty-six-year-old men had been in military service.[2]

VOLUNTARY RECRUITMENT

The system for procurement by voluntary recruitment consists of separate, decentralized, and relatively autonomous organizations. They are as old as each of the services they represent. Despite their relative independence, they have many comparable features.

The magnitude of the total recruiting effort is indicated by the fact that, in 1962, 3,368 recruiting stations were staffed by approximately 12,000 military personnel. However, there are other agencies performing voluntary recruitment functions that would expand this number. For ex-

---

[1] Louis Harris and Associates, "Public Opinion and the Draft," in June A. Willenz (ed.), *Dialogue on the Draft* (Washington, D.C.: The American Veterans Committee, 1967), pp. 64–65.
[2] *Review of the Administration and Operation of the Selective Service System*, 89th Congress, 2nd sess., House Report No. 75 (Washington, D.C.: Government Printing Office, 1966), pp. 9927, 10005.

ample, military personnel assigned to ROTC units at college campuses are implicitly part of the procurement system. So also are the numerous "in-service" recruiters who are primarily concerned with the re-enlistment of active service personnel. Finally, there are the Reserve components whose recruitment activities, although not related to those of the active services, absorb a large proportion of the potential enlistees.

The principle of decentralization that characterizes the local boards of the Selective Service System is also exemplified by the operational independence of the individual recruiting stations. While local board members come from the same community as the registrant, the local recruiting personnel must build a relationship between their service and the community. They become identified with the locale by establishing residence there and maintaining contacts with local public officials and service clubs.

Table 1

MILITARY PERSONNEL ASSIGNED TO RECRUITING AND ADMINISTRATION OF RECRUITMENT, 1962

Service	Officers	Enlisted men	Total
Army	261	2,751	3,012
Navy	356	3,233	3,589
Marine Corps	85	1,443	1,528
Air Force	361	2,734	3,095
Totals	1,063	10,161	11,224

Table 2

RECRUITING STATIONS, BY TYPE AND SERVICE

Service	Main	Branch	Total
Army	70	1,148	1,218
Navy	40	895	935
Marine Corps	49	419	459
Air Force	—	756	756
Totals	150	3,218	3,368

SOURCE: Department of Defense, *A Study of Military Compensation, 1962.*

But they remain, first of all, senior and exemplary servicemen, with an active and responsible affiliation with their services.

The recruiter also differs from the local board in the degree of his accessibility.[3] While the local board maintains a secretive, official image, the recruiter's role is supported by an extensive informational system. National media carry their advertising as a public service. Promotional material is provided routinely to high school guidance counselors. These devices are reinforced by the obvious identification of the recruiter himself as a competent and credible representative of his service.

Applicants for enlistment come from two general sources. One is the result of active contacts between the recruiter and various community agencies involved in youth activities. Thus, recruiters appear on high school "Career Days" to present descriptions of the opportunities in the armed forces. They also explain legal responsibilities for registration. The screening of applicants with delinquency records brings recruiters into contact with police and probation officers who often suggest potential enlistees. The other general source is the self-selected "walk-in" at the recruiting station, which offers a variety of inducements for enlistment.

Potential enlistees appear to constitute a unique population. A comparative study of Navy recruits and high school seniors (using Project TALENT data) suggests some characteristics of the universe from which recruits are drawn. In terms of fathers' occupations, Navy recruits resemble the general high school senior population. However, only 24 percent of them take the college preparatory curriculum, compared to 46 percent of the grade-12 boys. The recruits have generally lower occupational aspirations than other boys. While 47 percent intend to go to some kind of college upon completion of service, only 10 percent would score high enough to be admitted to most public universities in this country, compared to 32 percent of other boys. On the basis of aptitude test scores, the Navy recruit group most resembles high school graduates one year out of high school who are in the structural trades or in agricultural occupations. The Project TALENT report notes that the recruiting pool is initially depleted by the 49 percent of high school youths who enter college

---

[3] One indication of the accessibility of the recruiter is that in the Chicago area all branch recruiting stations are located on the ground floor, usually in store-front office space, while offices of the Selective Service System are on the second floor.

immediately after graduating from high school, a group that tends to be relatively high in aptitude and achievement levels. It continues :

> This is intensified by the fact that the hard-core industrial groups have also been pulled out of the group. Thus the ones available for recruitment represent the high school graduate who enters neither college nor hard-core industrial occupations. On the other hand, the non-graduates who do not enter hard-core industrial occupations tend to include a considerable number of low aptitude students.[4]

Criticisms of the voluntary recruitment systems generally include their emphasis on the quota system, the competitive relations between services, and the lack of operational coordination with the local boards of the Selective Service System.

First, the quota system, by which each branch station recruiter is given a specific recruitment goal to attain, tends to put more emphasis on obtaining enlistees of any kind rather than those with special skills or aptitudes. The emphasis on numbers tends to orient recruitment activities toward population categories that involve the least competition with the labor force, especially high school youth before and after graduation. This tendency is reinforced by the fact that the actual recruiting quota is based on Selective Service data of the number of registrants who are classified as "available and qualified." The use of the category 1-A as a measure of the recruiting potential of an area thus has the effect of concentrating recruitment activities in a manpower pool that has already been identified by Selective Service.

Second, the fact that recruiting is one of the least unified operations of the Department of Defense promotes excessive competition among recruiters of the four services, and militates against operational coordination. One effect is an extensive duplication of effort in competition for a limited segment of the pool of potential enlistees. However, a more important result is that the failure to define common elements and the special advantages of each service requires potential enlistees to "shop" for information essential to a well-considered career choice. In 1966, a policy

---

[4] Marion F. Shaycroft, Clinton A. Neyman, Jr., and John T. Dailey, *Comparison of Navy Recruits with Male High School Students on the Basis of Project TALENT Data* (Washington, D.C. : American Institute for Research, June, 1962), p. 51.

to consolidate branch recruiting stations was initiated to alleviate this situation.

Third, there is no effective contact between recruiting stations and the local boards of the Selective Service System. Occasionally recruiting materials are made available in the waiting rooms of the local boards, and clerks are aware of the locations of recruiting offices. Local boards and recruiters may be located in the same building, usually the post office or other federal building. But spatial proximity does not insure operational coordination. Although recruiters have vastly superior information about the requirements and opportunities of the military services, this information is rarely utilized by the local Selective Service boards. High school students probably get most of their information about their draft obligations from recruiters rather than from representatives of the Selective Service System.

THE SELECTIVE SERVICE SYSTEM

While recruiters attempt to merge their identification with the armed forces with local community affiliations, the Selective Service System has cultivated the image of a civilian agency, balancing local community needs and the manpower demands of military organization. The system is exclusively civilian only at the local board level; it is heavily military in executive personnel. This tends to foster a view of its function as that of a personnel procurement agency of the Department of Defense rather than that of an independent agency.

The quasi-military nature of the System is epitomized by the title of the National and State Directors' Offices as "headquarters." The directors of each state and other major subordinate jurisdiction usually carry some military title; in 1964, only seven were listed in the *Annual Report of the Director* without a military rank. Other executive positions in each headquarters, such as Deputy Director and chiefs of major staff sections, are occupied by 249 commissioned Reserve officers of the armed forces, 57 of whom are assigned to National Headquarters and 192 to subordinate headquarters. Salaries (except those of directors) are paid by the respective services, and are reimbursed by funding from the Selective Service System. In addition, the System maintains a Reserve component training program for 695 Reserve and National Guard officers, consisting of correspondence courses and periods of annual active duty training.

Although staff titles foster a military image, in practice there is little of the operational coordination characteristic of military organization. The major point of contact is in the reporting of registrants by local boards and the subsequent allocation of quotas by the National Headquarters. Of the data reported to the National Headquarters, the most important are the number of registrants classified as 1-A and 1-A-O. These data are used as the basis for estimates of the total military manpower pool, by voluntary recruitment agencies as well as by the Selective Service System.

However, the category "I-A," on which the induction quota is based, consists of two significant subcategories: those who have already been examined and are known to be qualified, and those who have been so classified but not yet examined. The first category can be counted; the second must be estimated. The number of unexamined who would qualify is then estimated on the basis of the average national preinduction examination rate for the preceding six months and added to the known qualified. From this total a final estimate is made of the ultimate number of men who will qualify on the final examination by applying the average induction examination acceptance rate for the preceding six months.

These calculations provide an estimate of the number of men in each state who would be available and qualified if all were called. The proportionate contribution that each state makes to the national pool is then used to distribute the requirements of the Department of Defense. Thus a state that contributes 3 percent of the total estimated "available and qualified" is allocated a quota of 3 percent of the men demanded. The quota is then suballocated to local boards by the State Headquarters, using a similar formula. Calls are finally made by the Local Board Clerk from a roster of availability within each category of a schedule of priorities. Except for volunteers who are called in the sequence in which they have volunteered, in all other categories the sequence is based on age. (See Table 3, "Schedule of Induction Priorities.")

The State (or other major jurisdiction) Headquarters is primarily an accounting and representational echelon, although it does have some executive functions. Its major function is the suballocation of the quota to local boards. As priority categories are exhausted it announces the

Table 3
SCHEDULE OF INDUCTION PRIORITIES

1. Delinquents (registrants who have been so defined whenever they have failed to perform any duty or duties required of them under the Selective Service Law) who have attained the age of 19 years in the order of their dates of birth with the eldest being selected first.
2. Volunteers who have not attained the age of 26 years in the sequence in which they have volunteered for induction.
3. Nonvolunteers who have attained the age of 19 years and have not attained the age of 26 years and who do not have a wife with whom they maintain a bona fide family relationship in their homes, in the order of their dates of birth with the eldest being selected first.
4. Nonvolunteers who have attained the age of 19 years and have not attained the age of 26 years and who have a wife with whom they maintain a bona fide family relationship in their homes, in the order of their dates of birth with the eldest being selected first.
5. Nonvolunteers who have attained the age of 26 years in the order of their dates of birth with the youngest being selected first.
6. Nonvolunteers who have attained the age of 18 years and six months and who have not attained the age of 19 years in the order of their dates of birth with the eldest being selected first.

SOURCE: *Annual Report of the Director of Selective Service* (Washington, D.C.: Government Printing Office, 1963), p. 12.

necessity for reclassifying men in deferred categories, although the locus of decision remains with the local board. It also recruits and nominates members of local boards, and subsequently monitors the classification activities of the board.[5]

The third and most crucial level is the local board itself. The justification for its establishment was the assumption that popular acceptance of the draft would be promoted by a belief that members of the local community, familiar with its population and circumstances, were determining whose services could be spared. Thus the local board, by identification with the registrants' neighborhood, provided a readily accessible echelon in an otherwise remote bureaucratic structure. It also served to deflect criticism from the federal government.

Despite the crucial role of the local board, very little is known about

---

[5] *The Annual Report of the Director* scarcely mentions the functions of the State Headquarters, which may indicate something of their importance in the system.

its operations. The secrecy of its deliberations is reinforced by a policy of minimizing its prominence in the community. The title "local board" in reality designates two things. First, it means the members of the board as a relatively independent quasi-judicial body, who rarely meet more than once a month. Second, it denotes a branch or echelon of the Selective Service System in continuous operation under the direction of the board clerk. The jurisdiction of the local board is defined by existing political boundaries rather than demographic characteristics of the communities included. There is at least one board in every county (or comparable subdivision) in each state and territory, and more in metropolitan areas. Within multiple-board cities, jurisdictions are defined in terms of political wards and precincts.

Members are selected from volunteers and nominees from civic and veterans' associations, recommended by the State Director, nominated by the Governor, and appointed by the President. There are usually five members. Each is required to be a resident of the county in which his board is located, but not necessarily within its jurisdictional area in the case of a multiple-board city. A member must not have any active military affiliation. Tenure is usually continuous until resignation. The identity of board members is often concealed—especially in metropolitan areas—on the grounds that they might be contacted outside of regular channels. They receive no compensation for their services.[6]

However, in the daily routine activities of the Selective Service System one of the most important roles is that of the Clerk of the Local Board, a paid employee of the System. Local board clerks are employed from the Civil Service Register, and only administrative qualifications and experience are required. The Clerk maintains the continuity of the local board operations between meetings by receiving registrations, preparing files for action by the board, announcing the classifications, issuing the calls, and answering all correspondence directed to the local board. Clerks also tend to have long tenure and develop extensive administrative and legal knowledge of the System. However, their perspective is usually limited to the administrative processes in which they are involved. The fact that they lack the service recruiter's extensive knowledge of service life,

---

[6] *In Pursuit of Equity: Who Serves When Not All Serve?* (Washington, D.C.: The National Advisory Commission on Selective Service, 1967), p. 21.

and consequently are unable to answer questions about "life after induction," tends to foster an impersonal, procedure-dominated atmosphere in the local board office.

In one sense, the Clerk performs more of a judicial role than does the local board. Only that minority of registrants who dispute the initial classification actually appear before the board. For the majority, the Clerk is the decision-making echelon, and his decisions are accepted by registrants without appeal. When the board actually meets, the number of cases to be decided within the limited time of three to four hours is so large that the Clerk has to prepare the cases for decision before the meeting and present them to the board for validation. Between meetings, guidance in making complex decisions is more likely to be sought from State Headquarters than from members of the board.[7]

A survey of local boards and classification actions in the Chicago area in 1966 by the author revealed that more than 90 percent of the actions could be determined on the basis of information on the Classification Questionnaire, or from the reports of the Armed Forces Examining and Entry Station, and consequently required no adjudication. Only three categories comprised 80 percent of the decisions: initial registrations (0 to I-A), disqualified by examination (I-A to I-Y or IV-F), and over liable age (V-A). Adjudication was required only with reference to conscientious objectors (I-A-O or I-O), hardship (III-A), and the reclassification of marginal college or graduate students (II-S). (See Table 4, "Selective Service Classification.")

The dominant role of the Clerk does not imply that his influence substantially affected the decisions of the board, but rather suggests that board action was unnecessary in most cases. However, the "Minutes of Local Board Proceedings" reported even the initial classifications of new registrants to I-A, or the reclassification of old registrants to V-A, as if they were individual actions decided by vote when no significant decision was actually involved. Board records rarely indicated a decision by anything less than a unanimous vote in these or any other classifications. Thus the credibility of the board's judicial role was jeopardized by the number of moot issues that they were required to represent themselves as deciding

[7] *Ibid.*

Table 4

SELECTIVE SERVICE CLASSIFICATIONS

CLASS I

Class I-A : Available for military service.

Class I-A-O : Conscientious objector available for noncombatant military service only.

Class I-C : Member of the Armed Forces of the United States, the Coast and Geodetic Survey, or the Public Health Service.

Class I-D : Qualified member of Reserve component, or student taking military training, including ROTC and accepted aviation cadet applicant.

Class I-O : Conscientious objector available for civilian work contributing to the maintenance of the national health, safety, or interest.

Class I-S : Student deferred by law until graduation from high school or attainment of age 20, or until the end of his academic year at a college or university.

Class I-W : Conscientious objector performing civilian work contributing to the maintenance of the national health, safety, or interest, or who has completed such work.

Class I-Y : Registrant qualified for military service only in time of war or national emergency.

by vote. Another effect was to foster the development of an atmosphere and momentum of consensus that might severely limit the chances that a registrant's appeal would be sustained when a substantial issue was presented. Perfunctory validation of administrative decisions arranged by the Clerk might thus undermine the judicial role of the local board.

The Chicago study also indicated that the board had lost its standing as a group of "friends and neighbors." More often the members were strangers whose identities could be established only if they were recognized by the relatively small number of registrants who personally appeared before the board. The chance of such recognition in a metropoli-

SELECTIVE SERVICE CLASSIFICATIONS	
CLASS II	
Class II-A :	Occupational deferment (other than agricultural or student).
Class II-C :	Agricultural deferment.
Class II-S :	Student deferment.
CLASS III	
Class III-A :	Extreme hardship deferment, or registrant with a child or children.
CLASS IV	
Class IV-A :	Registrant with sufficient prior military service or who is a sole surviving son.
Class IV-B :	Official deferred by law.
Class IV-C :	Alien not currently liable for military service.
Class IV-D :	Minister of religion or divinity student.
Class IV-F :	Registrant not qualified for any military service.
CLASS V	
Class V-A :	Registrant over the age of liability for military service.

SOURCE: *Annual Report of the Director of Selective Service* (Washington, D.C.: Government Printing Office, 1963), p. 12.

tan area was, of course, very slight, since the only residence requirement was that the board member live in the same county as the local board jurisdiction. Since the member's appointment was to a specific board and his tenure was usually indefinite, the composition of the board usually lagged behind the demographic characteristics of a changing community. Thus, in Chicago, many board members who were originally appointed when they were South Shore residents had since moved to North Shore suburbs but still commuted to their original boards. Meanwhile, the population of these board areas had been markedly changed by the out-migration of whites to the suburbs and the in-migration of Negroes from the rural South. Under these conditions the local board was more likely to be perceived as identified with the Selective Service System than with the local community.

Finally, the validity of the board's decisions on occupational deferments rested on the assumption that at least one member had adequate knowledge of the occupational structure of the community. However, the complexity of the industrial structure of a metropolitan area was such as to minimize the chance that a board member would have adequate knowledge of a specific occupation and its relationship to an industry. Without such knowledge, decisions were more likely to be made on the basis of such spurious considerations as the prestige of the employer or industry in the community, or the ability to sense the issues to which the board would be responsive.[8]

Differential social impact

Military manpower procurement by means of voluntary recruitment and conscription are not equal in the degree to which they meet the three criteria suggested earlier for judging their appropriateness.

ADEQUACY

First, by itself voluntary recruitment has not been an adequate source of manpower, in numbers or in timeliness. In such inducements as wages, working conditions, and opportunities for advancement, the armed forces are at a disadvantage in competing for a share of the labor force. However, there would appear to be a consistent proportion of potential enlistees in the manpower pool whose tendency to enlist is related to such factors as the end of the school year, local employment prospects, and a variety of other social and economic factors. This pool is expanded by the inclusion of an unknown number of "draft-impelled volunteers" who, be-

---

[8] The various appeals echelons and procedures of the Selective Service System are omitted for the purpose of brevity. However, their existence is more important in a functional analysis than their effect. For a thorough discussion see *ibid.*, p. 28.

ing vulnerable to the draft, seek to gain some choice in their service assignment by enlisting voluntarily, even though this entails a longer term of service than is required of the draftee. In a Department of Defense survey of first-term active duty and Reserve personnel in October and November, 1964, 38 percent of the regular enlistees, 41 percent of the officers, and 71 percent of the Reserve enlistees (without active service) answered "no" to the question "Would you have entered service if there had been no draft?"[9]

Enlistees appear to have superior attributes for trainability. They are younger than draftees (see Table 5). Relatively more of them are in Armed Forces Qualification Test mental groups I and II (as measured by the Armed Forces Qualification Test, "AFQT"), while draftees score more frequently in mental groups III and IV (see Table 6). At entry, only 41 percent of the Army enlistees, as compared to 53 percent of the draftees, are high school graduates (see Table 7). However, an additional 20 percent of the enlistees are awarded high school equivalency credits on the basis of the General Educational Development (GED) test, as compared to only 3 percent of the draftees (see Table 5). Finally, enlistees are more likely to re-enlist than draftees, and consequently are the principal source in all services of permanent cadre personnel with long-range commitments (see Table 8).

Although the criterion of adequate manpower would appear to be fully met by the total manpower inventory maintained by Selective Service, the actual pool from which inductions are made is only slightly larger than that from which enlistees are drawn. Thus, in September, 1966, about 586,000 of the 32 million registrants were actually classified as available for military service.[10] The population on which the quota is based is only a small segment of the total local manpower pool. Thus, men who have been deferred continuously since high school graduation are never examined, and do not affect the experience rate. Similarly, enlistees who are obviously qualified do not directly affect the acceptance/rejection experience because they are reclassified I-C after entry into active service.

Consequently, although Selective Service achieves numerical ade-

[9] *Review of the Administration and Operation of the Selective Service System*, House Report No. 75, p. 9935.
[10] *In Pursuit of Equity*, pp. 136–138.

Table 5

PERCENTAGE DISTRIBUTION OF ARMY INDUCTEES AND ENLISTEES AND OF TOTAL MALE ACCESSIONS (ALL SERVICES) BY AGE AND YEAR OF BIRTH

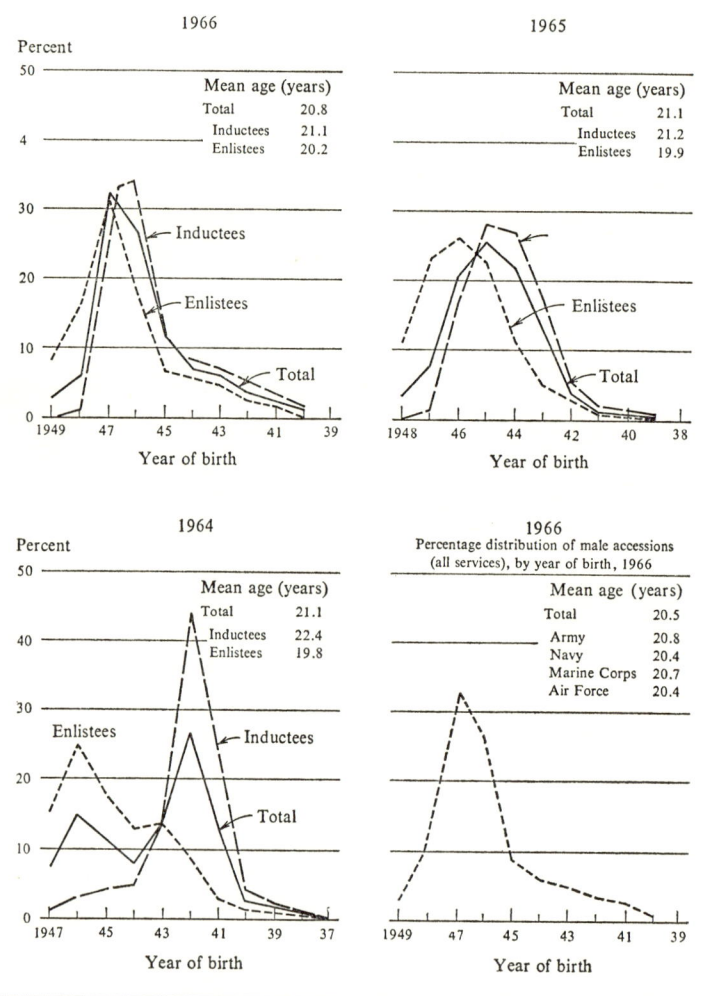

SOURCE: Office of the Surgeon General, United States Army, Supplement to *Health of the Army,* "Results of the Examination of Youths for Military Service, 1966" (Washington, March 1967). Charts for Army Inductees and Enlistees from p. 44, Chart for all Male Accessions from p. 59.

quacy, the pool of men from which inductions are made tends to constitute the same limited segment of the total population as that from which enlistees are drawn.

UNIVERSALITY

The second criterion relates to the universality of the chances of service, and the equitable distribution of such chances throughout the society. The Selective Service System explicitly incorporated this criterion in the earlier title of the legislation, establishing it as "The Universal Military Service and Training Act." In two respects, a goal of universality is achieved by Selective Service : by the registration of all youths at age eighteen, and by the accumulation of a registrant pool of several age groups so that periodic fluctuations in manpower demand do not discriminate against specific age groups.

Voluntary recruitment methods deviate from this criterion by the nature of the population to which they must appeal. The motivational ap-

Table 6

ACCESSIONS BY MENTAL GROUP, ENTRY MODE, AND SERVICE BRANCH, 1966

AFQT (Mental group, score, and expected percent)	Draftees	Enlistees				
		Total Enlistees	Army	Navy	Marines	Air Force
I (93–100) 7%	4.8%	8.2%	8.0%	10.0%	5.6%	8.4%
II (65–92) 28%	27.3	38.8	32.9	49.7	34.0	41.5
III (31–64) 34%	42.8	40.1	37.8	36.1	47.2	42.2
IV (10–30) 21%	23.2	12.9	21.3	4.2	13.2	7.9
Administrative Acceptees : (9–0) 10%	1.9					
Total	100.0%	100.0%	100.0%	100.0%	100.0%	100.0%

SOURCE : Office of the Surgeon General, United States Army, Supplement to *Health of the Army,* "Results of the Examination of Youths for Military Service, 1966" (Washington, March, 1967). Data for draftees from Table 21, p. 42. Data for Enlistees from Table 33, p. 52. For a full discussion of the development and use of the Armed Forces Qualification Test (AFQT) see p. 9.

peals that are effective inducements for enlistment are promises of opportunities for training and education not otherwise available except by military service. These appeals are most effective among those who are as yet unskilled, unattached, and unplaced in the social structure. Consequently, although voluntary recruitment tends to channel neglected elements of the social structure into the service, in so doing it provides opportunities for occupational mobility to which enlistees would not otherwise have access.

Under the conditions of total mobilization prevailing during World War II, when Selective Service developed, the principle of universality was functionally effective. Such conditions required that some occupational roles be viewed as alternative forms of national service. Universality

Table 7

A COMPARISON OF ENLISTEES AND DRAFTEES BY EDUCATIONAL ATTAINMENT

Educational level	Component	
	Regular Army	Selective Service
College graduate and higher	1.5%	3.1%
College, 3–4 years, nongraduate	1.3	2.8
College, 2 years	3.4	7.1
College, 1 year	5.5	7.6
High school graduate	41.3	53.0
High school, nongraduate, 4 years	1.9	2.6
High school, 3 years	6.4	6.2
High school, 2 years	7.2	6.5
High school, 1 year	5.5	4.1
Elementary school graduate (Grades 1 through 8)	3.8	2.8
Elementary school, nongraduate	1.8	1.4
Equivalency G.E.D. Credits		
2-year college level	0.2	0.1
High school graduate	19.9	2.7

SOURCE : Adapted from *Sample Survey of Military Personnel* (RCS AG-366), as of August 31, 1965, "Survey Estimate of Educational Level of Male Enlisted Personnel by Grade and Component," Department of the Army. Regular Army personnel, Grades 1–5, are assumed to be comparable to Selective Service personnel of the same grades, in length of service. In the original reports, percentages are calculated by educational level and specific grade, but comparability is not established.

rested on the assumption that the civilian role in question was equal in significance to military service. However, Selective Service was reactivated in 1948 under nonmobilization conditions as a supplementary manpower resource. Under these conditions, the deferment method was used for a different purpose: rather than representing a balancing of the relative values of specified civilian and military services, deferment was used as a solution to the problem of an expanding and increasingly superfluous manpower pool.

In World War II and the Korean conflict periods, the classification schedule was a simple organizational device for sorting the manpower pool into categories of relative availability and utility. The classification

Table 8

RE-ENLISTMENT RATES, BY BRANCH OF SERVICE AND PROCUREMENT SOURCE, 1950–1967

Procurement period [a]	First-term regulars					Inductees (Army)
	Total	Army	Navy	Marine Corps	Air Force	
1955	15.8%	38.9%	9.0%	16.5%	14.4%	3.0%
1956	22.8	28.2	11.5	23.7	29.3	3.5
1957	24.7	18.9	15.6	17.0	36.5	2.7
1958	27.6	17.2	22.6	24.2	39.8	4.7
1959	30.0	21.5	23.4	20.2	45.7	5.1
1960	21.2	23.5	21.3	11.1	24.1	9.1
1961	25.3	26.0	27.8	18.3	23.5	11.6
1962	27.4	23.8	28.3	20.0	35.3	20.1
1963	24.9	22.2	25.1	15.5	35.1	11.2
1964	25.2	27.9	22.5	14.4	29.5	3.6
1965	24.0	25.7	21.4	16.3	25.5	8.4
1966	23.2	28.0	22.8	16.3	18.9	10.2
1967	18.8	23.7	18.9	10.6	16.8	20.8

[a] Data for Fiscal Years rather than calendar years, indicating a 12-month period beginning on July 1 of the previous calendar year and terminating on June 30 of the year indicated.
SOURCE: Adapted from Selected Manpower Statistics, Directorate for Statistical Services, Office of the Secretary of Defense, April 15, 1968, p. 51.

action was unlikely to alter the social structure because the decision was based on the occupational or dependency status of the registrant at the moment of his classification. The basis for the deferment was unlikely to change during a short emergency period. However, such a classification schedule tends to acquire a different meaning in a longer perspective when permanently established. The schedule is interpreted as a set of approved behavior patterns, motivated by the desire to avoid service. Each category thus becomes an attainable status that can be maintained during the registrant's period of military liability.

The original conception of deferment as a sorting device has been formally redefined and established as the deliberate policy of "channeling." It is officially defined and explained as follows:

> ... the term "channeling" refers to that process through which registrants are influenced to enter and remain in study, in critical occupations, and in other activities in the national health, safety, and interest by deferment or prospect for deferment from military service. Selective Service channels thousands of young men through its deferment procedures into those fields of endeavor where there are shortages of adequately trained personnel. Many would not have continued their education at the undergraduate and graduate college level if there had not been a college student deferment program.[11]

Thus, although the definition of "channeling" complies with short-range goals, the long-range effects of the policy could be to distort basic social patterns. All educational goals would appear to be equally acceptable as bases for deferment. One effect of this might be that educational careers would be arranged on the basis of their "deferment potential" rather than intrinsic occupational aspirations. Recruitment into some professional fields might be correspondingly distorted.

The success of the effort to achieve an equitable distribution of liability for military service is indicated by the higher educational attainment levels of draftees as compared to enlistees (see Table 7). The number of draftees with two or more years of college is more than twice the number of enlistees at that level. To the extent that level of educational attainment is an index of social class, it can be said that Selective Service has distrib-

---

[11] *Annual Report of the Director of Selective Service*, 1963, p. 12.

uted the chances of service more widely throughout American society than would have been the case if voluntary recruitment had been the sole source of manpower. The local board method of adjudicating exceptions from national criteria has also served to maintain a closer relationship between military organization and the larger society than would probably prevail under a system of recruiting agents reporting only to their respective services and unresponsive to the local community.

It is important to note that quotas are not allocated to local boards on the basis of the age distribution of the board's area nor even according to the number of registrants. The quota base is the number of men who have been classified I-A and consequently excludes men who have been classified into deferment categories. Thus an upper-middle-class district with a high proportion of college students will have a correspondingly low quota because that proportion of the registrants attending college are classified as II-S and are not included in the quota base. A lower-class area with a small proportion of college students would have a larger quota but it would be distributed among the larger pool of men classified as I-A because they are ineligible for classification as college students. Consequently, a lower-class youth in a middle-class area has about the same chance of selection as other youths in a lower-class area who are classified as I-A. Thus, lower-class youths are more likely to be selected because they do not attend college, not because of the demographic characteristics of their local board area. The inequity is not in the method of allocating the quota, but rather in deferment policies that exclude or postpone the vulnerability of college students from the middle and upper classes. A national selection system would not eliminate the present inequities unless it were accompanied by an elimination of deferment categories.

MINIMAL IMPACT ON SOCIETY

A third criterion of an efficient procurement system is the extent to which it can operate effectively without seriously interfering with other essential functions of the larger society. However, this criterion can be overemphasized to the point that the value of universal involvement is sacrificed and recognition of the civic obligation of military service becomes blurred.

Voluntary recruitment exemplifies this dilemma. So long as procurement is limited to voluntary recruitment, social life can continue normally. The pool of voluntary recruits, composed predominantly of unskilled youths with no family responsibilities, is relatively fluid and unorganized. Their departure for military service involves no serious interruption of work or family life. The community is not obliged to provide welfare services to dependents as a substitute for their presence. The voluntary recruit is hardly missed in his community except by his parental family. But voluntary recruitment also excuses the larger society from a continuing concern for national military policy and the objectives for which military personnel are being used. Only a limited segment of the society has a real personal stake or involvement in military activities, and it is predominantly located in the class structure where its influence with community leaders is unlikely to be effective. Purely voluntary military service also is more likely to be perceived by members of the larger society as a conventional occupational career, freely chosen with full awareness and acceptance of the associated risks.

The Selective Service System presents a similar dilemma between minimizing the social impact of induction, and distributing the chances of service. The dilemma emerges from the expanding pool of surplus registrants. As the number of 18-year-old registrants has increased, the demand for military manpower has declined. With the expanded registrant pool, the interval between registration and induction has also increased, so that it is more likely that a registrant will have established himself in an occupation and family life by the time he is eventually called. One solution to this problem is to invert the order of call so that younger registrants are called first, when they are relatively unskilled and unattached. Age status is an objective criterion, unaffected by criteria of social class, region, or ethnic origins.

However, the solution adopted by the Selective Service System has been one of using the system of classification and deferment to reduce the number of persons who must be considered for induction. This policy, in effect, makes the draft applicable only to persons who cannot qualify for deferment categories, a criterion which is more likely to be influenced by factors associated with social class, region, or ethnic affiliation. Military service thus becomes concentrated in segments of the society rather than being distributed generally according to the objective criterion of age.

Effects of the professional military viewpoint

The process of military manpower procurement includes the relevant policies of the armed forces themselves. Such policies reflect, in part, the viewpoints of professional soldiers who view military service in the long-range perspective of an occupational career. These viewpoints may be in conflict with military service as a short-term experience, induced either by legal compulsion under Selective Service, or the expectation of specialized technical training with transfer value to civilian occupations by enlistees.

The combination of voluntary recruitment and Selective Service has produced adequate numbers of personnel. However, the assurance of a supplementary compulsory resource has had the negative effect of retarding innovations in personnel practices among the professional military. Such innovations as the lowering of entry requirements or the modification of internal conditions might have been stimulated by the prospect of a personnel deficit and the necessity for competing with other institutions of the larger society for a share of the labor force. When the inducements of procurement agencies were insufficient to attract men for positions requiring exceptionally skilled personnel—such as physicians and dentists—innovations such as special pay and career arrangements were introduced. However, in the opposite case, when the manpower pool included those of marginal physical or mental qualifications who were nevertheless capable of service under less stringent requirements, no changes were made. So long as the military organization had access to a more than ample pool of manpower that met existing standards, there was no necessity for developing criteria that would permit utilization of marginal personnel.

A second effect of an assured supply of manpower on professional military perspectives has been an exaggerated emphasis on entry requirements and procedures at the expense of long-range plans for job mobility, career flexibility, and rehabilitative programs within military organization. Dependence on a large continuing flow of new personnel required the development of mass testing programs to assign entrants to positions or schools as early as possible for maximum utilization during their limited term of service. Such programs required elaborate and rigid classification and assignment programs relatively insensitive to factors other than those derived from the tests. After assignment in terms of the results of such tests, subsequent performance on the job was largely irrelevant. The effect of reliance on mass testing was to exclude many men from opportunities for technical training in which they might well have succeeded. Thus, in an Air Force study of 11,000 men whose aptitude test scores were too low to qualify initially for technical training in any career field, it was found after four years that 77 percent of the high school graduates, but only 42 percent of the nongraduates, had performed successfully in such diverse types of work as transportation, utilities, supply, and air police. However, if test scores alone had been the criterion, the high school graduates would have been rejected for enlistment.[12]

A third effect emerges from the exaggerated use of cost accounting methods to evaluate personnel programs. Thus, the preference for the longer-term enlistee is based on the rationale that each additional month of service "pays for" the initial cost of procurement and training. Conversely, it is often asserted that the two-year draftee is less efficient because he serves for a shorter period. However, this rationale fails to consider the differences between populations of enlistees as compared to draftees. It would appear that the self-selection process operating among enlistees tends to obtain a population with a relatively larger number of "inefficient" personnel whose aggregate performance detracts from the values derived from the longer term of service.

Thus, one study of the job performance of men with low mental test scores concluded:

> Of RA (enlistee) Category IV [lowest acceptable grouping of test scores on the entry mental test instrument—Armed Forces Qualification Test] men in combat MOS, 50 per cent attained an acceptable level of performance and 43 per cent met standards of performance for career level. Percentages for the RA lower Category III men were virtually the same.

[12] Mary Agnes Gordon and Eli S. Flyer, *Predicting Success of Low-Aptitude Airmen,* Technical Documentary Report PRL-TDR-62-14, August, 1962, p. 6. Comparable results are reported for Navy enlistees in John A. Plag *et al., Age, Years of Schooling and Intelligence as Predictors of Military Effectiveness for Naval Enlistees* (Washington, D.C.: Naval Medical Neuropsychiatric Research Unit, July, 1965). The Army Experience is reported by W. A. Klieger *et al.,* in *Prediction of Unacceptable Performance in the Army,* Technical Research Note 113 (Washington, D.C.: U.S. Army, Human Factors Research Branch, TAG Research and Development Command, June, 1961).

More inductees (US), however, despite the fact that their AFQT [Armed Forces Qualification Test] scores ranged as low as the 10th percentile, were rated acceptable (63 per cent) and of career level (56 per cent). ... In technical MOS (Military Occupational Specialty), the RA Category IV men were lowest, the RA lower Category II substantially higher, and the US enlisted men decisively higher than either.[13]

Similar contrasts between enlistees and inductees appear in appraisals of combat performance and of delinquency records. Thus, on the basis of data collected on 2,291 men in combat during the Korean conflict, enlistees and inductees were compared in terms of the type of discharge awarded upon completion of service, and the number of court-martial convictions (see Table 9). These data suggest that because inductees are less likely to be delinquent, perform more efficiently during their service, and are more likely to complete their full term of service, their effective contribution is as great as that of the enlistee whose commitment to a longer period is less likely to be fulfilled.

The longer term required of enlistees may even aggravate their comparatively poor performance in relation to draftees. The two-year term required of inductees is more compatible with the time conceptions of the age group from which enlistees are procured. Studies of this age group have described them as being in the "trial work period" when occupational choices are made on a tentative and experimental basis. Their time perspective is such that they either avoid or subjectively ignore long contractual obligations, while attributing greater significance to shorter time intervals, such as one or two years, than is true later in life. This is indicated by the responses of grade-12 boys in Project TALENT to the question: "What is the *longest* period of *active* duty time for which you would consider enlisting in each branch of the service?" The results below indicate the significant preference for the two year term (see Table 10).

One of the major supporting arguments for the existing term of service (either two or three years) is that after sixteen weeks of basic and individual training, only twenty months of useful service remain. An additional two months of this time is consumed by leave and transportation. However, substantial changes in these time requirements are feasible.

[13] William H. Helme and Alan A. Anderson, *Job Performance of Enlisted Men Scoring Low on AFQT*, Technical Research Note 146 (Washington, D.C.: U.S. Army Personnel Research Office, May, 1964).

Table 9

COMPARISON OF ENLISTEES AND DRAFTEES BY TYPE OF DISCHARGE

Criterion category	Enlistees		Draftees and others	
	No.	Percentage	No.	Percentage
Honorable discharge—no court-martial convictions	894	62.4%	812	94.6%
Honorable discharge—one or more convictions	292	20.4	29	3.4
Other-than-honorable discharge	247	17.2	17	2.0
Total	1,433	100.0	858	100.0

SOURCE: A. U. Dubuisson and W. A. Klieger, *Combat Performance of Enlisted Men with Disciplinary Records,* Technical Research Note 148 (Washington, D.C.: U.S. Army Personnel Research Office, June, 1964).

Thus, an experimental program in basic training as early as 1956 demonstrated that the same performance levels could be achieved after four weeks of basic training as after eight weeks, especially with high-aptitude men. The report concluded:

> ... Trainees *at all levels of aptitude* learn as much military information in four weeks (when the Prevue Review technique is used in their training) as is normally learned in eight weeks by men of comparable intelligence. On performance tests, men of *middle* and *low* aptitude do benefit by the full eight weeks of training, although the high-aptitude men apparently make only minor gains in the additional time.[14]

A fourth effect has been to foster inequities within military organization, especially in exposure to the risks of combat and the chances of survival. This outcome is also partly an effect of personnel classification and assignment procedures. Functionally, it is essential that persons with scarce and critical skills be so located that the chances of their loss to the organization will be minimized. Persons who lack scarce skills of value to military organization are more likely to be assigned to positions where technical specialization is minimal, usually infantry. Typically, service in

---

[14] Victor B. Cline, Alan Beale, and Dennis Seidman, *Evaluation of Four-week and Eight-week Basic Training for Men of Various Intelligence Levels,* Technical Report 32 (Washington, D.C.: Human Resources Research Office, The George Washington University, 1956), p. 5.

such units involves more field service with risk, hardship, and prolonged discomfort, combined with monotonous and repetitive tasks with no transfer value to civilian life. Thus men are assigned to such positions because they lack specialized skills, while the lack of specialization at this echelon prevents them from ever acquiring such skills during their period of service.

It is also at this level that casualties are most likely to occur among enlisted men during active combat. They are replaced by men most recently inducted or enlisted and trained, rather than by rotation of those originally assigned to lower-risk echelons. Thus there is a continuously high demand for unskilled men to maintain the force level of high-casualty echelons, but attrition among men who have received specialized training and assigned to risk-remote echelons remains low. Consequently, replacement needs for those echelons is low, school quotas remain stable, entry standards remain high, and relatively fewer men are likely to be selected. These factors enhance the prospect that men with less education or who do not get high scores on aptitude tests are more likely to become casualties.[15]

Such policies are also derived from the preeminent value attributed to education in our society. Thus, deferments of college students insure that at the time of ultimate entry they will have an educational—and consequently an assignment—advantage over noncollege youths who entered after high school or less. Deferments for participation in officer procurement programs have a similar effect because officers have a relatively low casualty experience. Voluntary recruitment policies assure high school graduates of specialized technical and clerical schools if they are otherwise qualified by aptitude tests and thus remove them from the chances of selection as infantry replacements.

Conclusions

A basic consideration in the transformation of the Selective Service System is the definition of who shall serve. An effective resolution of this issue requires innovations in organizational format as well as military man-

---

[15] The only published data on this important point is that of Albert J. Mayer and Thomas F. Hoult, "Social Stratification and Combat Survival," *Social Forces*, XXXIV (December, 1955), 155–159.

Table 10

COMPARISON OF LENGTH OF SERVICE PREFERENCES OF HIGH SCHOOL SENIORS BY LENGTH OF SERVICE *"What is the* LONGEST *period of* ACTIVE *duty time for which you would consider enlisting in each branch of the service?"*

	Army		Navy		Air Force		Marine Corps		Coast Guard	
	No.	Per-centage	No.	Per-centage	No.	Per-centage	No.	Per-centage	No.	Per-centage
I would not consider enlisting in this branch	902	31.7%	753	26.4%	694	24.4%	1,035	36.3%	1,123	39.5%
Six months	342	12.0	283	10.0	213	7.5	271	9.5	303	10.7
Two years	609	21.4	562	19.8	510	17.9	435	15.3	436	15.3
Three years	230	8.1	267	9.4	289	10.2	218	7.7	175	6.2
Four years	170	6.0	304	10.7	406	14.3	214	7.5	168	5.9
Six years	60	2.1	119	4.2	180	6.3	109	3.9	81	2.8
Item omitted	531	18.7	556	19.5	552	19.4	562	19.8	558	19.6
Total	2,844	100.0%	2,844	100.0%	2,844	100.0%	2,844	100.0%	2,844	100.0%

SOURCE: Marion F. Shaycroft, Clinton A. Neyman, Jr., and John T. Dailey, *Comparison of Navy Recruits with Male High School Students on the Basis of Project TALENT Data* (Washington, D.C.: American Institute For Research, June, 1962), p. D-23.

power policy if there is to be more complete fulfillment of the criteria of adequacy, universality, and minimal impact on the larger society.

Failures to achieve these criteria are due to neglect of the relationship between policy and organizational format. The experience of both voluntary recruitment and Selective Service exemplify in different ways the discrepancy between these two factors. Voluntary recruitment has adapted to the necessity of competing with economic institutions of the larger society for a share of the labor force by appealing to such values of American youth as the desire for technical training and education. Selective Service has attempted to minimize interference with activities of the larger society by educational and occupational deferments, thus exploiting the same values. However, as a result of organizational format both systems ultimately compete for the same limited segment of the total manpower pool.

This analysis has emphasized the potential complementarity of voluntary recruitment and Selective Service. The lack of operational coordination, however, has contributed to the general criticism of the methods of military manpower procurement. Whatever policy changes may emerge from the political process, fundamental organizational changes are also required.

First, there is a critical need for a greatly expanded informational program. Selective Service has avoided this function, because of a policy of avoidance by local boards of prominence in the community, but such avoidance has fostered the accumulation of a vast amount of misinformation and allegations of intrigue in the absence of accurate knowledge of the operations of the System. To many, the failure of Selective Service to assume responsibility for guidance as to service alternatives has also appeared to be an abdication of responsibility for the results of their decisions. On the other hand, the informational activities of voluntary recruiters have been interpreted as promotional of their respective services rather than generally oriented to the guidance of youths in respect to their military obligations. A combined effort would eliminate both of these deficiencies and contribute to the attainment of their mutual objectives. The recruiting services should be charged with responsibility for an informational and guidance program in which the values of induction are given equal weight to those of voluntary enlistment.

Second, the physical location for both operations should be merged to eliminate organizational competition and to foster collaboration. A joint military manpower office would facilitate and encourage the exploration of service alternatives. The reluctance of Selective Service to effect such a consolidation has been based on an erroneous assumption of local community hostility toward the federal government. Such a conception is a vestige of the Civil War experience and is no longer justified. The Department of Defense in 1966 initiated a program of consolidating the recruiting efforts of the separate services. This program should be extended by including the activities of local offices of Selective Service as well. In addition to the enhanced effectiveness of procurement are the considerations of greater efficiency and economy.

Third, the Cadet Corps (or "High School ROTC") could be more effectively utilized as a recruitment source as well as an informational vehicle. Its current modest enrollment of about 90,000 is not an accurate measure of its potential usefulness in the preliminary training of youths for military service, especially in urban areas. It could be more fully exploited by awarding some measure of credit toward the fulfillment of the active service obligation in summer camp tours, and by greater exposure to an effective informational program.

A fourth organizational innovation would be the creation of a more effective relationship between the Reserve and active forces. Traditionally the Reserves have maintained a separate identity by assimilating veterans of recent wars with recruits without active military service. Their role in national defense was supplementary. Since 1960, however, they have assumed an increasingly competitive role with respect to the active forces. Many recruits are initially trained for relatively brief periods of six to ten months on active service and thereafter are deferred for active duty except in emergencies. Consequently, membership in the Reserves has increasingly developed as an abbreviated substitute for the obligation of a full tour of active service.

More important to the issue of manpower procurement, however, is that in the Reserve programs military organization has fostered the develment of a category of exemption from active service under its own auspices. The lack of an ethic of universality comparable to that prevailing under Selective Service has led to widespread allegations of preferential treatment of applicants with local prominence, especially athletes. Since the number of applicants has far exceeded the number of vacancies, competition for admission has been intense, but actual admission has depended heavily on the personal criteria of Reserve units as military formations resembling local armies, with minimal control by the federal government. The present inequity could be resolved by retaining Reservists in the order of call under Selective Service, but reducing their initial obligated term of service, if ultimately called, by the amount of time already served.

Organizational innovations alone, however, will not be adequate unless they are guided by substantial changes in military manpower policy, which has been dominated in the recent past by the dilemma of disposing of an accumulating surplus. Consequently, such short-range policies as increasing the selectivity of entry requirements have predominated. However, an adequate solution requires confrontation of the two most important elements of military manpower policy in a democratic society : eliminating qualitative barriers to participation and increasing the rate of participation.

Qualitative barriers to participation now prevail at both extremes of the educational continuum. Stringent entry requirements established by military organization currently exclude a third of the available manpower. Periodic re-examinations of the rejected have indicated that many could serve effectively by a minor change in the definition of the criterion. Their successful performance, once having overcome the hurdle of entry requirements, suggests that the technical demands of military organization can be effectively met with lower standards. More important, however, is that the permanent exclusion of such a substantial proportion of each age group from military service correspondingly deprives them of the opportunity for significant participation in a highly valued and vital place in American life.

At the opposite extreme, educational and occupational deferments, established as special categories by Selective Service upon the recommendations of what they interpret to be the representatives of higher education in America, are equally pernicious. As a minimum, they postpone the chances of service until so late a point that recently acquired technical or intellectual skills are either wasted by induction or exploited as a justification for continued exclusion from service. At another level of significance, however, is the historical fact that participation in military organization has been an essential credential for leadership in American society. The exclusion of the college graduate from military service now correspondingly limits his acceptability for political leadership in the future by removing him from participation in significant events of his age group.

Another major direction in which changes are required in military manpower policy is recognition of the significance of the declining rate of participation in military organization. The quantitative explanation is simple : the manpower needs of military organization have remained relatively stable while the available manpower has increased. Recognition of the accumulating surplus has fostered the development of devices for disposing of the surplus, through such artifices as permissive deferment policies. Such improvised solutions fail, however, to take into account the significance of military institutions in American society and the universal obligations of citizen participation in them.

The developing problem confronting military manpower agencies is whether military service can be retained as a component of the civic ethic when it is meaningful only to a dwindling fraction of American men. Through more flexible training and assignment policies and adjustment of the term of service to the available manpower, the participation would be increased and the significance of these institutions in American society would be revitalized. The solutions that we have proposed are intended to avoid the crisis that present policies portend : that membership in American military organization will increasingly represent or comprise a minority group in American society.

Historical background of Selective Service in the United States

HARRY A. MARMION

THIS CHAPTER presents a brief and concise summary of the emergence of conscription as a solution to the recurrent problem of military manpower procurement during critical periods in national defense. Special emphasis is placed on developments of current relevance such as student deferments and the Reserve components.

European origins

The first modern conscription law was adopted by France during the French Revolution. During the nineteenth century most major European nations adopted the practice of conscription in connection with various conflicts. The rationale was that the number of men under arms and the ability to produce an inexpensive musket as a weapon would be the deciding factors in any war.

The first hundred and fifty years

The early colonists in America brought with them from England the militia concept. This meant that every able-bodied person should be armed and ready to fight whenever the occasion demanded. From the earliest settlement at Jamestown in 1607 until 1775, when the American Revolution began, conscription of one type or another was called for in a number of laws and ordinances passed by the various political subdivisions of the time.[1]

The Revolution and the War of 1812

In both the American Revolution and the War of 1812 the voluntary system of procuring men for the armed forces failed. To stimulate enlistment, bounties of various types were offered, including clothing, land, and even money. In 1777, Massachusetts and Virginia resorted to conscription. By February, 1778, only about two-thirds of the authorized Continental army had been recruited and Washington recommended to the Continental Congress that the necessary men be obtained by universal conscription in all of the Colonies. At this point, however, aid from France to the struggling young nation eliminated the necessity for extending conscription.

Near the end of the War of 1812 the ranks of the army were depleted and the Congress considered conscription. Again such action was dropped when the war ended.

The Civil War

Until the Civil War the use of conscription in America had been limited. Both sides resorted to the practice out of necessity. In the North it became quite obvious that a system of voluntary enlistment was not adequate. On March 3, 1863, Congress passed the first conscription act. It was not a

---

[1] For a more detailed discussion of this period, see *Outline of Historical Background of Selective Service and Chronology* (Washington, D.C. : Selective Service System, 1965), and *Backgrounds of Selective Service* (Washington, D.C. : Selective Service System, 1947), Vol. 1, pp. 55–62.

model law, and much public resentment resulted. Basically the law required all men between the ages of 20 and 45 to register. The requirements of the Army were foisted on the states in proportion to their population. The states subdivided the required numbers to various districts. Credit was given to those districts that could show previous enlistments. A man could buy an exemption for $300 or procure a substitute for an agreed-upon amount. For the rich, avoiding conscription was a relatively easy task, and the heavy burden fell upon the poor.

The first drawing of names in 1863 led to riots in such widely separated cities as Boston, Massachusetts; Wooster, Ohio; Portsmouth, New Hampshire; Rutland, Vermont; and New York City. In New York City the riots were severe, causing many deaths and great property damage. The rioters concentrated on the federal provost marshals, who were in charge of drawing the names.[2] This deep-seated feeling about conscription, particularly among the poor, coupled with the bounty and substitute provisions of the law, was responsible for sweeping changes in the legislation providing necessary military manpower prior to World War I.

The principal advantage of conscription was an increase in volunteers. Volunteers received a bounty; conscriptees did not. Actually, out of almost 800,000 names drawn, less than 50,000 served.

The South started conscription earlier—in 1862—and held its men for one year as opposed to three to nine months' service in the North. It allowed sweeping occupational exemptions, which led to abuses and fostered discontent between rich and poor. Exempted groups increased and special interests clamored for more of the same. The Southern legislation was not any better than the law enacted in the North; both were relatively unsuccessful.[3]

After the war, in 1866, the administrator of conscription in Illinois, Brigadier General James Oates, wrote a report about the deficiencies of the conscription law in the North. He made certain recommendations for

[2] For a good description of the draft riots, see William B. Hesseltine, *Lincoln and the War Governors* (New York : Knopf and Co., 1948), Chap. 14, pp. 273–307. For a discussion of the system in a particular state, see Eugene C. Murdock, *Ohio's Bounty System in the Civil War* (Athens, Ohio : Ohio University Press for the Ohio Historical Service, 1963). It should be understood that the evils and corruption in Ohio are not peculiar to that state alone.

[3] An interesting discussion of conscription is contained in Samuel Eliot Morison, *The Oxford History of the American People* (New York : Oxford University Press, 1965), pp. 666–667.

future legislation. This report was not acted upon for more than fifty years until Enoch H. Crowder, the Judge Advocate General of the Army, utilized the material in preparing legislation for President Wilson.

World War I and the National Defense Act of 1916

In order to appraise the first modern draft legislation enacted, the differences between the contending positions must be established. The professional military desired an effective standing army with additional emergency strength from recruitment of volunteers. This approach generally followed the pattern of the previous hundred years in America. On the other hand, President Wilson took the position that in a crisis the nation must not depend on a standing army but upon a citizenry trained and accustomed to arms. The professional military won and the National Defense Act of 1916 set up a blueprint for an increased regular military establishment.

While the debate on the National Defense Act was going on, some were already preparing for war. Grenville Clark suggested to General Leonard Wood the idea of men voluntarily engaging in military training for a month. The "Plattsburg idea," as it was called, gave elementary military training to a large number of men. Those who volunteered became advocates of national defense when they returned to their communities.[4]

Early in 1917 it became obvious that the nation must begin to prepare for war. President Wilson asked the War Department to prepare a "draft law" and Colonel Enoch H. Crowder, the Judge Advocate General of the Army, wrote the original text in February of 1917.[5] The day after war was declared in April, 1917, the bill entitled "An Act To Authorize the President To Increase Temporarily the Military Establishment of the United States" (commonly referred to as "The Selective Service Law") was presented to Congress. There followed a bitter six-week debate in Congress. Arguments against the bill alleged unconstitutionality, soldier

[4] For an interesting discussion of this period, see Frederick Palmer, *Newton D. Baker—America at War* (New York : Dodd Mead & Co., 1931), Vol. 1.
[5] At some point between the Civil War and World War I, the word "conscription" appears to have declined in popularity and the word "draft" substituted.

slavery, an attempt to Prussianize America, and that before machinery could be set up the country could raise half a million men voluntarily.

One of the most important provisions of the Act was Section 4, which said in part : "The President is hereby authorized ... to create and establish ... local boards which shall consist of three or more members, *none of whom shall be connected with the military establishment* [emphasis added] ... such boards shall have power within their respective jurisdiction to ... determine ... all questions of exemption under this act. ..." Some other provisions of the act were as follows :

1. Selective Service from the beginning of the conflict
2. Service for the duration
3. No bounties, substitutes, or purchased exemptions
4. Registration by voluntary act at designated places (usually polling places) in local communities
5. Age limit : 21–31, later amended to 18–45

If one were to sum up the 1917 legislation, it could be accomplished by one phrase—"Supervised Decentralization." President Wilson signed the bill into law on May 18 and the first registration was held on June 5, 1917, when 10 million men were registered. After the registration was accomplished the order of selection was established by a central lottery located in Washington. The first drawing was held on July 20, 1917, and the greatest lottery in history fixed the order of call for 10 million Americans. The law registered 24 million Americans, selected and inducted nearly 3 million, and was so successful that it required only three minor revisions during its period of applicability.[6]

Student deferment

Prior to World War I no serious thought had ever been given to deferment of students in America, except for their often being considered too young for service.[7] During the first World War consideration was given for the

---

[6] David A. Lockmiller, *Enoch H. Crowder* (Columbus : University of Missouri Studies, 1955), a biography of the first head of the Selective Service System, contains a detailed and informative history of the 1917 Act, especially Chaps. X through XIII.

[7] The material in this section comes from *A Working Paper : The Student Deferment Program in Selective Service,* prepared in the Planning Office, Office of the Director, National Headquarters, Selective Service System, February, 1952.

first time to the importance of education and the possibility of a type of deferment. At no time during this period were local boards even close to the bottom of the manpower pool available. Thus, there was no great public reaction to approximately 145,000 youths involved in the Student Army Training Corps. In 1917 this program was devised to allow students under the age of twenty-one to be relieved from active military duty to attend college for three years. There were more than five hundred college units established in the country but before the first enrollees began their courses of instruction, Congress lowered the draft age to eighteen. After this change the period of instruction for these students was reduced to nine months. The first students were activated in early October, but the Armistice was signed in November and all trainees demobilized before the end of the year. Because the program was so short-lived, there can be no real assessment of its worth. The precedent of some type of student deferment, however, had been established.

Post-World-War-I period

The planning and study for future emergencies began in 1926, when the Joint Army and Navy Selective Service Committee was convened. A nucleus of an organization to administer a future Selective Service law was established. Prior to the declaration of a limited national emergency in 1939, the committee had studied, revised, and drafted a proposed law. By the summer of 1940, a national headquarters had been set up and all state groups alerted so that when the Selective Training and Service Act of 1940 was passed, a nationwide organization was ready to be put into operation.

The act entitled "An Act To Provide for the Common Defense by Increasing the Personnel of the Armed Forces of the United States and Providing for Its Training" called for registration of all males between the ages of 21 and 35. In the first registration more than 16 million men registered. Inductions began in November, 1940. The act was strictly a peacetime measure that provided for a training period of a year or less, with no service beyond the limits of the Western Hemisphere, except in our territories or possessions. It provided that no more than 900,000 men could be in training at the same time.

President Roosevelt appointed a civilian, Dr. Clarence Dykstra, the first Director of Selective Service in late 1940. The President felt that legislation calling for induction of men in peacetime needed a civilian director to inspire public confidence. Dr. Dykstra, the President of the University of Wisconsin, commuted to Washington for six months while continuing to hold his position at the university. After six months Dr. Dykstra resigned for several reasons, including health and a board of trustees that were concerned over his absences. President Roosevelt appointed Lieutenant Colonel Lewis B. Hershey to be Director in July, 1941.

During the period of emergency from November, 1940, to October 31, 1946, more than 10 million men were inducted. Large numbers of students were also in uniform. Both the Army and Navy operated educational programs at colleges and universities and more than 200,000 men were maintained as military students.[8]

Expiration of the Selective Training and Service Act

President Truman recommended to Congress in March, 1947, that the Act be permitted to expire on March 31, 1947. Congress passed a law establishing the Office of Selective Service Records, charged with maintaining records, data, and files on the entire Selective Service process. General Hershey was named Director of the agency. A nucleus of Selective Service personnel was retained for protection against national emergencies necessitating almost instant manpower mobilization. For the first time since 1940 the United States depended solely on enlistments for maintaining the posture of the services. This hiatus was to last for fifteen months.

Truman and the 1948 Act

President Truman tried unsuccessfully for four years to have Congress pass a Universal Military Training Act. The proposed legislation would provide one year of training for all American men. This issue always fostered bitter debate, but the adoption of a policy of national defense de-

[8] National Manpower Council, *Student Deferment and National Manpower Policy* (New York: Columbia University Press, 1952), Chap. I, pp. 23–38, discusses student deferment.

pending upon air-nuclear deterrent cost the universal training concept most of its Congressional support. Because of the Cold War crisis, Congress did enact the Selective Service Act of 1948. Thus, for the first time in American history, men were drafted into the armed forces during peacetime. Again General Hershey was appointed Director of Selective Service.

Peacetime inductions immediately presented new problems for the Selective Service System in a completely new context. The experience during two World Wars was not really relevant. Since in 1948 there was no real war effort, the previous formula of who should serve, based on individual contribution to the war effort either in a military or civilian capacity, was not now pertinent.

The provisions of the 1948 Act were essentially the same as the World War II legislation. The period of service was, however, set at 21 months. All men between the ages of 18 and 26 were required to register. Youths in the 18-year-old category were allowed to enlist for one year (limit of 161,000 per year) and avoid the draft by joining the Reserves for six years.

The law provided that high school students could continue their study, if their work was satisfactory, until graduation, or until they reached the age of 20, whichever was first. College and university students could have induction postponed until the end of the academic year. The law further authorized the President to issue regulations that could defer persons whose activity was found essential to the national interest. This included study, research, and medical or scientific endeavors. The initial registration found over 8 million men eligible for service. Subsequently, men were required to register within five days after their eighteenth birthday. After January, 1949, the armed forces were able to obtain the required manpower and the draft calls were canceled.

Korean period

The value of having Selective Service apparatus available was shown in June, 1950. Although draft calls had ceased, local boards had continued registration and classification of eligible males. Inductions were begun within 60 days after the beginning of hostilities in Korea.

Universal Military Training and Service Act of 1951

The Selective Service Act of 1948 was succeeded by the Universal Military Training and Service Act of 1951. There were a number of significant changes in this Act which in general increased the sources of manpower available for induction. Some of the significant changes were as follows:

> 1. It canceled the deferment for married men without children. (In 1953 this provision was amended to cancel deferment for fatherhood, with some exceptions.)
> 2. It lowered the age limit of liability for military service from 19 to 18½.
> 3. It extended active duty period to 24 months and instituted an eight-year total obligation for combined active duty and membership in the Reserve.
> 4. Conscientious objectors, in lieu of military service, could perform certain civilian tasks in the national interest.
> 5. It extended to age 35 the liability of most men deferred after June 19, 1951.
> 6. Deferment by law was provided for college students to the end of the academic year or until they ceased satisfactorily to pursue their studies, whichever occurred earlier.
> 7. The Korean Bill of Rights was enacted in 1952.

President Truman appointed a National Security Training Commission to study UMT and to provide Congress with a detailed plan for implementation. The plan was presented in late 1951. The Universal Military Training provisions of the Act were debated but never passed.[9] During the three-year period of the Korean War more than a million and a half men were inducted through Selective Service procedures.

Proposals for student deferment

The reinstitution of the draft, together with a growing concern over shortages of scientific and other specialized personnel, made draft deferment in the 1950's a real issue for the first time in our history.

[9] See *Congress and the Nation 1945–1964*, pp. 266–272, for a good synopsis of the Congressional action on the draft and Universal Military Training.

James H. Conant and Vannevar Bush urged a Universal Military Training proposal later known as the "Conant Plan." The proposal would have inducted all qualified males at 18 with no deferments for anyone. After a two-year hitch a man would pursue a civilian occupation, or go to college, subject, if necessary, to call up as a member of the Reserve. Conant later modified his proposal with respect to medical students. He recommended that they be deferred until after graduation.

The Association of American Universities agreed with the Conant Plan insofar as induction at age 18 was concerned. They proposed, however, that after a period of training (four to six months), the armed forces would select certain students by examination. Those selected would be furloughed in order to attend college. After graduation, Selective Service would determine who would be recalled and who would be deferred.

The Scientific Manpower Advisory Committee of the National Security Resources Board (known as the Thomas Committee) also submitted a plan for student deferment. It recommended four months of training for all qualified 18-year-old males. High school students would be deferred until age 19 or until graduation, whichever came earlier. After this period of training some men would be selected for college enrollment (program to be determined by the student) in Reserve Officer Training Corps programs. Another group would be selected for college enrollment in a Reserve Specialist Training Corps to provide education in science, engineering, medicine, and other fields. After graduation these men would be available for either civilian or military activities essential to the public interest. Both these avenues would provide a continuous flow of manpower into the military (ROTC) and critical civilian fields (RSTC). The selective process would be made on the basis of "competitive examination."

Finally, the "Trytten Plan," a composite of reports of six Advisory Committees to Selective Service, was presented in late 1950. This plan was essentially the student deferment program finally adopted by the Selective Service System through Executive Order of the President.

The plan called for the maintenance of an uninterrupted flow of students through college.[10] Students would be selected for deferment on a

---

[10] M. H. Trytten, *Student Deferment in Selective Service* (Minneapolis: University of Minnesota Press, 1952), although outdated, carefully analyzes the need for deferment in a period of "less than all out national emergency."

basis of their performance in college and a nationwide test administered by the Selective Service System. After graduation students would be given four months to secure "essential employment." Those who at the end of that period were not eligible for further deferment would be inducted. (This portion of the Trytten Plan was not enacted.)

Student deferment in the 1950's

As stated earlier, high school students doing satisfactory work must be deferred until graduation or their twentieth birthday, whichever occurs earlier. A full-time college student who is ordered to report for induction must be deferred, at his request, until the end of the academic year. This form of statutory deferment may be secured only once.

Presidential Executive Orders may provide for further deferment of individuals whose education or employment may be in the national interest. Local draft boards have no obligation to defer students based on federally established guidelines. Each individual case may be examined in light of conditions facing local boards. Any man who obtained a deferment extends his liability for military service to age 35.

1955 amendments

As was stated earlier, more than 1.5 million men were inducted through the Selective Service process during the Korean War. In fiscal 1954 and 1955 after the truce, less than half a million were inducted. The Universal Military Training and Service Act was extended until July 1, 1959, by legislation signed by the President in June, 1955. The principal expiring provision was the authority to induct men who had not acquired extended liability through deferment.

Reserve Forces Act of 1955

One of the lessons learned as a result of the Korean War was that the Reserve forces of the country were inadequate to meet any significant aggressive challenge. President Eisenhower advocated the passage of the

Reserve Forces Act, which would provide a large number of men, essentially for the Reserve. The most important provision of this act provided for a "critical skills" Reserve program with local boards assigned *the responsibility for selecting men eligible to enlist* [emphasis added]. Men believed to be in "critical skill capacities" by local boards were required to enlist for three to six months of active duty for training and then were assigned to the Reserve for a balance of an eight-year enlistment. This program was discontinued after August 1, 1963.

The so-called "six months program" was also established; it provided (with certain quotas) that men before age 18½ and before they received orders for induction could join a Ready Reserve unit. They would be required to spend eight years in the Reserve, including from three to six months of active duty for training. Later, in 1957, this program was made available to those over 18½ years of age. This program was highly beneficial to the Reserve. No figures are available to determine what proportion of young men who availed themselves of this option were college students.

Extension to July 1, 1967

Public Law 88–2, approved March 28, 1963, extended the Universal Military Training and Service Act until July 1, 1967. It should be noted that the extension of the draft law was accomplished with perfunctory hearings and little debate.

Student deferment policies in the early 1960's

At present a student may further postpone service by passing the Selective Service Qualification Test (grade of 70) or attaining the required class standing for his appropriate academic year.

In effect, the law provides that all college freshmen be deferred for one academic year and that at their request they may be deferred further if the local draft board follows the recommendation of Selective Service and the student meets the stated guidelines. There is no provision in the law that protects part-time students. Graduate students may be deferred if they graduated in the upper quarter of their college class, are accepted into graduate school, and pass the Selective Service Qualification Test with a higher grade (80) than required of an undergraduate student.

During the period from 1951 to the spring of 1963, more than 600,000 students had taken the test. From 1963 until the spring of 1966 nearly all boards deferred students making satisfactory progress toward a degree, and the test was discontinued. Escalation of the war in Vietnam changed the student deferment picture. The Selective Service Qualification Test has been reinstituted and was offered during May, 1966.

Men found not acceptable

Although not directly concerned with student deferment, one other aspect of the draft regulations deserves mention.

Supposedly because of advanced technology, the services desire to obtain and retain higher quality manpower. The 1958 Amendment to the Universal Military Training and Service Act gave the President authority, which is delegated to the Department of Defense, to increase the standards for induction. This resulted in an increase in rejection rates among those eligible to serve. The result of this, in turn, is that the armed forces are now in competition with all other manpower users for a smaller group of men—*the most desirable manpower in the nation.*

During the period from July, 1950, to June, 1965, 47.9 percent of those otherwise eligible for induction into the service were found not qualified at the preinduction examination. (See Table I.) In Table III of the 1965 Report, the breakdown by cause for those men found not qualified at the preinduction examination (June, 1950–June, 1965) is summarized as follows:

	Percentage	No.
Failed mental requirement	43.1%	1,471,218
Failed physical requirement	47.1	1,567,895
Other	9.8	359,760
	100.0%	3,398,873

Table 1

ARMED FORCES INDUCTION NOT-QUALIFIED RATES, BY MONTH, NOVEMBER 1948–JUNE 1965[a]

Month and year	Induction examination			Month and year	Induction examination		
	Number delivered by local boards	Number found not qualified by Armed Forces	Percent found not qualified		Number delivered by local boards	Number found not qualified by Armed Forces	Percent found not qualified
November 1948– February 1956	2,259,596	127,384	5.6	1961			
1956				January	9,602	2,868	29.9
March	16,930	1,278	7.5	February	4,836	1,711	35.4
April	7,008	530	7.6	March	2,983	1,060	35.5
May	12,420	1,050	8.5	April	1,800	767	42.6
June	13,158	1,179	9.0	May	353	255	72.2
July	14,582	1,441	9.9	June	226	161	71.2
August	14,865	1,455	9.8	July	13,049	2,936	22.5
September	16,340	1,402	8.6	August	15,261	2,940	19.3
October	19,432	1,683	8.7	September	29,370	5,560	18.9
November	19,112	1,757	9.2	October	24,710	4,199	17.0
December	17,742	1,620	9.1	November	25,166	4,130	16.4
1957				December	20,754	2,937	14.2
January	19,588	1,720	8.8	1962			
February	17,234	1,543	9.0	January	20,005	3,378	16.9
March	16,513	1,373	8.3	February	12,090	2,461	20.4
April	14,901	1,214	8.1	March	9,409	2,313	24.6
May	14,255	1,211	8.5	April	8,444	2,133	25.3
June	12,311	1,135	9.2	May	8,181	2,177	26.6
July	14,001	1,341	9.6	June	8,498	2,308	27.2
August	12,446	1,497	12.0	July	7,141	1,973	27.6
September	9,488	1,326	14.0	August	7,163	2,006	28.0
October	8,089	1,228	15.2	September	7,257	1,867	25.7
November	7,844	1,256	16.0	October	6,413	1,898	29.6
December	7,821	1,143	14.6	November	6,249	1,951	31.2
1958				December	7,983	2,308	28.9
January	11,679	1,473	12.6	1963			
				January	6,126	1,799	29.4

Month	Col A	Col B	Col C	Month	Col A	Col B	Col C
February	14,947	1,824	12.2	February	6,239	1,843	29.5
March	15,056	1,771	11.8	March	11,929	2,952	24.7
April	14,723	1,581	10.7	April	13,071	3,158	24.2
May	15,457	1,774	11.5	May	13,062	3,381	25.9
June	12,475	1,443	11.6	June	6,338	2,091	33.0
July	12,385	1,457	11.8	July	9,791	2,912	29.7
August	13,534	2,643	19.5	August	15,192	3,909	25.7
September	15,307	2,936	19.2	September	15,053	3,956	26.3
October	14,378	2,805	19.5	October	20,665	4,485	21.7
November	13,927	2,741	19.7	November	22,934	3,806	16.6
December	13,333	2,507	18.8	December	15,724	2,567	16.3
1959				*1964*			
January	12,149	2,511	20.7	January	20,970	3,503	16.7
February	11,865	2,268	19.1	February	17,446	3,417	19.6
March	10,480	2,113	20.2	March	18,164	3,305	18.2
April	7,181	1,302	18.1	April	16,193	3,209	19.8
May	6,561	1,234	18.8	May	10,627	2,551	24.0
June	6,645	1,339	20.2	June	7,736	2,067	26.7
July	10,508	3,043	29.0	July	10,812	2,701	25.0
August	12,190	3,382	27.7	August	5,859	1,943	33.2
September	13,838	3,815	27.6	September	7,323	2,269	31.0
October	13,475	3,891	28.9	October	9,220	2,863	31.1
November	13,048	3,660	28.1	November	11,126	3,037	27.3
December	9,374	2,603	27.8	December	10,294	2,519	24.5
1960				*1965*			
January	10,437	3,108	29.8	January	8,226	2,411	29.3
February	6,272	1,999	31.9	February	5,470	1,877	34.3
March	5,933	2,223	37.5	March	11,433	3,153	27.6
April	10,015	3,593	35.9	April	17,717	3,920	22.1
May	10,417	3,285	31.5	May	18,495	3,831	20.7
June	14,612	4,968	34.0	June	21,623	3,736	17.3
July	9,047	2,244	24.8	Total	3,625,142	394,908	10.9
August	10,280	2,711	26.4				
September	11,682	3,142	26.9				
October	13,037	3,502	26.9				
November	10,367	3,009	29.0				
December	11,061	2,774	25.1				

[a] See 1957 Annual Report for monthly figures from November 1948 through February 1956.

SOURCE: *Annual Report of the Director of Selective Service, 1965*, Appendix 15, p. 68.

In fiscal 1965 "preinduction examinations were given to 581,716 registrants 19 years of age and over ... among these, 287,582 or 49.5 per cent were found qualified while the remaining 50.5 per cent were not." [11]

One can say that this high rate of rejection greatly affects the overall manpower situation.

The current controversy over Selective Service

Widespread criticism of the draft system is a recent phenomenon. During the two World Wars the system worked well because of complete national commitment. During the Korean conflict, there was little outcry against the draft. As late as 1963, when the law was extended, there was little or no opposition expressed by Congress or any significant segment of the population.

The unpopularity of the Vietnam War, the escalation of the conflict in the spring of 1965, and relatively recent student militancy in the country have currently brought the entire Selective Service System under close scrutiny from many quarters.

In June, 1966, hearings on the administration and operation of the Selective Service System before the Committee on Armed Services of the House of Representatives clearly revealed a myriad of conflicting opinions on this issue. The hearings also produced a summary of the long-awaited study of the present draft system undertaken by the Department of Defense two years earlier. The evidence of concern was heightened when, concurrently with the hearings, the President established a National Advisory Commission on Selective Service. In November, 1966, Congressman L. Mendel Rivers, ever mindful of the legislative prerogative of Congress, appointed a Civilian Advisory Panel on Military Manpower Procurement to advise the House Armed Services Committee, of which he is the Chairman. In March, 1967, both panels had reported their findings. Shortly after the report of the President's Commission the President sent a message to Congress that included the following recommendations, which closely paralleled those recommended by the Commission he appointed:

[11] *Annual Report of the Director of Selective Service 1965*, p. 22.

Historical background of Selective Service

1. The current law be extended for a four-year period
2. Men be inducted on a "youngest first" basis
3. Deferment policies be tightened so as not to become exemptions and that postgraduate deferments be discontinued, except for medical and dental school[12]
4. Firm rules be formulated to apply uniformly throughout the country in determining eligibility for all other types of deferment
5. A system of random selection be established
6. Improvement of the Selective Service System be immediately effected to assure better service to the registrant in counseling and appeals; also better information to the public about the operation of the System and broader community representation on the local boards
7. The proposed reorganization of the structure and organization of the Selective Service System be studied
8. The life of the Advisory Commission on Selective Service be continued for another year
9. Enlistment procedures for the National Guard and Reserve units be strengthened to remove inequities

The Report of the Civilian Advisory Panel on Manpower Procurement also supported the concept of taking youngest men first but rejected any form of lottery. It supported the deferment of students until they received their undergraduate degree or reached age 24. Graduate deferments would continue only in critical areas as determined by a special National Manpower Board. The panel also urged the President to order Reserves to active duty to distribute the burden equitably between draftees and Reserves.

The Advisory Panel opposed most suggestions that would change the present system. The only really innovative suggestion was to take youngest first but even on this point the Panel did not take the next logical step, namely some form of random selection. With the pool of those reaching the age of 18 increasing rapidly, an increase of over one million between 1952 and 1966, the arithmetic indicates some form of random selection is necessary.

---

[12] With regard to undergraduate deferments, the President admitted that he had not decided what course to take. In his words: "I hope and expect that the Congress will debate the questions this issue poses for the nation's youth and the nation's future."

Summary

For almost two hundred years the United States had no experience with compulsory military service except in connection with major wars. Thus, compulsory service had been closely associated in the public mind with total national emergency.

In 1948 this situation changed and even though military strength requirements were not large, these requirements were not being met by voluntary enlistment. The situation was complicated by the aggressive tendencies of some nations, which necessitated countermeasures by the United States. In 1948, for the first time in American history, Congress authorized the induction of men for a period of military service in peacetime. This presented Selective Service with a completely new set of problems with previously attained experience no longer totally relevant. Also, the postwar complexity of society and expansion of knowledge, technical and otherwise, indicated a need for thoughtful consideration of deferment programs for undergraduate and graduate students. The unpopularity of the Vietnam War, the changing character of American college students, and the tenor of Congressional reaction have caused the entire Selective Service process to be subjected to intense scrutiny. Certainly the draft law will undergo a great deal of stress after its expiration on July 1, 1967.[13]

---

[13] See *Outline of Historical Background of Selective Service and Chronology* (rev. ed., 1965), for a thorough outline of historical background on this matter.

A social profile of local draft board members: the case of Wisconsin

JAMES W. DAVIS, JR.
KENNETH M. DOLBEARE

Introduction

DESPITE THE SIGNIFICANCE of the Selective Service System in American society, it has been the subject of virtually no systematic research.[1] Even answers to such apparently routine questions as who serves on the local board, how they are appointed and by whom, how long they serve, and how they relate to their communities are difficult or impossible to find. This paper attempts to provide partial answers to these questions. In addition we will try to sketch some of the links between Selective Service and the society and economy in which it operates. The data on which the paper rests include background and attitudinal details obtained in the Fall

[1] When we began our research the only substantial thing we were able to find was one doctoral dissertation, which examined the attitudes of 121 local board members in the New York City area; see Donald D. Stewart, "Local Board : The Place of Volunteers in a Bureaucratic Organization" (unpublished Ph.D. dissertation, Columbia University, 1950). During the 1950's and early 1960's, Selective Service attracted little attention, but it became the object of much attention and criticism when draft calls began to mount in 1965. The National Advisory Commission was appointed in July, 1966, and during the fall, conferences were held at Antioch College, the University of Chicago, and New York University, among other places. Papers on the draft have been presented at such disparate places as a meeting of the American Veterans Committee and the Industrial Relations Research Association.

of 1966 through a mail questionnaire that elicited 81 percent response from the 389 local board members of the State of Wisconsin.[2] We also interviewed 40 board members from a variety of boards, and about 30 Selective Service personnel from the State Director of Local Board Clerks.

Our inquiry was limited to the State of Wisconsin, but we think that it has reached all the essential characteristics of the System. In conjunction with data developed by the National Commission on Selective Service, whose work permits us to develop national generalizations but does not include the detailed attitudinal background and operating characteristic data available through an in-depth inquiry, it should provide a base for evaluating some of the complaints and prescriptions concerning the System.[3] We will look first at patterns of selection of local board members, then at the results, and finally at the significance of the profile of membership established.

Recruitment of local board members

Classification and selection for induction are carried out by local boards composed of citizens who are part-time volunteers. There are eighty boards in Wisconsin, each with five members except for scattered vacan-

[2] This paper is based on research conducted as part of an inquiry into the relationships, present and potential, between Selective Service and poverty; it was supported by funds granted to the Institute for Research on Poverty at the University of Wisconsin pursuant to the provisions of the Economic Opportunity Act of 1964. The authors acknowledge their indebtedness to the Institute for its assistance, and to Marilyn Wenell, Barry Gaberman, and James Thomas, graduate students in the Department of Political Science at the University of Wisconsin, for capable and resourceful research assistance. The study would not have been possible without the full, frank, and open cooperation of all elements of the Selective Service System. We are particularly indebted to Colonel Bentley Courtenay, State Director, who, with the approval of National Director General Lewis B. Hershey, made available the nonconfidential records of his State Headquarters and assisted us in securing the cooperation of local board members and other personnel of the System. Naturally, he bears no responsibility whatsoever for the judgments expressed here.

[3] This inquiry differs from that of the National Commission in that it rests on individual questionnaires to local board members, which tap background characteristics, community activities, and attitudes; it relates the foregoing to the classification, induction, and enlistment performance of local boards and the socioeconomic characteristics of their jurisdictions; and it draws on interviews at all levels of the Selective Service System.

cies; they commonly meet once a month for three or four hours, although this varies with the size of calls. By law, only the local board can decide upon deferments or inductions, and the national guidelines established are advisory only. Until the law was amended in 1967, membership on local boards carried no term or maximum age limit, so that a man might serve as long as he wished.

The statutory provision for nomination by the Governor and appointment by the President is implemented by widely varied actual practices. In California, for example, Superior Court Judges recommend local board members to the Governor; in Texas, the recommendation is made either by the State Director or by local committees acting in his name. In Wisconsin, the State Director secures nominees from a variety of sources and recommends them to the Governor. The sources employed here suggest that the real selection process may take one of two basic forms. The first is selection by the local board itself, perhaps limited by understandings about geographic or occupational representation on the board. The retiring member, another member, or the chairman may secure the approval of the other members for a man he proposes and send the name on to the State Headquarters for forwarding to the Governor. Of our 314 respondents, 39 percent said they had been recruited by the local board. Thus, many boards are essentially self-perpetuating bodies. The second major selection pattern is through the efforts of State Headquarters personnel, usually the field staff known as "auditors." Occasionally, a local board may decline to choose a replacement and fairly often it has difficulty finding one; sometimes the State Headquarters may seek to change the character of the board. In these cases, the auditor—normally responsible for liaison with Local Board Clerks and oversight of their operations —takes on the additional job of locating a new member. The standard sources are the local postmaster, service and veterans' organizations, and prominent local people. In some instances, officers of the State Headquarters themselves may take part in the selection process. Eleven percent of our respondents said they had been chosen by the State Headquarters in some way, and 32 percent said the most recent addition had been selected in this way. Many board members are unaware of the manner in which they or others were selected, so that these totals are rough approximations only.

These observations may be summarized by suggesting that the recruitment of local board members is highly situational. It varies over time within local boards, it varies among local boards, and it varies from state to state. The present requirement of gubernatorial nomination and Presidential appointment says little about how board members actually are found. And without field research on a state by state basis it is impossible to say. From our experience, we would be loathe to say anything about the selection of local board members in Illinois or Minnesota or New York.

Turnover on local boards

How long do draft board members serve? Until 1967 they served without limit of time and this means that many served a very long time indeed. Table 1 shows the length of tenure of board members, and compares our sample response with data on all board members compiled for us by the State Headquarters.

Table 1 indicates that our respondents are closely representative of all board members, with perhaps a slight overrepresentation of older members and underrepresentation of newer members. More than half of all board members have served more than 10 years, and further breakdown indicates that more than 10 percent have served more than 20 years. Clearly, there is not much turnover. There are several reasons for the long tenures of draft board members. One reason no doubt is that when draft

Table 1

LENGTH OF TENURE OF BOARD MEMBERS 1966

Years of service	Questionnaire respondents	All local board members
0–4	27%	30%
5–9	14	17
10 and over	57	53
No response	2	
	100%	100%
	$N = 314$	$N = 389$

calls are low the job is not a taxing one. More important, perhaps most important, is that board members almost to a man say that they get satisfaction from doing a job that has to be done and that they think is an important one. For many, this service seems to be a means of participating in something that extends beyond their own community and gaining a sense of integration with the nation as a whole. They are proud of their job and some feel they gain status from being on the local board. Needless to say, this feeling of doing an important job is cultivated by both State and National Headquarters. Unable to offer monetary rewards, the Selective Service System tries to maximize the psychic rewards that a board member may get. This is one reason, surely, that local boards are sent only general guidelines and advice and reminded that final decisions on individuals are in their hands.

Other reasons for the long service of board members may be suggested. One is that the State Director and his staff try to keep board members contented so that they will not resign. The State Director, for example, does not like to take appeals from local board actions because he does not want to give the appearance of questioning what a local board has done. For the same reason, unless a case contains procedural inadequacies he is unlikely to send a case back to a local board before it reaches the Appeal Board. He does not want the board to think he is questioning their judgment. Perhaps another reason for long service on the part of board members, though less important, is that long service is obviously rewarded by the system. Men with 10, 15, 20, and 25 years of service get appropriate certificates and pins accompanied with all due ceremony. Long service in the Selective Service System has developed into an organizational norm. It is a norm that is operative all the way from National Headquarters down to rural local boards. General Hershey has been director since 1941, and there are State Directors and local board members who have held their posts as long. Once developed, the norm itself has supplemented or reinforced the other determinants of long service.

Until 1967 Selective Service did not have a fixed retirement age, even though retirement ages have been established elsewhere in the federal government. We can suggest only tentative reasons. It is not always easy to recruit new members, and when replacements are not readily available it is functional to encourage incumbents to stay on. Another reason for encouraging long periods of service may be that it makes the job of the State Director simpler. With relatively little turnover he deals with boards he knows and whose actions and reactions he can intuitively predict. With higher turnover he would not know his organization as well. To this can be added the fact that the continuity of local boards provides an island of stability in a sea of change. When draft calls go up and down and deferments tighten and loosen unpredictably, familiar and experienced men on local boards may make the Headquarters job less stressful. Paradoxical as it seems, it may be that encouraging long service is a way of coping with the stress of change.

This low turnover may be an obstacle to innovation in the organization; a stable work force may lead to an inflexible organization and excessive support for the status quo. This statement must of course be qualified. Selective Service has never failed to respond to higher or lower calls for men. It has frequently adjusted its deferment practices as conditions changed. Clearly, in this area of induction and deferment it is flexible. But in organization structure, in data handling, in selection procedures, and in personnel procedures, the System operates today essentially as it has since 1940. One can at least wonder if it would be so stable if it had higher turnover.

Two other consequences of low turnover are possible. Social and economic changes in a community, particularly those that result in population moves, may mean that the local board becomes quite unrepresentative of the community. Members chosen in the early 1950's, to say nothing of the 1940's, may not reflect the current population in an area. A third consequence is that low turnover may yield in time an organization with disproportionate numbers of elderly men, particularly in an organization where there have been no age limits. (We will present age data shortly.) The result of this may be that the men, unable to keep up, expect more and more assistance from their clerk. To be sure, when Selective Service is relatively dormant, as it was until 1966, it may make no difference that the organization is composed of superannuated men. But when the organization is working under pressure it may make a difference. A problem for Selective Service, though perhaps one unrecognized publicly, has been to keep the organization "fit" when times were slack so that it could work when there was work to do.

The characteristics of board members

Who are these local board members and what are their social characteristics? As we suggested in the first section and in agreement with the length of service figures, draft board members are middle-aged and elderly. By law they are required to be at least 30 years old and since 1967 they cannot be over 75. In fact, very few are under 45; more than twice as many are over 60 as under 45. Table 2 shows the age groupings of Wisconsin board members and compares our respondents with State Headquarters' data on all board members in the state, and also with the state population and with two other groups of public officials.[4] The extent of superannuation within Selective Service is clearly revealed in these comparisons : Over 40 percent of local board members are over 60 years of age, and further breakdown shows that 26 percent are over 70. The age distribution of Wisconsin board members is only slightly higher in the older categories than the national distribution of ages of board members in the remaining 4,007 local boards of the country, but is distinctively older than any of these comparative populations. The state population, the members of the state legislature, and even the U.S. Congress, are all substantially lower in age than local board members.

We have found that men stay on as local board members long after they have retired from their jobs, and some have even come on their local boards at that point in life. Agreement is general throughout the system that superannuation is a problem, but it is difficult to handle. Men who have volunteered their time for several years and who find that attending board meetings gives them a sense of function in their late years are not anxious to retire, and the State Headquarters finds it difficult to detach them. The problem is further complicated by the delicate relationship that exists between the State Headquarters and the legally autonomous volunteers whose cooperation is essential. Volunteers cannot be issued orders; the work of the System must be accomplished with tactful suggestions and invitations. It may be just too costly in terms of continued working relationships to precipitate a confrontation with respect to an elderly member.

---

[4] This exhausts the available comparative materials of the State Headquarters, but gives us confidence that there is no discernible bias to the 81 percent returns that our questionnaire produced.

Table 2

AGE OF LOCAL BOARD MEMBERS, COMPARED TO STATE POPULATION AND SELECTED OTHER OFFICIALS 1966

Age group [a]	Local board questionnaire respondents, 1966	All Wisconsin local board members, 1966	Wisconsin state population, 1960 [b]	Wisconsin state legislators, 1966 [c]	U.S. Congress 1966 [d]
30–44	16%	17%	38%	30%	29%
45–59	40	41	33	41	46
60–69	18	42 [e]	17	21	19
70 and over	26		12	8	6
	100%	100%	100%	100%	100%
	N = 314	N = 389	N = 960,305	N = 117	N = 534

[a] In all instances, percentages are based on the populations which are over 30 years of age (the minimum age requirement for service on a local board) in order to maintain comparability.

[b] SOURCE: U.S. Census, 1960 (Male population over 30 used as base).

[c] SOURCE: Wisconsin Blue Book, 1966 (N = 117 because 16 members rejected because under 30 or age unknown).

[d] SOURCE: Congressional Quarterly (1st session 89th Congress, N = 534 because one member under 30).

[e] Figure includes all over 60.

A local board member is also likely to be a veteran with no more than a high school education and to be in a white-collar occupation. Alternatively, he may be a farmer, which is hardly surprising in Wisconsin. Table 3 shows the detailed breakdown in veteran status, occupation, and education. About half of the local board members are veterans of either World War I or World War II. There are only a few veterans of other conflicts. Perhaps surprisingly, more than a third of the local board members are not veterans.

The occupational distribution tends to confirm our characterization of board members as representative of the middle class. The proportion of businessmen is generally consistent with studies of influentials in other communities, although the character of businesses represented is distinctive.⁵ There are few bankers or managers of larger corporate enterprises among local board members, most of whose businesses are of the local retail or service variety. Comparisons with other profiles of community influentials and of those highly active in their communities probably provide better indications of the special nature of Selective Service than do comparisons with the state's population, but both approaches are revealing.⁶ The underrepresentation of blue-collar workers is worth noting, for example, even though the proportion is not much different from the level of blue-collar civic activity usually found.

Similarly, while the educational level of board members is above that of the population, this is consistent with other findings to the effect that better-educated people take part disproportionately in civic affairs. The percentages in the lower educational categories are relatively high as a result of the generally advanced ages of local board members. Racial minorities are represented on all boards where the minority group constitutes at least 10 percent of the population. There are currently four such boards, and in each case the minority group is represented on the board in rough proportion to the population under the board's jurisdiction. This is certainly not true in all states.⁷

The civic and community activity of these local board members is very high. Consistent with our middle-class characterization, they are

---

⁵ One transcommunity study that may serve as the closest comparative work here is William V. D'Antonio, William H. Form, Charles P. Loomis, and Eugene Erickson, "Institutional and Occupational Representations in Eleven Community Influence Systems," *American Sociological Review,* XXVI (June, 1961), 440–446. This study compares six Southwestern U.S. cities and two Mexican cities with data from Floyd Hunter, *Community Power Structure* (Chapel Hill : University of North Carolina Press, 1954), and Delbert C. Miller, "Industry and Community Power Structure : A Comparative Study of an English and an American City," *American Sociological Review,* XXIII (February, 1958), 9–15. It finds businessmen dominant in all cities, with financiers and manufacturers well represented. It also notes the presence of newspaper editors along with lawyers, but our inquiry did not turn up a single member of any communications industry.

⁶ This approach of comparing the population under study both with the general population from which it is drawn and with the analogous special population in other communities is applied and discussed in Robert E. Agger, Daniel Goldrich, and Bert E. Swanson, *The Rulers and the Ruled* (New York : John Wiley & Sons, 1964), pp. 274–282. In the four communities there examined, lower classes were severely underrepresented, but at varying levels.

⁷ See *Report of the National Advisory Commission on Selective Service* (Washington, D.C. : Government Printing Office, 1967), Table 1.8, p. 80.

Table 3

SELECTED CHARACTERISTICS OF LOCAL BOARD MEMBERS, COMPARED TO STATE POPULATION

Characteristic	Local board members	State population [a]
OCCUPATION [b]		
Managerial, sales	26%	16%
Self-employed, not professional	13	3
Professional		
lawyers	4	7
others	2	
Government	10	9
Post office employees	8	
Education	4	1
Agriculture	23	14
Blue-collar workers	10	47
	100%	97%
	N = 314	N = 1,011,324
EDUCATION		
Less than high school	19%	61% [c]
High school graduate	33	23

[a] Proportions reconstructed from occupational detail on male labor force, 1960 census (3 percent not reported).

[b] Occupational categories were shaped to fit the pattern found, e.g., post office employees are listed separately because of the relatively high number found. Our impression is that this is due to the propensity of Selective Service personnel to seek

most active in church affairs, then in veterans', fraternal, and business and professional associations. Indeed, the levels of associational memberships, activity in community affairs, and public office-holding reported by these local board members suggest that they are thoroughly embedded in the social and political structures of their communities. If level of activity in these three dimensions is any measure, we would have to class them as "influentials" in their communities.[8]

[8] The identification of "influentials" is itself a subject of academic disagreement. The inventory of the literature made by Wendell Bell, Richard J. Hill, and Charles R. Wright, *Public Leadership* (San Francisco: Chandler Publishing Co., 1961),

SELECTED CHARACTERISTICS OF LOCAL BOARD MEMBERS, COMPARED TO STATE POPULATION

Characteristic	Local board members	State population [a]
Some college	26	8
College graduate	10	8 [d]
College graduate plus	12	
	100%	100%
	$N = 314$	$N = 1,068,342$
VETERAN STATUS		
Nonveteran	38%	63% [e]
World War I	16	5
World War II	37	19
Korea	4	7
Other	3	6
W.W.I and II	1	not given
No response	1	
	100%	100%
	$N = 314$	$N = 1,342,416$

names for new local board members from the local postmaster, frequently finding success at the first stop.

[c] Based on 1960 Census, which uses male population over 25 years old as base.

[d] This figure represents 4 or more years college completed.

[e] Based on 1960 Census, which uses male population over 14 years old as its base.

In an attempt to measure the extent of involvement of local board members in community social and political life, we asked respondents to list the groups or associations to which they belonged, the public offices (elective and appointive) which they had held, and to indicate the extent to which they had been active in each of the various stated forms of com-

---

employs five approaches to the study of leaders : positional, social participation, reputational, opinion leadership, and decision-making or event analysis. Local board members would appear to qualify by either of the first two definitions; we do not wish to solve the problem by definition, but rely on subsequent evidence to strengthen what may at this point appear to be an assumption.

munity activities.⁹ Table 4 shows that local board members are quite remarkable joiners : more than half belong to three or more voluntary associations, and there were as many board members who belonged to seven or more groups as belonged to none! This activity seems the more noteworthy in the light of national data indicating that a very small proportion of adults in the United States belong to two or more associations.¹⁰ The groups to which board members belong are geographically localized groups that normally participate in the daily public life of their communities. Absent from their lists are reform groups, unorthodox associations, minority group organizations, and unions.

Our measures of activity were designed to supplement the mere listing of memberships and provide some sense of the intensity of engagement in community affairs. The data in Table 6 confirm that local board

---

⁹ The questions asked were : "To what groups or associations do you belong? (please include civic, veterans, religious, business, and fraternal groups)." "Have you held any public office other than that of draft board member? If so, please state what office(s) (include elective offices and appointive offices, such as mayor, city council, county board, school board, postmaster, county agent, etc.)." "Please indicate the extent to which you have been active in each of the following community service activities :" (followed by list in order shown in Table 4).

¹⁰ While authorities differ, it seems clear that the number of memberships held by these board members is distinctive. A comparison of recent studies of the U.S. adult population is illustrative :

Number of Memberships	Wisconsin Local Board Members 1966	U.S. Adults 1960 ᵃ	U.S. Adults 1954 ᵇ	U.S. Adults 1955 ᶜ
None	5%	43%	45%	64%
One	14	25	30	20
Two	22	14	16	9
Three or more	59	18	9	7
	100%	100%	100%	100%
	N = 314	N = 970	N = 2000	N = 2379

ᵃ Gabriel Almond and Sidney Verba, *The Civic Culture* (Princeton : Princeton University Press, 1963), p. 264.
ᵇ American Institute of Public Opinion survey.
ᶜ National Opinion Research Center survey.
Both surveys are reported in Murray Hausknecht, *The Joiners : A Sociological Description of Voluntary Association Membership in the United States* (New York : Bedminster Press, 1962), p. 23. While local board members are all males, and males show slightly higher incidence of associational memberships, this can hardly account for these totals.

Table 4

NUMBER OF GROUPS TO WHICH BOARD MEMBERS BELONG

Number of groups to which members belong	Percentage of board members giving this answer
None	5%
1 or 2	37
3 or 4	33
5 or more	25
	100%
	$N = 314$

SOURCE: For the question from which the data are taken, see footnote 10 to the text.

Table 5

TYPES OF GROUPS TO WHICH BOARD MEMBERS BELONG

Types of groups to which board members belong	Percentage of board members belonging	Percentage of U.S. adult population with such membership, 1960
Church and religious	60%	19%
Veteran	46	6
Fraternal	39	13
Business and professional	35	8
Community service	21	14
Service clubs	17	
Social and recreational	13	13
Farm	12	3
Unions	3	15

Totals exceed 100% because of multiple memberships.

SOURCE: National data drawn from Gabriel Almond and Sidney Verba, *The Civic Culture* (Princeton: Princeton University Press, 1963), p. 247. Entry under our "community service" combines their "charitable" and "civic-political" categories. All other categories in the two studies bore the same labels.

members are highly involved in church and religious affairs, as was suggested by the membership data. Other public service activities follow closely, but politics is comparatively low on the list. It appears that local board members are active and probably influential members of their communities but not the openly partisan office-holding types.

Table 6

COMMUNITY ACTIVITY OF LOCAL BOARD MEMBERS

Activity [a]	"Fairly often active"	"Occasionally active"	"Never active"	No response [b]	
Youth work	36%	27%	14%	23%	(100%)
Charity work	43	35	7	15	(100%)
Church affairs	58	23	7	12	(100%)
Service clubs	32	20	26	22	(100%)
Politics	21	26	32	21	(100%)
Business and professional	26	23	29	22	(100%)
					N=314

[a] Higher percentages in regard to activity than in memberships (Table 5) are assumed to be the result of the cumulative nature of the question which is the basis of this Table and the fact that some of these activities would not require group membership.

[b] "No response" category was created to distinguish these respondents from the more convincing affirmative indications in the "Never" column, but lack of response is assumed to be the equivalent of "never" in most instances.

The remarkably high proportion of two-thirds of the board members have had some form of public office experience. Relatively few members, however, have held partisan or elective office: as Table 7 shows, their offices were mostly appointive or "good government" or nonpartisan type offices. Interviews suggest that State Selective Service Headquarters attempts to avoid involvement of its personnel and operations in partisan politics whenever possible. It seeks instead "the right kind of people," who turn out to be the civically active merchants and managers.

Our developing composite portrait of the local board member as a white-collar civically active joiner may be sharpened somewhat by comparing boards in varying social and economic contexts. Not unexpectedly, rural board members differ from urban board members in background characteristics and degree of involvement in their communities. The urban boards reflect the industrial occupations of their areas, and also have more attorneys and other professionals, higher levels of education, and a number of Negroes proportionate to Negro population in the major city of the

Table 7

PUBLIC OFFICES HELD BY LOCAL BOARD MEMBERS

Type of office held [a]	Percentage of all respondents ($N = 314$) who report having held this office
County Board	13%
City Council	9
School Board	26
Appointive boards	18
Post Office	6
Civil Service	5
Other public office [b]	32

[a] Of these offices, only the County Board is normally filled by partisan election, and in several counties there is no contest in the final election. City Councils are normally nonpartisan, although this may be only form in some cases. School Boards, while elective, are almost always nonpartisan in fact as well as form.

[b] These positions include a wide variety of employment such as County Veterans' Service Officer, public utility engineer, state employees, and local government employees.

state. Outside the highly urbanized areas, there is not much difference in board members' backgrounds. And there is little difference between urban and rural boards as to the age of members, length of service, veteran status, or number of organizational memberships.

There are some noticeable differences between urban and rural board members that are not quite so predictable as those so far noted. For example, although there are no differences in the number of groups to which members belong, nor any differences in the proportion who are veterans, there is a distinctly greater tendency for rural members to be members of veterans' organizations. Table 8 points up the fact that only 28 percent of urban members are members of veterans' groups while twice that many, or 57 percent, of rural members are; we surmise that the local veterans' groups are instruments of recruitment in rural areas but not in the urban areas, although veteran status is still thought desirable in the urban areas.

Another decisive difference may be noted in regard to the public office experience of board members. Rural board members are much more likely to have held public office, perhaps reflecting the relatively larger number of offices available to capable and active members of the rural community. This effect is particularly noticeable in regard to that office most commonly held by draft board members, namely the School Board. There are relatively many urban residents per available School Board office, of course, and this is part of the explanation for low public office experience. The urban board member may be as active, but his activity probably takes more of a youth work, charity, or professional orientation and less of a community-governing form. Aside from these differences the profile of board membership shows considerable homogeneity across the state. This might well be expected under a self-perpetuating and standardized recruiting system.

There is another difference between urban and rural board members that warrants attention. Our data make it very clear that a local draft board is a "little group of neighbors" in rural areas and in small towns, but not in cities. This is indicated by the figures in Table 8, which show

Table 8

DIFFERENCES BETWEEN URBAN AND RURAL LOCAL BOARD MEMBERS, SELECTED CHARACTERISTICS

Characteristic	Degree of urbanization			
	City (95% urban)	Small city (40–70% urban)	Small town (20–39% urban)	Rural (below 20% urban)
Membership in veterans' groups	28%	45%	44%	57%
Public office held	28	59	62	83
School Board service	0	21	28	38
Contact with registrants[a]				
frequent	3	15	19	13
occasional	26	47	55	48
rare, never[b]	72	37	26	39
	N = 39	N = 71	N = 100	N = 84

[a] Measured by response to question, "Some Local Board members frequently see registrants or get phone calls from them. Others hardly ever have contact with registrants except at Board meetings. Would you say that you have contact with registrants (either in person or by phone) Rarely—Occasionally—Frequently—?"
[b] Includes negligible number of nonresponses, which are taken to be negative answers.

that members of large city boards are not nearly as likely to have frequent contact with their registrants as members of rural or small town boards. And members of large city boards are much more likely to say they rarely or never have contact with their registrants.

We think this difference between city and noncity boards is important since one of the rationales for the local board is that its members know the local men and their situations. It may well be that in the small towns of America this is the case, but we doubt that it is true in urban America. Our data indeed suggest that the rapid urbanization of America has substantially negated one of the basic justifications for the local board system of conscription.

In addition to the size of the population in a local board area there are other variables that are related to frequency of contact with registrants. They are, as might be expected, length of service on the board, public office experience, and number of organization memberships. In brief, board members who have been on the board over five years are more likely to have frequent contact with registrants than members who have been on less than five years, and they are less likely to say they rarely or never have contact. Doubtless this is so because the longer a man serves the more likely it is that registrants will know he is on the draft board. Board members with public office experience are also somewhat more likely to have frequent contact with registrants than members without such experience, and less likely to say they never have contact. One explanation for this fact is probably that men in public life are more likely to be known and identified as draft board members than men who are not so exposed to public view. It may also be that men in public life find registrant contact more acceptable. They are probably more accustomed to citizen and voter contact. Finally, men who belong to several organizations are more likely to have frequent contact than men in none or only a single organization, probably because they are better known and more exposed.

In this section, we have reviewed findings that appear to reflect at least three different perspectives on local board members. We saw them as civically active men representing the social and political structures of their communities; as a special type of locally based public official exercising control of a national function; and as a body of men operating in the context of community expectations and pressures and serving to link their localities with the rest of the nation. These are complementary, not mutually exclusive, perspectives that help to give depth and meaning to our findings.

In each of these approaches to an understanding of the part played by local board members in their communities across the state, we would draw distinctions between urban and rural contexts. In our assessment of who served on boards, we noted that the activities of board members gave indications that they were community influentials, but this would have to be qualified by adding that the evidence is strong that in rural areas they are much closer to the governing function than in urban areas. We do not draw our tentative conclusions about status as influentials from mere memberships in community organizations, but also from levels of activity in various civic affairs and the striking incidence of public offices held. We saw that partisan politics was not as frequent a form of activity as nonpartisan public service type activity. The primary source of board members, perpetuated through the described recruitment patterns, is the local business community : local merchants and managers in rural areas and white-collar men in the urban.

In looking at rural local boards and their environment one is reminded of the conditions described in *Small Town in Mass Society*.[11] One finds, as in Springdale, the self-image of neighborliness and self-reliance, the domination of the community by small businessmen, and an unrecognized but pervasive politics. As might be expected in a Springdale, in some rural areas the draft has been converted (perhaps unconsciously) into part of the social control system of the community. Some board members will promptly and enthusiastically reclassify a man when a change in his status coincides with a violation of community norms—as in the case of failure to keep up child support payments, leaving one's family, or not getting a job in timely fashion.

The complexity of the urban environment means that urban members are not only more removed from their registrants but also from participation in public affairs. They have a different background of associational activity and more professional backgrounds to draw on for what

[11] Arthur J. Vidich and Joseph Bensman, *Small Town in Mass Society* (Garden City, N.Y. : Doubleday & Co., 1958), especially Chap. 2 and pp. 111, 136, and 104. The extent of the conflict between assumption and reality is emphasized in Maurice Stein, *The Eclipse of Community* (Princeton : Princeton University Press, 1960), pp. 289–294.

we have hypothesized to be more impersonal, standardized application of deferment and classification policies. They are not representatives of the major influentials in the large city; they are anonymous, and for the most part invisible.[12]

As public officials, these local board members were distinguished by their age and length of service. A very large proportion of them had some other kind of public office experience, of a similar nonpolitical kind; again, urban members were low in this experience but still far above the average for the population. Almost to a man, they gained strong satisfactions from their service, perhaps because it served as a means for them as individuals to feel more fully involved in the larger society. Their very low turnover and their large number of other localized activities and memberships leads to the impression that draft boards become the permanent property of these lifetime residents; in this way they become the managers of the national government's function. Once again, we are reminded of Springdale, this time in regard to the way in which local political forces took over the making and administration of agricultural policy. The takeover in the urban area is more individualized and less systematic. As participation in a governmental function, the only near parallels are in OPA or TVA.

Positions on the local boards seem to be part of a network of similarly nonpartisan offices with overlapping occupancies distributed among active members of the community. They do not appear to be "first offices" for the advancement of public careers, and this plus the strict avoidance of partisan politics practiced in the recruitment process seems to assure that partisan politicians will not be found on boards.[13] We may reasonably hypothesize that the motivations of these men will be distinguishable from those that send other men into elective public offices.[14] We know of no studies that compare the background characteristics and motivations

---

[12] We have found no community power study or other work from the fields of political science or sociology that includes draft board members.

[13] The concept of "first offices" is drawn from Joseph A. Schlesinger, *Ambition and Politics: Political Careers in the United States* (Chicago: Rand McNally, 1966), pp. 176–181.

[14] For a distinction between the motivations of those who seek elective office and those who seek appointive office—in this case the school board—*see* Rufus P. Browning and Herbert Jacob, "Power Motivation and the Political Personality," *Public Opinion Quarterly,* XXVIII (Spring, 1964), 75–90, especially 86–87.

of appointive, nonpartisan officeholders such as these across several communities, and the existing literature suggests obliquely that the explanation for the appearance of these particular characteristics among local board members probably lies in some configuration of the opportunity patterns,[15] social structure,[16] political cultures,[17] and motivational contexts within communities.[18]

In the third approach, we see local boards as entities or groups of men operating in a way not always understood by their communities but thoroughly conditioned by community expectations as they are felt by board members. As do some other public officials, board members tend to feel that the public does not understand or appreciate the work they do; they are acutely aware of the public's scrutiny, however, and take actions in particular ways for the sake of appearances. They are defensive with outsiders and the press because of the damage that misinformation may do to their self-image (which they would like to project out to the public) of fairness and scrupulous adherence to policy set from above. When registrants are present for personal appearances, board members try to see that all procedures are correctly followed, but they still pride themselves in rural areas on being able to make decisions based on their personal and extraofficial knowledge of the registrant; in many boards, the member who knows the registrant best will be granted deference in the decision.

Members are sufficiently well known in rural areas that they may be informally requested by local employers to act in particular ways. Boards are authorized to permit employers to appear with registrants who are seeking occupational deferment, and many employers regularly do. Farm

---

[15] See Schlesinger, *op. cit.,* Chap. V, especially p. 50.

[16] Linton C. Freeman, Warner Bloomberg, Jr., Stephen P. Koff, Morris H. Sunchine, and Thomas J. Fararo, *Local Community Leadership* (Syracuse, N.Y.: Syracuse University, University College Paper No. 15, 1960), make some useful suggestions about the relationship between societal complexity and specialization of leadership in several communities.

[17] In a forthcoming work based partly on empirical studies of four of the cities from which these local board members were drawn, Robert Alford makes the case for the relevance of political culture.

[18] The data on which this paper is based are part of a larger study including opinion samples from clientele groups and the general public as well as more detailed data on jurisdiction of boards. See Davis and Dolbeare, *Little Groups of Neighbors: The Selective Service System* (Chicago: Markham, 1968).

organizations are probably the groups most frequently urging particular concerns upon boards, while teachers are the type of local registrant whose deferral or induction is most clearly a matter of general public concern. (Many of the decisions that rural boards have to make on occupational deferments, of course, concern men who have left the community some years before and are now working in some industrial area at a job whose characteristics and necessity to the national interest are unknown to the members.) Local board decisions are thus high in impact on their local communities and local perception of this is readily conveyed back to the board members. The result for some boards is to lean heavily on guidance from State Headquarters as a means of avoiding the onus of responsibility, and paradoxically for some others to take special pride in their independent discretionary behavior. In either case, the local board is one more means—and a relatively intimate one—of bringing national government actions, policies, and demands down to the level of the local community. In rural areas, the link is open and highly visible; in urban areas, the public may remain quite unaware both of the selection of its young men and of the processes by which they are selected.

Attitudes of local board members toward Selective Service

Perhaps more significant than the social profile of local board members is an analysis of their attitudes toward specific deferment policies and other aspects of Selective Service. We sought to measure attitudes toward the desirability of deferring certain groups of men through responses to the question, "How important do you think it is that each of the following be deferred from the draft?" To some extent, responses reflected current deferment policies, but the variations suggested that individual opinion was being sounded effectively. Table 9 presents these data.

It is clear that board members have little use for the conscientious objector. They are lowest in the "very important" category and highest in the "should not be deferred" category. No doubt this partially reflects the inordinate amount of time board members must invest in personal appearances for registrants who do not meet the statutory limitations for objector

Table 9

ATTITUDES OF LOCAL BOARD MEMBERS TOWARD DEFERMENT OF VARIOUS TYPES OF REGISTRANTS[a]

Group	Very important to defer	Fairly important to defer	Should not defer	Depends	Don't know, no response	
Fathers	35	25	4	29	7	100
College students	23	32	10	30	5	100
Farmers	16	21	6	44	13	100
Graduate students	12	24	20	38	6	100
Married men	5	13	49	26	7	100
Conscientious objectors	5	7	55	24	9	100
						$N = 314$

[a] Responses were indicated by checkmarks under the appropriate heading in exactly this format. The question was phrased, "How important do you think it is that each of the following be deferred from the draft?"

status but who are still determined to fight their cases up through the appellate system to the courts. The complexity of the law and the facts in individual cases mean that appeals and litigation are quite probable, and so some boards tend to deny the claim as a regular practice and let the Appeals Board handle the case.

The effects of the policies and practices of 1966 regarding deferments are apparent in the general pattern of rankings as to importance of deferment. Scientists and fathers were deferrable, while marriage alone was not a basis for deferment; the large proportions in the "depends" category probably reflect the individualist orientation of the deferment standards, which require that each registrant establish facts warranting deferment classification. College student deferment was less automatic, and some board members appeared to have reservations about the practice. Graduate students, even though officially entitled to the same status as other students, were clearly considered less entitled to deferment. The heavy proportion in the "depends" category in regard to farmers was probably due to the elaborate criteria that have been set up in this state to measure productivity before granting an agricultural deferment.

We also sought to obtain board members' reactions to several evaluative statements about the operations of the Selective Service System. This was done by asking board members to indicate the extent of their agreement or disagreement with six variously worded (but frequently heard) comments about the System. Table 10 summarizes the responses to each statement.

The first four statements have to do with the relationships of the local board to higher authority within the System and seek to develop some sense of the realities behind the legal autonomy which local boards enjoy. Our assumption was that we could identify alternate patterns of self-reliance or guidance-seeking, the latter in order to reduce the tensions that accompany responsibility. We appear to have found that board members exhibit both at the same time, for they seek more precise policy statements and guidance at the same time as they value their discretion. In more detailed breakdowns it was possible to locate boards where one view or the other predominated, but we did not find that sharply different classification performance patterns resulted.

The last two statements in Table 10 represent two of the most frequently heard complaints about national deferment policies, and we wanted to learn how the board members felt on these issues. The context from which the board member responds to these statements is a combination of his own personal experience, his awareness of complaints, reading of national media, and the regular communications that he receives from the National Headquarters. The Selective Service System *Newsletter,* sent monthly to all board members, and other internal communications as well, tend to be rather defensive about complaints generally, and decidedly negative on these two points particularly.

In the light of the foregoing, it seems significant that a full 74 percent of board members see the Reserves and National Guard as, in effect, means of avoiding the draft. This is the greatest area of consensus in attitudes that we found anywhere in our analyses. Perhaps even more surprising is the fact that more board members agreed than disagreed that wealthier registrants were less likely to be inducted; the breakdown was

Table 10

LOCAL BOARD MEMBERS' RESPONSES TO EVALUATIVE STATEMENTS ABOUT THE SELECTIVE SERVICE SYSTEM

Statement	Response	
1. "Regulations and other policy statements from National and State Headquarters should be more specific, more detailed, and less vague."	21%	Agree strongly
	39	Agree
	16	Don't know, depends
	17	Disagree
	3	Disagree strongly
	4	No response
	100%	
	$N = 314$	
2. "State Headquarters personnel should provide more guidance so that Local Boards are not required to guess at what they should be doing."	15%	Agree strongly
	37	Agree
	20	Don't know, depends
	22	Disagree
	4	Disagree strongly
	2	No response
	100%	
	$N = 314$	
3. "The discretion which Local Boards have is a valuable factor in tailoring regulations to individual registrants' situations."	27%	Agree strongly
	51	Agree
	10	Don't know, depends
	6	Disagree
	2	Disagree strongly
	4	No response
	100%	
	$N = 314$	

47 percent to 40 percent, with 14 percent undecided or not responding. This judgment from such a source and in such a context lends significant support to the allegation; our own classification and selection data rather clearly indicate that the allegation is true, and that the cause lies in national deferment policies and not local board discretionary action.[19]

With this background in board members' attitudes, we may search out differences between types of board members and their expressed opin-

[19] James W. Davis and Kenneth M. Dolbeare, "Selective Service: Present Impact and Future Prospects," *Wisconsin Law Review*, 1967, pp. 892–913.

LOCAL BOARD MEMBERS' RESPONSES TO EVALUATIVE STATEMENTS ABOUT THE SELECTIVE SERVICE SYSTEM

Statement		Response	
4.	"Local Boards should be consistent in their judgments, even if it occasionally means that a borderline claim to deferment must be denied."	26% 42 17 12 1 2 --- 100% $N = 314$	Agree strongly Agree Don't know, depends Disagree Disagree strongly No response
5.	"The Reserves and National Guard are frequently a means whereby registrants successfully avoid the draft."	31% 43 11 10 3 2 --- 100% $N = 314$	Agree strongly Agree Don't know, depends Disagree Disagree strongly No response
6.	"Registrants from wealthier families are less likely to be inducted under present policies than registrants from less favored families."	17% 30 11 24 16 2 --- 100% $N = 314$	Agree strongly Agree Don't know, depends Disagree Disagree strongly No response

ions on various aspects of these questions. Even where correlations between background characteristics and attitudes are found, of course, we would still have to show the relevance to actual performance on the part of the board members in order to attach great significance to our findings. But this is the direction in which our analysis must head if it is to shed light on the reasons for particular local board actions, or if we wish to judge whether some recruitment practices are to be preferred over others. If board members' characteristics do not suggest something about their attitudes, or if attitudes themselves do not result in particular classification or induction actions, then we may dispense with this inquiry except for the intellectual satisfaction of having acquired certain facts.

There are not many striking variations in board members' opinions that are traceable to background characteristics. Certain correlations, however, as well as some of our negative findings, are directly relevant to the issue of what difference it makes who serves on local boards. We found a distinct association between the extent of board members' education and their attitudes toward deferment of college students and graduate students. Table 11 eliminates "don't know" responses and presents attitudes by educational attainment. Those who are themselves college graduates or who have had some graduate training are much more likely to attach some degree of importance to student deferment and much less likely to be opposed to such deferments. The same pattern of attitudes exists in regard to graduate student deferment although in less decisive form.

We found another minor example of board members' "looking out for their own" in regard to agricultural deferments. Members of farm organizations were more likely to think farm deferments are very important than other rural board members and even than other unorganized farmers generally. In absolute numbers there are relatively few farm deferments in the state, however, so that this could have little impact in any event.

The negative side of our findings appears to be revealing in itself. Such factors as age, length of service, occupations, public office experi-

Table 11

ATTITUDES TOWARD STUDENT DEFERMENT BY EDUCATION LEVEL OF LOCAL BOARD MEMBERS

Attitude toward student deferment	Educational level			
	Less than high school	High school graduate	Some college	College graduate and graduate training
Very important	24%	23%	23%	29%
Fairly important	25	31	30	49
Should not defer	21	11	12	2
Depends	30	35	35	20
	100%	100%	100%	100%
	$N = 59$	$N = 97$	$N = 77$	$N = 66$

ence, and organizational membership or activity seemed to have no systematic effect on attitudes in the areas we have discussed. Not even veteran status, which we had expected to correlate with stricter attitudes toward deferments, gave rise to any clear contrast with nonveteran attitudes. Nor did the attitudes of those most active in church affairs show any greater sympathy for the conscientious objector than the inactive members; only tenths of a percentage point difference between the two groups was visible in most categories.

The implication of these largely negative findings is that, in general, the background that a member brings to local board service does not carry over into clear distinctions as to his attitudes toward deferments and other aspects of the draft. Of course, we have not probed every attitude that may be relevant, but we have touched upon enough to lead us to this tentative conclusion. We have noted only one major and one minor exception. These limited (though still probably important) differences in attitudes suggest that board members have developed considerable consistency of viewpoint during their service on their boards. Perhaps, considering the nature of the recruitment processes, they already shared many of the same views before they came on their boards.

Our negative findings were largely repeated when we examined the relationship between local board area variables (percentage urbanized, median income, and the like) and the attitudes of local board members. There were two exceptions, but hardly major ones. One exception, which is shown in Table 12, was that board members in poorer areas were more

Table 12

RESPONSE BY INCOME LEVEL OF BOARD AREA TO QUESTION: *"Registrants from wealthier families are less likely to be inducted under present policies than registrants from less favored families."*

Response of local board member	Income level of board area	
	Under $5000	$5000 and over
Agree and agree strongly	54%	38%
Don't know, depends	9	13
Disagree and disagree strongly	34	47
No response	3	2
	100%	100%
	$N = 179$	$N = 135$

likely to think that the well-to-do could avoid the draft than were board members in richer areas. This finding is particularly interesting in view of the fact, reported in another paper, that the burden of service does fall more heavily on poorer people.[20] The perception (or prejudice) of board members in poorer areas is more accurate than the perception of board members in richer areas. Why? Perhaps one reason is that board members in richer areas may be less willing to perceive and admit that the well-to-do get off. It is easier for them, more satisfying, to believe that the draft bears equally on all and does not have economic bias built into its deferment policy. Members of boards in poorer areas, on the other hand, are confronted with the reality of having to classify men I-A because no alternative classification is available. They know whom they are taking : men not going to college.

But granted the differences between board members in richer areas and poorer areas it is also true that a third of the members in poorer areas thought that the wealthy did not get off and over a third in richer areas thought that they did. Perhaps the simplest way to account for this disparity is the lack of data in the Selective Service System concerning its economic impact. Local board members have little beyond their own eyes and their own hunches to tell them who is being drafted and they have no knowledge of any but their own local board. It is no wonder that there is disagreement among men in comparable economic areas, given this situation.

We found one other revealing attitudinal difference, this time reflecting urbanization differences. Board members from cities proved to be distinctly more sympathetic to conscientious objectors than were rural board members. In the urban areas, 26 percent of board members felt that it was fairly important or very important to defer conscientious objectors, while 39 percent thought they should not be deferred; in the most rural areas, only 4 percent could see it as fairly or very important, while 7 percent said they should not be deferred. Perhaps this reflects the greater experience of urban boards with such claims, but it suggests that tolerance of the unorthodox is significantly higher in the city.

We have noted some differences in attitudes of board members that

---

[20] *Ibid.*

seem to correlate with their backgrounds and life experiences, but for the most part we have seen homogeneity of attitude within the organization. The recruitment processes or the socialization effects of service on local boards seem to have led to the development of generally shared views toward the System and its operations. This analysis does not preclude the possibility of the existence of sharply deviant individual boards, but it does suggest that such would be an exception rather than the rule.

This finding that boards are not widely variant attitudinally is of major significance when we come to an effort to understand why variation in performance is so great. It says in effect that the major cause of intrastate variation in classification and induction must be the nature of national deferment policies themselves and the differential ways in which they bear upon the different types of board jurisdictions.[21]

Conclusion

In his prepared testimony before a subcommittee of the House Appropriations Committee, General Hershey described local boards as "little groups of neighbors."[22] This paper has tried to go beyond that characterization and to describe in some detail the membership of local boards. One of our main conclusions is that draft boards, if they are anything, are little groups of local notables. The local board is one of the groups to which local community leaders gravitate. On the basis of our research we cannot say what effect this has on the operations of the system. But we can wonder whether the local board concept is viable. Local boards are clearly not representative of all segments of the community, to say nothing of being representative of those affected by the law.[23] So far are board members from being "neighbors" that, in cities, board members rarely if ever have contact with registrants outside of board meetings.

The local board system is presumably an attempt to obtain local par-

---

[21] *Ibid.*
[22] Hearings before a Subcommittee of the Committee on Appropriations, House of Representatives, 89th Congress, 2nd sess., February 1, 1966; see prepared testimony, p. 19.
[23] This point is illustrated most forcefully in some Southern states in which there was not a *single* Negro on *any* local board in 1966.

ticipation in the execution of national policy. But our data show that local participation is likely to mean only participation by the influential if not the dominant members of the community. Our data provide an enlightening illustration of one form of participatory democracy : it may not be too much to say that the local board system allows local elites to execute policies that bear most heavily on the nonelites.

A major theme of this paper is the contrast between the "little groups of neighbors" image of Selective Service purveyed by the System and apparent reality. In the past, because not much attention was directed at the operations of Selective Service, the contrast passed unnoticed. But as Selective Service receives more attention the divergence between image and reality will be noticed; perhaps the contrast may be a force for change—both in the reality and in the image.

Decision-making in local boards: a case study

GARY L. WAMSLEY

THE ANNUAL Report of the Director of Selective Service for 1965 states: "The 4,016 local boards are the basic units where the fundamental operations of the System are performed." [1] This chapter seeks to present and analyze empirical observations of local board behavior in one metropolitan area.

After the disastrous draft riots of the Civil War, the Report of the Provost Marshal General recommended an educational policy to bring the people to a more rational view of the nature and necessity of the draft. The report did not specifically recommend civilian boards as a means of doing this.[2] The idea evolved naturally in the planning of the 1917 System by Provost Marshal General Enoch Crowder. Though little-noted at the time, the move was later hailed as the major reason conscription was accepted.[3] This move had great symbolic meaning in the America of

[1] *Annual Report of the Director of Selective Service 1965* (Washington, D.C.: Government Printing Office, 1966), p. 8.
[2] *Final Report of the Provost Marshal General*, Vol. II, pp. 1–50.
[3] David A. Lockmiller, "Enoch H. Crowder: Soldier, Lawyer, Statesman 1859–1932," *The University of Missouri Studies,* Vol. 27 (Special Number, 1955), pp. 54 and 153.

1917. E. A. Fitzpatrick, who was director of Selective Service in Wisconsin during World War I, makes clear by his eloquence the powerful symbolism of the boards.

> The civilians were neighbors. They were, as it were, indigenous to the soil. The men were well-known in the neighborhood. They were often personal friends or family friends of the men who were to be sent to war. They had the intimate knowledge of family histories and of individual histories.[4]

Within the conceptions of authority current in 1917 boards of "friends and neighbors" seemed to legitimate the decisions entailed in conscription. This study focuses on the operation of local boards in the changed social and political context of 1966.

Access

This study is based on interviews and observation of Selective Service operations between March and October, 1966. During these six months, research was conducted at National Headquarters, the State Headquarters, and among seventeen local boards of a metropolitan area I shall call Hill City.

Hill City is a city usually considered to be Eastern but with many of the characteristics of the Midwest. It is a center of heavy industry and transportation. Hill City's population is a little over a half million and the population of the metropolitan area numbers two and a half million.

Initial negative contacts with Selective Service gave way to permissive access when my status as a captain in the Air Force Reserve was made known. Whether this was the key to access is not certain, but persons at all levels seemed aware of my military status and the impression was unavoidable that it facilitated interviews.

I was permitted to conduct any interviews, observe any proceedings, and to see any materials except the confidential files of registrants. All clerks were interviewed at least once. My constant presence soon led to interaction beyond the level of interviews, and I was largely accepted as

[4] E. A. Fitzpatrick, *Conscription and America* (Milwaukee: Richards Publishing Co., 1940), pp. 46–47.

a normal part of the clerks' environment. All interviews and observations made in a day were placed on tape or written from memory and notes.

Boards were observed simply on the basis of which board was scheduled to meet. For this reason research was conducted among all of the boards, but the actual meetings of only nine were observed, some of them more than once. Limitation of time eventually forced a decision as to whether or not to observe all 17 boards at least once. It was felt that a point had been reached where no new understanding of board decisions was being gained. Since the research at the local board level was only part of a larger analysis and since full coverage of the boards would not alter inherent limitations of method and sample, it was decided to expend research effort at other levels.

The search for purpose

The function of Selective Service is to procure military manpower. But what is the specific purpose of the boards as decision-making mechanisms? Selective Service regulations quite clearly state that they are to make military manpower procurement decisions so as to provide for the "maintenance of the national health, safety, or interest."[5] While the responsibility is clearly indicated, the means of meeting it are not at all clear. It is most easily met in a war of total mobilization. It is least disruptive when men are plentiful and world tensions low. It can be most difficult in times of partial mobilization and contention over the "rightness" of the war.

In addition, the board is supposed to adjust the processes of the draft to the individual and his circumstances. Boards have had to alter their thinking after years of manpower surplus during which they sought to rationalize deferments by saying that they were "channeling" men into occupations in the national health, safety, or interest.[6] Boards observed in this study spent the preponderance of their time arguing about, discussing, and puzzling over the concrete meaning of "national health, safety, or in-

[5] *Code of Federal Regulations,* 1622.25, 1622.22.
[6] *Review of the Organization and Administration of Selective Service System,* Hearings before the Committee on Armed Services, House of Representatives, 89th Congress, 2nd sess., 1966, p. 9622.

terest." The words were used constantly in granting or refusing deferments, and registrants were often asked to show how their deferment would be in the national health, safety, or interest. Letters were built around the theme of national interest by companies having continuous contact with boards in seeking occupational deferments. An example was an air brake company seeking deferment for an employee, which wrote:

> Braking systems for railroads and mass transit systems have been judged as essential to the welfare and safety of the nation and our contribution as a primary supplier has been considered vital for Selective Service purposes. Local boards have consistently granted the appropriate occupational deferment for our technical people.[7]

Although Selective Service was willing to take credit for the "fruits" of a national manpower policy that did not officially exist, when criticized for not making that policy explicit and applying it uniformly by better guidance to boards, it retreated to the older implied function of boards—adjustment of process to the individual on the basis of intimate knowledge of him and his environs. For example, in defending the lack of any official definition of a full- or part-time student, General Hershey said:

> That is one of the reasons why the local boards could do things I could never do here, and nobody else could do because they know whether that is truth, and they know enough about him to know whether he is putting something over on them.[8]

The uncertainty as to the proper purpose of the boards was felt by the board members. In observing boards over a six-month period, it seemed that the frustration of the members over the lack of clear purpose increased markedly as calls remained high, requests for interviews mounted, and letter requests for deferments were received. Typical excerpts from discussions are:

> BOARD MEMBER A (looking at a letter): Here's a guy who's working on hydraulic pumps—an engineer. Company says it builds pumps for sewage treatment plants and for drainage systems in missile complexes—

[7] Observation Report No. 27.
[8] *Review of the Organization and Administration of Selective Service System*, p. 9694.

Decision-making in local boards : a case study   87

> therefore, deferment requested because the job of the man is in the national health, safety, and interest.
> BOARD MEMBER B : Sewage plants! Aw c'mon—the national health?
> BOARD MEMBER A : Hell, how do we know; maybe our national health is in jeopardy. How do they expect us to know?
> BOARD MEMBER C : Yeah (with sarcasm). Can't let our missiles get wet either—have enough trouble getting them to light as it is.[9]

Or the remark of a new member, attending his first meeting :

> NEW MEMBER : I'd like to ask a question if I might. We're supposed to decide these cases on the basis of whether deferment is in the national health, safety, or interest?
> CHAIRMAN : Yes. That's what the regulations say.
> NEW MEMBER : How can we do that?
> CHAIRMAN : Well, you get the hang of it after a while. You see, it's sort of like an accordion. Sometimes you stretch it out and get generous with deferments and then other times you squeeze it up tight.
> NEW MEMBER : Well, I guess I've got a lot to learn. ...[10]

Perplexity and frustration were not confined to the new members. One member with twenty-four years' service, after a forty-minute discussion of a case, exploded :

> If they expect us to decide what's in the national health, safety, and interest, why in the hell don't they give us something we can make a decision on—something in writing. They tell us one damn thing and then another and it's always "Headquarters says." Let's turn this down and if they don't like it, let Headquarters appeal it.[11]

Thus, although board members were expected to decide cases on the basis of national health, safety, and interest, they lacked adequate information to make such decisions efficiently. The Critical Skills List, published in 1955, was not used at meetings by any of the boards in this study.[12] On two occasions members asked the Clerk if an occupation was on the list, but most clerks never used the list, though they had heard of

[9] Observation Report No. 15.
[10] Observation Report No. 7.
[11] Observation Report No. 32.
[12] *Selective Service Operations Bulletin,* No. 228.

it. Members' decisions were based on what they had read or heard in the news, what they believed the national interest should be, and what they knew from their own experience or occupation.

During this study, I saw no instance in which board members knew a registrant or his family.[13] Board members took pride in knowing the physical area of their jurisdiction. When a registrant appeared before a board, he was first asked where he lived or worked. Board members then proceeded to discuss this location until they had pinpointed it sufficiently for one of them to announce that he "knew where it was." Clerks often spoke of how their board members "knew their areas," but, with only one exception, when questioned the clerks revealed that they did not mean a knowledge of the registrant, his family, or personal circumstances.

Upon comparing addresses with jurisdiction lines it became evident that fully one-third of all the board members in this study did not live within the jurisdictions of their boards:

Total board members for 17 boards	74
Members residing in their jurisdictions	50
Members not residing in jurisdictions	18
Members not residing in their jurisdictions but in a location that could be loosely construed as "in the area"	6

A major departure from the "friends and neighbor" concept was found in a board covering a Negro neighborhood. There were no Negro members on the board and none of the members lived in the jurisdiction. The chairman was the only member who could be said to live near the jurisdiction. He lived in perhaps the last "all-white block" to be found near the neighborhood, and had stated on numerous occasions that he would resign before allowing a Negro to sit on the board.

Perhaps the passing of the time when a local board could know the registrant and his personal condition was best pointed up by a clerk who was asked if board members knew many of the registrants. She replied:

> Oh, no. They're familiar with the district, but they don't know the kids that come in. You know the induction notices used to read—"Your friends and neighbors have selected you"—and it got so it made people

---

[13] From clerks and boards there were occasional stories (perhaps 10) of cases in which members knew registrants. Usually the instances were during World War II.

so mad that they dropped it. One fellow came in here boiling mad and said "Who are these friends and neighbors? I want to see them right now!" [14]

The clerks and decisions

The clerks often described themselves with some accuracy as part clerk, social worker, top sergeant, policeman, recruiter, and substitute parent. They were overwhelmingly women, mature in years, with a devotion to their work that was incredible.[15] They comprised an insulated and relatively autonomous personnel system within the Selective Service System.[16] The clerks were in positions of far greater responsibility and power than most of them would have expected to achieve given their socioeconomic background, educational level, or their salary of $4,600.[17] They were immersed in their roles and dedicated to their work. Many worked late into the night and on weekends, despite low pay, a lack of in-grade pay increases, no overtime, and more compensatory time built up than they could ever be permitted to use.

Congressman Chet Holifield of California said during the draft hearings:

> The Civil Service Commission clerks are running these boards, not the members ... the bulk of the work, I would say 85 per cent of the work of screening and classifying these boys are done by Civil Service clerks and then when the board meets that night, they hand it to them and they run through them and the clerk says "this bunch on the top ought to go" so they sign their names and they go. In many instances we are not achieving the principle that we thought we were achieving of having local businessmen and leaders in the community express evaluative judgment on the merits of specific cases. It is being done by low-paygrade clerks.[18]

[14] Interview No. 8; the form was SS 252, printing date of 1951.
[15] Sixteen of the 17 in our study were women. See also Hearings before the Subcommittee on Civil Service, House of Representatives, 89th Congress, 2nd sess., 1966, p. 6.
[16] The other systems are the Reserve and National Guard officers who staff State and National Headquarters, and the board members.
[17] This is an average figure for the nation. See Hearings before the Subcommittee on Civil Service, p. 9.
[18] *Review of the Organization and Administration of Selective Service System*, p. 9764.

Does this study support Holifield's conclusions? Basically, the answer is yes. The role of the clerks is far more significant than spokesmen for the system admit, but some explanations and qualifications will show that role to be a great deal less important than critics imply.

First, the volume of classifications was so great that a board could not possibly handle them all, let alone review each one extensively. However, the records did not valuate whether a classification action had required discussion or had been reviewed by a board. There was no requirement that board members sign board actions, although clerks were urged to get their signatures. Clerks usually saw to it that potentially controversial cases were signed by at least one board member; nonetheless the claim that "the power to classify rests solely with the boards" seems to have meaning only in symbolism.[19]

The vast majority of classification actions were so routine that they were quite unlikely to have required board review. For example, the following routine classifications make up the great numerical bulk of classification decisions:

I-A or IV-F to I-Y (available for emergency)
III-A dependency to V-A (over-age) (or any other classification changed to V-A)
I-Y to IV-F (or any other change to IV-F)
I-A to I-D (reserves), or I-C (active duty)
I-D or I-C to IV-A (veteran)
I-A to I-SH or II-S (students)
I-SH to II-S (high school to college)

Some boards processed certain classifications routinely without review, while other boards did not follow such procedure. For example, some boards instructed their clerk to defer automatically anyone working in the field of science so that all I-A's or II-S's to II-A's were not reviewed, while these same actions were carefully gone over by another board. Or a I-A to III-A (dependency) might be done automatically by one clerk on the basis of a pregnancy slip or birth certificate, while such a case might be

---

[19] The claim that only boards classify is found throughout Selective Service publications. See *ibid.*, pp. 9623, 9624, 9667.

thoroughly discussed by another board. The following were most likely to receive review of a board :

I-A to I-O or IA-O (conscientious objectors)
I-A to III-A (dependency)
I-A to II-A (critical occupation)
I-A to II-C (agricultural)
II-S to II-A (student to critical occupation)

The public record of board classification actions gives no clues as to how a classification was made but the total number of actions for each meeting offers evidence that the majority were never reviewed by the boards.

Several boards of varying sizes were selected at random and a review of classification actions over five months was made. Typical was a board with 13,000 registrants that had 215 actions in March, 176 in April, 219 in May, 348 in June, and 217 in July. The size of these totals clearly shows that they were not all reviewed in a two-to-three-hour monthly meeting. Boards with larger numbers of registrants sometimes met twice a month. The largest board among the 17 was the second largest in the state. It had 24,000 registrants and met twice a month. Its monthly classifications ranged from 450 to 1,334, obviously beyond the ability of any board to discuss each case thoroughly, even in two meetings.

The typed minutes of board meetings kept by clerks were not a public record. It was also unclear whether a board reviewed the cases and made a decision, but usually a clerk would record in the minutes those she felt were important enough to take into a meeting even if the board never discussed all of them. The minutes of meetings confirmed direct observations. A board rarely was able to conduct interviews with more than three or four registrants in a meeting. The number of files they were able to review depended on whether they divided the work, how well they worked together, and the types of cases. Many boards divided files and each member decided the cases in his stack. Others divided them and each man presented a summary of each case to the others, who indicated approval or disapproval of his proposed actions.

Generally, a clerk carried 20 to 30 files into a meeting, 10 to 15 might be discussed for widely varying amounts of time, and there might be three or four interviews. The other files might be signed without discussion or perhaps even this would not be done. Clearly, 175 to 350 cases were not reviewed.

The second qualification that must be made is that it was unnecessary for a board to discuss most cases separately. The great majority of classifications were routine and automatic. When a man sent in a pregnancy slip he could only become III-A; papers proving enlistment in the active Armed Forces could only result in I-C; the Reserves, in I-D; over 26, in V-A, and so on.

Third, the clerks *did* sort and stack files for board meetings and some lightly penciled in a recommended classification on the file cover, but they did not necessarily place on top the ones they felt "ought to go." Rather they usually set aside for first consideration those that were most controversial or sensitive, whether they seem headed for induction or deferment —cases they would not dare handle automatically or routinely because an appeal would probably be taken and they wanted legitimation by the board. Clerks were not necessarily interested in induction, though their exasperation at the registrant who was clearly trying to evade his obligation may have tended to a "pro-induction" attitude toward such individuals. However, these instances were exceptions. Generally a clerk had a thoroughly bureaucratic outlook toward the registrants and wanted only to put them "into some slot." In other words, they seldom cared whether or not a man was inducted as long as he was no longer problematic for them.

While it was entirely possible for clerks to influence decisions, their intervention was not always detrimental to the registrant. As one clerk said:

> You have to protect the registrants from the board as much as you do the board from the registrants. They [members] can't keep up with the rules and regulations. They only come in once a month and maybe they read something that made them decide "no more grad students deferred." Well, you can't have that sort of thing. We're supposed to report things like that to headquarters but you can't do that either. You have to live with these men. So I pull files like that one out and say they are on a hold or pending or I say "We have a new regulation on that." Then when they have cooled down I put them back into the pile. Every clerk has to do things like that.[20]

---

[20] Interview No. 7.

Most board members made comments about how much they relied on the clerk. Clerks were in a position to control information that came to a board. Before each interview clerks customarily briefed members of the board on the contacts and experiences they had had with the registrant or recalled the highlights of any past interaction between the registrant and the board. In doing this they could (and from my observations often did) set the general predisposition of the board toward the registrant. Throughout this study, however, there were no briefings that I felt prejudiced a board in a direction they would not otherwise have taken after the interview.

The role of the clerks can be summarized by saying that they were far more significant in classification decisions than is admitted by spokesmen for the System, who denied that they had any part in classifications. But viewed against the automatic nature of most decisions and the shared values of clerks and board members, the role seemed less than critical.

The decision premises of boards

If boards did not have the information for national manpower policy and could not adjust process to individual on basis of personal knowledge, what *did* they base their decisions on?

There seemed to be three major sources from which members derived such values and notions—middle-class values, a "veteran's outlook," and the lack of information and absence of clear purpose for decision.

The first thing to be noted about board members was the predominance of middle-class values and attitudes. Registrants were often lectured or quizzed on the values of thrift, hard work, obedience to the law, morality, concern for parents; aliens were shown little sympathy in classification actions; college education was highly valued; efforts at self-improvement, materially, socially, or educationally, were lauded. Members were cognizant of persons above them in class status ("the real wheels," "those who have real money," "the prominent families") and manifested even more awareness of those below them in status ("the other half," "the poor devils").[21]

[21] Sociologists do not pull their knowledge of class values and attitudes into clear profiles for classes. Most, however, would attribute the foregoing traits to the middle class. It might be added that I had no preconceptions of the class make-up of the boards. It came as a surprise.

The occupations of members revealed a heavy preponderance of those occupations and professions of middle-class status.[22] They ranged from firemen up to a vice president of a medium-sized public utility company, which probably represented the highest community standing found in the study. Most of them were the less-prominent attorneys, dentists, ministers, lower and middle management personnel, small business owners, accountants, department managers in large retail stores, and the like. Though Hill City is noted for its heavy industry, only one board member was a blue-collar worker.

Aside from an ex-Congressman, a County Fire Marshal, and a politically appointed Director of Veterans Affairs for the county, none of them were political office-holders nor, so far as could be ascertained, active in politics.

The second major source of decision premises for board members stemmed from their status as veterans. Among the 77 board members included in this study veterans outnumbered nonveterans better than seven to one. One clerk of 25 years' service admitted that until recently she had erroneously believed that the regulations required that members be veterans. Most board members belonged to veteran organizations, especially the American Legion. Experience as veterans provided them with a unique outlook on military service and the use of military power in pursuit of foreign policy.[23]

The most consistently expressed sentiment of board members was that military service was a valuable experience for any young man. Members referred to it as a means of acquiring skills and training that would be useful in civilian life; a maturing experience; a manhood ritual all should go through; and above all a service one owed his country. In part, this attitude expressed a defensive rationale developed in support of the nega-

[22] Sociologists are not fond of taking occupational rankings such as the 1947 North-Hatt NORC study and dividing them up as indicators of class strata. It may be informative to point out that board members in this study had scores ranging from 90 to 67. The NORC study is mentioned in virtually any treatment of stratification. See Robert Hodge *et al.*, "Occupational Prestige in the United States," *American Journal of Sociology,* LXX (November, 1964), 290.

[23] The term "veteran's outlook" is used here for want of something better. For a brief description of the American Legion's outlook on world affairs, see Gabriel A. Almond, *The American People and Foreign Policy* (New York: Praeger, 1960), p. 171.

tive task of the boards. It might also be an effect of the methods used in recruiting board members.

Board members themselves recruited replacements. Quite often a man was first placed on a reserve status and began receiving a monthly in-house news organ titled "Selective Service," which contains "editorials" by General Hershey. One member of the National Headquarters staff admitted that "it gives sort of an informal policy" to the thousands of members.[24] The reserve board member was then called upon occasionally to fill in for absent members. If he had, or acquired, values that meshed harmoniously with the others, he eventually replaced a retiring member or more likely one that died. The values that a man had to acquire, or bring with him, stemmed largely from his status as a veteran.

The veteran status was functional in another way : in legitimation of decisions, an essential support for the board's negative task. Members, clerks, and other officials were proud of this preponderance of veterans because "none can say they haven't served their country"; "they know what they are sending these boys off to"; and "the boys have more confidence in them."

A third factor influencing decisions was the lack of information and clear purpose on which to base decisions. Without personal knowledge of the registrant, information on national manpower needs, or ability to investigate claims of registrants, the members were constantly torn between universalistic and particularistic considerations. Because they were expected to carry out some generalized national manpower policy, they tried to act on the basis of universalism and to treat similar cases in a uniform manner. At the same time they were expected to adjust the processes of Selective Service to specific individuals. Because they lacked informational resources to do either, they usually acted in a highly particularistic manner—by treating registrants in accordance with the relationships they developed with them in the interviews or from letters in the files. Consequently, seemingly insignificant things like posture and dress become important in decisions.

In pursuit of uniformity of treatment, boards attempted to follow universalism : they endeavored to determine what sort of registrant they

---

[24] Interview No. 23.

had before them and then treat him in some way similar to other registrants of his type. But these efforts foundered because (1) they were given few if any general norms necessary for universalism (or they were given norms that led to seemingly inequitable decisions); and (2) they were forever plagued by the half-mythical, half-real institutional goal of adapting process to the individual—the demand for particularism.

For example, a board attempting to act on the basis of universalism had finished processing a stack of files, granting occupational deferments as usual. Then they began to encounter requests for deferments from men who had just joined firms after leaving college:

> BOARD MEMBER A : I can't see letting these guys dodge their commitment like this. You know what they're gonna do—get kids or stay there till over 26. I don't think it's fair.
> BOARD MEMBER B : Well, I agree, but some of these guys are going into defense work.
> BOARD MEMBER A (referring to a file) : This guy's going to work at GM in auto engineering and testing—how in the hell is that connected with defense? And besides—how critical can any man be just out of college and on the job three weeks? You can't tell me these guys are critical to anyone—defense or not.
> CHAIRMAN : Thing we have to remember is that Colonel Blank (State Headquarters) said to let these guys go from college to industry and get started.
> BOARD MEMBER A : I know. But it doesn't make sense to me. Hell yes, he'll be valuable to someone after he's on the job a while.[25]

The argument continued at some length and grew quite heated before the board reluctantly agreed to defer such men. Thus they had groped for some universal criteria on which to base their actions but could find only a vague suggestion from State Headquarters that made no sense to them on the basis of their information and that led them to a conclusion that seemed unfair to them.

Their frustration, however, was not yet at an end. As they proceeded through more files, they were confronted with requests to defer men on the basis of jobs they would accept within a month. At this, the whole argument erupted again, with one board member angrily declaring, "I'll

[25] Observation Report No. 9.

be damned if I am going to defer some man as critical who isn't even on the job yet!" He then launched into a long and bitter tirade against "sending all these poor kids from the West End of town while all these others with money go to college and then get a critical occupation." He concluded, flushed and angry, with—"I've had it! I say turn down this request for deferment. If Headquarters doesn't like it that's too damn bad. I'm not afraid to tell them where to go! I told F. D. R. I'm ready to tell them." [26] Finally the chairman brought all of them back to the frustrating reality that went with trying to be universalistic when he said, "Well, we let all the others go. How are we going to treat this one any differently?" Of course, they could not.

In this case the frustrated board reluctantly based its decisions on universalism, but it would be difficult to prove they arrived at any more equity in doing so. In other instances, boards often balked at the inequity universalism seemed to create, or despaired of finding the information needed for a decision, and opted for particularism. However, the excerpts below illustrate that there was no more equity to be found when decisions were based on particularism. For example :

> BOARD MEMBER A : A deferment to study architecture in graduate school!?
> BOARD MEMBER B : Isn't this the rich kid that's given us all the trouble?
> CLERK : That's the one.
> BOARD MEMBER A : As far as I'm concerned he shouldn't be allowed to keep going to school. It's so obvious he's trying to get out of serving! Remember that bad knee story he came in here with?

Often they reacted in a particularistic manner to items in the file such as the wording of a letter which seemed to imply disrespect for the board. Or, more often, they reacted in a particularistic way to the registrant in his interview with the board.

> CLERK : If you're ready I'll bring Mr. X in.
> CHAIRMAN (with a smile) : Has he gotten rid of this (gesturing to indicate a beard)?
> CLERK : Oh, yes—slick as a whistle. (Other board members chuckle.)

[26] *Ibid.*

Or another board :

> CHAIRMAN (holding up a file and speaking to the researcher) : You ought to see this guy. Were you ever in the military, Captain [sic]? Well this is the sort of guy you would take down to the latrine and scrub down with a wire brush. I mean, I've seen these Hell's Angels out in California —seen them on the television and he's worse looking than any of them. Just plain scurvy. (To the clerk.) Let's make this baby I-A. We'll fix his trolley.[27]

Discussion following an interview often dwelt only partially upon universalistic aspects of the case. As much time was frequently spent in particularistic commentary.

In the absence of guidelines and information, dress, mannerisms, bearing, forthrightness, grooming, and the like, all took on exaggerated importance. Because manpower demands changed constantly and because they were given no comprehensible or manageable norms, universalism was often untenable. Obviously the board members themselves did not consider "national health, safety, and interest" to be useful norms.

One Hill City board had developed its own higher norm and thus solved the problems that plagued the others. Its higher norm was that "everybody had to serve." No one was in a critical occupation for any longer than it took to replace him and an employer was given a specified time to do just that. Deferments, they said, were deferments, *not* exemptions. Considerable tension existed between the board and State Headquarters as a result of this drastic method of simplifying decision rules. Probably the most exasperating thing to State Headquarters was the fact that the board's interpretation of the law and regulations was perfectly legitimate.

Because board members were given few specific things on which they could legitimately base their decision, they probed into many irrelevant aspects of the registrants' lives in an effort to find something on which to base a decision. Typical queries were such as these :

> "What do you do with your spare time?"
> "You don't like to submit to authority, do you?"
> "What kind of car do you drive?"
> "Were you ever in the Boy Scouts?"

[27] Observation Report No. 14.

If one cannot somehow limit the scope of his concern with an object, he cannot be universalistic and treat the objects uniformly in accord with higher norms. And yet if the scope of concern is too restrictive, one cannot adjust the general administrative process to the individual.

Board decision: the problem classifications

Both necessity and common sense dictated that boards handle only cases that were problematical. These tend to be dependencies, occupationals, conscientious objectors, and (in the last year) students.[28]

DEPENDENCIES

The boards seemed most effective and their decisions seemed to contain less logical contradiction in cases of dependency. They were relieved of any pressure to search for higher, universalistic norms. Here they were adapting general process to the individual and both particularism and diffuseness were more clearly acceptable patterns of action and decision. It is true that they lacked knowledge of the individual and of his environment, but they did humanize by inquiry a sensitive area which a thoroughly bureaucratic approach would have aggravated by impartiality. Their inquiry was unlimited and they felt no compulsion to be anything but diffuse. Furthermore, the variables in dependency cases were so great, the exigencies of situations so numerous, that efforts to make decisions more bureaucratic would have been disastrous. It is difficult to see how rules could be written and universal norms applied in these cases.

> Is a widowed mother financially secure but emotionally dependent on her son?

> If the family that lost a father does not need the oldest son financially, do the younger children still need him as a form of father substitute?

> A well-to-do widow may have enough money to live on without her son's support but at what level should she be forced to live? If she is used to

[28] I assume that in some areas boards concern themselves with agricultural deferments, though they may, like Agdustria, have an elaborate point system developed by agricultural interest groups. A man is given so many points for producing x bushels of wheat for market, so many for eggs, and the like. In such a situation the clerk may merely compute or verify the points.

living at $15,000 a year, should she have to live on half that? Sell her house?

However, the boards' capabilities in dependency cases would have been improved by better information. Often the decision to induct was centered around whether or not dependents would receive as much support in the form of military allotments as they did from the registrant as a civilian. Yet some boards seemed to be unaware that allotments were paid; others did not know how much they amounted to.

CONSCIENTIOUS OBJECTORS

There were not many such cases and only a few were observed. Clerks offered information on other cases. Persons seeking a I-O or I-A-O whose denominations have a long history of pacifism were processed routinely and from obtainable information the deferment was granted without board interviews. Jehovah's Witnesses were invariably spoken of deprecatingly. Perhaps this was a reflection of their socioeconomic status, or perhaps the perceived extremity of their views and a belief that they had an uncooperative attitude toward Selective Service. But if they had certification as a minister of certain degree they were readily deferred.

Often board members and clerks spoke with scarcely concealed disdain of Black Muslims who sought deferments as conscientious objectors. The impression gained from limited observation and interviews is that conscientious objectors failing to fit established and accepted patterns, such as the Muslims, were brought before the boards as the first test of the religiosity of their objection.

Board handling of these cases was efficient, not because they had any more information about the individual or his circumstances but because they had a clear norm to guide them. Conscientious objection must be based on religious grounds rather than a mere objection to a particular war or foreign policy. Board members seemed as capable as anyone else of determining the sincerity of religious beliefs. A case involving a conscientious objector taken on appeal will eventually come before a Department of Justice hearing officer. Thus, it would receive a review that differs from the one given other cases that go to the appeal boards.

STUDENTS

The boards did not view the student classification as a problem until the demands of Vietnam grew more acute. In 1966 the boards were directed both formally and informally to "tighten up" on students.[29] Thus, during the period of this study, students began to request board interviews.

In the cases observed the boards bent over backwards to permit a man to stay in school. The function of the interviews observed was, according to clerks and board members, to "scare" the marginal student into enlistment or into full commitment to his studies. The boards probably were as competent as anyone to listen to the reasons for a registrant's failure to progress at a "normal" rate of speed toward a four-year degree.

As of 1966 one real problem in the handling of students was not in the board decisions but in the all-pervasive, indiscriminate pressure of the draft. The guidance to tighten up on students included specific directions to cancel induction orders if a student had returned to or entered a school and was in good standing at the time he was called. However, this information was never transmitted to the thousands of registrants who were ordered for preinduction physicals unless they asked. Assuming that induction was inevitable, many (there is no way to know how many) rushed to enlist or volunteer for induction. Undoubtedly this did serve to "pick up" students of marginal commitment, but there is no way of knowing how many serious students were panicked into enlistment. The Field Director for the State pointed out that by reviewing reports of local boards he could quickly spot a situation in which a board was making inequitable decisions or decisions that were contrary to policy.[30] This might have been true for nonvoluntary induction but there is no way of detecting the indirect pressure that causes enlistment and volunteering for induction.

OCCUPATIONS

In the matter of critical occupations (II-A) the performance of the boards seemed most vulnerable to criticism. Some boards automatically deferred anyone whose employer requested it. Some had the clerks automatically

---

[29] As is customary in Selective Service, this informal direction came from a variety of places. It was implied in the directions on drop-outs, transfers, and the like; in word-of-mouth direction from State and National Headquarters; and in General Hershey's editorials in *Selective Service*.

[30] Interview No. 21.

defer anyone in science and engineering; some boards inducted professional engineers with graduate degrees; some automatically forwarded all requests from the scientific field to the State Scientific Advisory Board; some were trying to induct all teachers with exception of those teaching science; some were automatically deferring all teachers; some boards felt that a critical occupation deferment should never be for more than six months. There simply was no uniformity among the boards.

The II-A's did not constitute a large number of registrants but they seemed to be a major source of institutional posture. The registrant seeking a II-A was valuable to someone—that "someone" often constituting a powerful interest group.[31] This situation seemed to be the major source of institutional posture that included informal, word-of-mouth policy direction and emphasis on the specific individual case with avoidance of general policy direction. Both appeared to be methods of institutional defense against pressure from interest groups.

The largest section of State Headquarters was the manpower division, where the great bulk of the Headquarters' work went on. They handled those appeals to the Director (state and national) that the system permits. This apparently happened for two major reasons. First, because the slow and cumbersome appeal board machinery of Selective Service could not cope with the burdens thrown upon it. This was particularly true because registrants were so little aware of procedural rights. When a registrant who had failed to use his appeal rights faced induction and his employer demanded consideration for deferment, it was felt that the clerks had to be able to refer the protest some place since no one wanted to give them the power to cancel induction on their own authority. Or if a registrant had utilized all his appeal rights but still brought his hysterical mother into the board office to protest induction, it was felt that the clerks should be able to deflect the problem, rather than having the board and the clerk trying to enforce an induction order or calling in the police or FBI. It was evidently felt that such compulsion was better handled by some agency further removed than the local board.

The second reason for this informal appeal procedure was to give higher headquarters a chance to correct some of the lack of uniformity

---

[31] Labor unions are appeased by an automatic II-A deferment for anyone engaged in an apprentice program that is on a list approved by the State Director. The list, of course, was prepared by the leading unions of Agdustria.

among boards. To attempt this through the formal appeals machinery would mean that policy would have to be specified, written, and turned over to the same sort of nonexpert, traditionalistic decisional mechanism as one finds in the local board. To do this would have been to invite the problem of negotiation with interest groups at state and national levels. Moreover, this would also have entailed the loss of the ability to react flexibly to changing manpower demands. Those skills considered critical would have to have been constantly renegotiated. Trying to settle definitively and in writing what occupations were in the national health, safety, and interest in the midst of fluctuating manpower requirements, such as those developed in 1965 and 1966, would have been an incredibly difficult task. The "appeals to the Director" procedure permitted a flexible but carefully camouflaged manpower policy. The decentralized system provided only dispersed and obscure targets for interest groups, and by treating each case individually there was always an answer to interest group protests. It could be claimed that no one had decided that draftsmen or hydraulic engineers were not vital to the national health, safety, or interest—simply that *a* case had been decided by *a* board. If there were continued protests involving a certain occupation or skill group some informal policy guidance could be passed on to the boards.

Evaluation

What sort of evaluation can be made of the local boards and their decisions, on the basis of these limited data?

Some might be disturbed by the pronounced middle-class attitudes and values of the boards. But would it be reasonable to expect to find application of anything else but the most widely held values in a society? Would it not be dysfunctional for Selective Service and in fact for our political system to staff boards with anything but representatives of middle-class values?

Some might ask that the boards include persons from different social strata. While this might serve some symbolic function, it is unlikely to alter many decisions. One need not be a social scientist to forecast that those of the lower strata will look "to their betters" for cues on decisions. And if the higher socioeconomic strata were included, would not their prestige and influence overshadow the others?

And what of the "veteran outlook?" One is led to much the same conclusion as the one about concern over middle-class values. If local boards are used in a conscription system, whether it be for purposes that are largely symbolic or as a decision mechanism, it is virtually inevitable that they become staffed with veterans. Not only will those directing the program find it desirable for purposes of legitimating decisions, but men without the status of veterans will be reluctant to accept positions on boards. The status of a veteran is a natural defense a man would want to have in making the unpleasant decisions conscription entails. Nonveteran members could be encouraged but perhaps only by requiring them by regulation or law. Even if nonveterans were sought out, it is likely that they would adopt the same attitudes as veterans.

The lack of information and clearly defined goals would seem to be the aspect of board decisions that deserves the most immediate attention and the area in which that attention can best obtain results.

Selective Service was designed to be nonbureaucratic, to have powerful symbolic meaning, to be primarily legitimating and secondarily efficient, and to win acceptance by means of nonuniformity. Its institutional ideology can be described as "finding the path of least resistance." I saw many cases considered "too hot," "too puzzling," "too troublesome," handled by granting a deferment with the statement that "he's got several years to go to reach 26, we'll try to nail him later." When any registrant or group of registrants became too shrill in their protests, Selective Service apparently eased the friction with deferments.

In the past all of this was functional for the institution. The question is whether or not this structure, process, and organizational style have become dysfunctional? Because of changes in our political culture and because Selective Service for a variety of reasons has been left to carry out a complex and unofficial manpower policy, its structure, process, and style seem incapable of winning acceptance for its task. Instead they complicate it.[32]

Clearly, acceptance at one time hinged upon nonuniformity and

---

[32] I have not tried to go into these changes in our political culture. Some of the obvious ones would be the decline of localism, changed notions of equity perhaps stemming from the civil rights movement and changed notions of national service. Other factors are the oversized manpower pool, and the nature of the Vietnam war. See other chapters in this volume.

consciously nonbureaucratic structure and process. But it is precisely these things that are hampering acceptance and challenging legitimacy today. In an age of less mobility and slower communications it was appropriate that cases would be handled differently in different areas. But this has changed. Americans now seem ready for more "legal rationality" in the matter of conscription, and for more definitive guidelines for boards and more expertise in clerks. Perhaps a professional hearing officer is called for instead of a board of "friends and neighbors."

Prescriptions and institutional defenses

It is hard to have contact with Selective Service without developing prescriptions to remedy its problems. There are a great many things that cry for improvement. But the reformer would do well to ponder the fact that he is confronting an institution rather than a mere organization. As Philip Selznick puts it, an organization is

> ... an expendable tool, a rational instrument, engineered to do a job. An "institution," on the other hand, is more nearly a natural product of social needs and pressures—a responsive adaptive organism.[33]

An institution, according to Selznick, is "infused with value." Those who would change an institution would do well to plan carefully and move cautiously. Its instinct and abilities for self-preservation are powerful.

Selective Service has built a variety of institutional defenses, each worthy of greater discussion. Selective Service has successfully portrayed itself as a decentralized institution. (This depends upon one's definition of decentralization.) State and National Headquarters can and do exercise detailed decision power. Usually they have permitted the boards to operate within broad control limits, constricted only if certain decisions became too contentious. They have exercised control through appeals to directors or by the directors taking appeals to appeal boards. As one official said, "If *we* take an appeal to the state appeal board, or to the national board, there isn't much doubt about how it will come out." [34]

[33] Philip Selznick, *Leadership in Administration* (New York : Harper and Brothers, 1957), p. 5.
[34] Interview No. 28.

Decentralization has had other functions that have become more important than "staying close to the people." It has dispersed the targets for interest groups. It has also isolated the individual in his relations with Selective Service. The relationship is reduced to the registrant and his board rather than students and Selective Service or chemists and Selective Service, and the like. The individual has found it difficult to marshal any political power and bring it to bear upon the area of uncertainty surrounding the anticipated board decision. Selective Service regulations were designed to further this condition by making the proceedings nonjudicial and informal, and by enabling the boards to refuse anyone but the registrant the right to appear on his behalf.

A second defense is successful self-portrayal as a civilian agency, independent of the Pentagon. This independence is real, but State and National Headquarters are in fact staffed with hybrid- or semimilitary men. These men are products of an insulated personnel system composed of National Guard and Reserve officers. As one officer in National Headquarters put it, "We are sort of a bridge between the civilians and the military and having us keeps the politicians out." [35] Such staffing minimizes responsiveness to ordinary political stimuli from both the civilian and military sectors but maximizes access to both.

Another defense is in successful self-portrayal as a "grass roots, voluntary organization" composed of patriotic citizens performing an unpleasant duty. An example of the utility of this defense can be found in the fact that every Congressman, no matter how critical he was of the System, would describe it in exactly such terms. That every Congressman had in his district some of the approximately 15,000 volunteer members of the System may partly explain this.

The System has successfully propagated the belief that each case is handled individually by the boards. As this study points out, this not only is untrue but probably impossible and unnecessary.

No list of defenses could leave out the charismatic institutional leadership of General Hershey. The devotion to him is exceptional. One has to descend all the way to board clerks before the simplest question is not answered with profuse praise for the General. He was a perfect model

[35] Interview No. 31.

of Selznick's institutional leader. His skillful relations with Congress indicated an acute sensitivity to politics and politicians. This sensitivity has been useful in defending the institution before Congress.

The strong institutional allies cultivated by Selective Service deserve mention. Included among them are some of the most powerful interest groups in America : the American Legion, the Veterans of Foreign Wars, the National Guard Association, and the Reserve Officers Association.

Finally, the pattern of interaction between the boards and socioeconomic strata has served as a defense; those registrants who were articulate enough to request board interviews were also most congenial with the reasoning and middle-class values of the boards and either accepted a board's decisions because of this congeniality or were most likely to be deferred by the boards. In contrast, those who felt the weight of the draft in proportionally the greatest numbers were most likely to accept the boards' decisions without challenge and were least likely to become part of any critical opposition to it.[36]

Summary

This study of local board behavior has suggested that boards are confused as to their purpose as a result of our changed political culture and situations like Vietnam. They lack the information and guidance to determine or act in line with national health, safety, or interest, and are only slightly less handicapped in adjusting the processes of conscription to the individual. The bulk of the boards' workload could be bureaucratized, and is in fact currently handled by the bureaucratic part of the system (the clerks), to a far greater degree than institutional myth admits. Board

---

[36] For some support for this hypothesis, see Arthur D. Klassen, Jr., *Military Service in American Life Since World War II : An Overview* (Chicago : National Opinion Research Center, University of Chicago, 1966), pp. 217–259. Klassen does not focus directly on the differential impact of the draft on socioeconomic classes, evidently because he is aware of the complexity of equity. Nonetheless, if one discounts the impact of Korea, and notes that the *lowest* classes often are rejected in great numbers, the data on Klassen's pp. 251, 252, and 253 seem to support the hypothesis. See also Karen Oppenheim, *Attitudes of Younger American Men Toward Selective Service,* Military Manpower Survey Working Paper No. 5 (Chicago : National Opinion Research Center, University of Chicago, March, 1966), pp. 15–20.

behavior and decisions are primarily influenced by their lack of clear purpose, status as veterans, and middle-class values. Board performance in handling some problem classifications, such as dependencies and conscientious objectors, suggests that if provided with purpose and information, boards might perform in some areas in a manner that would find greater acceptance than bureaucratic handling. There are institutional defenses developed over the years that may serve to insulate Selective Service from changes in social needs and pressures.

Juvenile delinquency and military service

MERRILL ROFF

Introduction

Although concepts of fairness would, in the abstract, require the entrance of 100 percent of the male population into the armed forces in times of declared war or serious emergency, the application of this is always tempered by the fact that some men are considered better qualified than others, and a minority are, for various reasons, considered not qualified at all.

The first and most general restriction is on the basis of age. It is obvious that there is, in general, some age at which males would be too young and some age at which they would be too old for service. In practice, during World War II the draft applied only to those between the ages of 18 and 45, and early in the war many draftees who had reached the age of 38 were released. (More recently, the upper level for the draft has been around 26 years—more because supply was ample in relation to demand than because those 30 years of age were too old.) There is inevitably a certain arbitrariness about any chosen cutting point. Certainly, many 15- and 16-year-olds or many 50-year-olds could contribute effectively in combat; in times of extreme emergency, such as the period early in World War II when England feared immediate invasion, the age standards were broadened substantially for those prepared to fight in England.

In general, however, ages of somewhere around 18 to 35 are considered optimal for men who are to be taken from their homes to become members of fighting units.

Within this preferred age range, substantial numbers are normally rejected because of physical inadequacies of various kinds. These include heart disease, deformities or other defects of bones and limbs, defective vision, ear trouble, allergic diseases, high blood pressure, and epilepsy. Standards for these are not, of course, within the scope of this discussion.

There are behavioral characteristics that are clearly disqualifying in their most extreme forms. Included here are the mentally deficient who require custodial care, hospitalized psychotics, and certain of the "worst" criminals. Just where the line should be drawn as we go up the scale of intelligence, toward the less severe psychiatric disturbances, or the less serious criminals, offenders, or delinquents is a matter on which we need more information than is now available. Decisions here are also influenced by the supply and demand situation.

With respect to psychiatric disorders, there has been a marked shift of attitude since 1940. This has taken the form of de-emphasizing psychoneurosis in the total psychiatric picture. It was believed by some psychiatrists in 1940 that if they only had enough psychiatrists to do the job, and if they were permitted to reject enough people as potentially neurotic, they could eliminate much if not most problem behavior in the services. Many psychoneurotics did not do too badly in World War II, with the result that there are at the present time very few rejections because of psychoneurosis, and in some locations there is no such entrance screening at all.

In contrast to this, penitentiary inmates and certain less severe offenders against the law are still regarded as undesirable, or at least as suspect, by the services. More research is needed to help decide just where the line should be drawn in this area. In this very complex, real-life situation there are inevitably many times in which policy decisions must be made before the factual information that would support or fail to support them is available. Facts do not automatically generate policy, but many policy decisions are influenced by factual material. The research reported here is a study of the adult outcome, particularly in a military situation, of individuals who had been juvenile delinquents during childhood or adolescence. It shows what actually happened with samples of former juvenile delinquents from two different states.[1]

Service regulations and practices

A partial outline of the regulations governing service admission of individuals with a history of law violations is given below, to indicate in some detail the way the requirements are described and the rigidities and flexibilities involved, including the points at which administrative decisions are permitted.[2] Until recently, only the Army contained drafted men. The other services depended instead on voluntary enlistment, but they recognized that their enlistments were markedly influenced by the presence of the draft. In all cases, for the recruiting personnel of the various services and at the induction stations and local boards of the Selective Service System, the requirements shift from time to time in accordance with the quota they have to fill. These sometimes operate differently at the same time for different services. A recruiting officer once pointed out that his opposite number in another service was accepting some individuals that the first one would not even consider, as least at that time.

A persistent problem for all the services is the practice followed by some judges, particularly in juvenile courts, of permitting an individual to avoid the normal penalty for his misbehavior by enlisting in one of the services. This meets various felt needs since it has the effect of getting the

---

[1] The work reported here was supported (in part) by Contract No. DA-49-007-MD-2015 with the Army Medical Research and Development Command, and by USPHS Grant No. M-2218, from the National Institute of Mental Health. Dr. S. B. Sells acted as a consultant on an important part of this work.

[2] This outline was prepared in 1964, just prior to the acceleration of military action in Vietnam, and reflects the situation at that time. Serious consideration was given to reworking it to reflect any changes that may have taken place since that time, but this course of action was finally rejected. In a changing set of circumstances, it is not possible to guarantee that any set of regulations will remain exactly constant from one month to the next. As this is being written, a directive has just been issued for the services to accept a substantial number of men who, for low aptitude or other reasons, have been in draft category I-Y (not acceptable under standards previously in force, but usable in an emergency). It is not yet clear just what the effects of this will be.

offender out of the community, and is in accord with the occasionally held opinion that all that a young man needs to get straightened out is a period in one of the services. It is hard to find out how often this is done, since no record is normally made of the transaction. The services have opposed this practice on the ground that they are not correctional institutions. Whether or not it would be desirable to have a correctional branch of some kind operating under the direction of the military, it would in any case be desirable to obtain information about the outcome of individuals with different preservice backgrounds.

The regulations of the various services show essential similarities but some differences as to who is and who is not acceptable and as to procedures for dealing with borderline cases in this area. The following general outline of regulations of the four services indicates the extent to which specific action is or is not prescribed for individuals with a history of conflict with the law, including juvenile delinquency :

1. All services ask the potential enlistee or inductee about his history of court convictions, including juvenile court adjudications.

a. The Army has a form for this purpose, which is to be completed at the recruiting station.

b. The Navy provides that Police Record Checks and juvenile court checks will normally be obtained for all places of residence since the 14th birthday, using a prescribed form. Each applicant is also required to sign a Fraudulent Enlistment Warning Sheet after being advised orally of the consequences of providing false information.

c. In the Air Force, a Police Record Check is normally required of all applicants at the time of first enlistment, using a prescribed form. The Air Force also provides that all applicants will be asked if they have ever been in the custody of juvenile authorities or have ever appeared in a juvenile court.

d. The Marines direct that the recruiter personally question each applicant for enlistment or re-enlistment as to whether or not he has ever been convicted of an offense by a civil court, including a juvenile court adjudication. Police Record Checks are to be obtained in each place of residence since the 12th birthday.

2. All applicants who have been convicted by a civil court for any offense punishable by death are barred by all services. Those sentenced to imprison-

Juvenile delinquency and military service

ment for a term exceeding one year are acceptable only upon approval or waiver by a higher headquarters.

a. The Army considers morally unacceptable any applicant having frequent difficulties with law enforcement agencies, criminal tendencies, a history of antisocial behavior, alcoholism, drug addiction, sexual misconduct or questionable moral character, or traits of character that render him unable to associate with other men. However, waiver may be requested for individuals in this group from the Armed Forces Moral Waiver Determination Board.

b. The Navy requires approval by higher authority of applicants who have been convicted of a felony or any offense involving sex, or who have committed two or more misdemeanors resulting in civil restraint other than a traffic violation; and of applicants who have committed four or more traffic violations within the preceding two years.

c. The Air Force lists as ineligible for enlistment with waiver persons having frequent difficulty with law enforcement agencies, criminal tendencies, a history of antisocial behavior, alcoholism, drug addiction, sexual perversion or questionable moral character that renders the person unfit to associate with members of the military service. Additionally, waivers are required for four or more traffic violations or one single violation involving drunken driving; for accidents resulting in fatalities or injuries, leaving scene of accident, and similar violations deemed of major consequence by local law enforcement agencies.

d. The Marines permit request for waiver when the offense is not a felony or one involving moral turpitude, or the maximum punishment prescribed by the applicable law does not exceed one year's imprisonment.

3. All services provide that individuals currently involved in a criminal court action are unacceptable pending completion of the case.

4. All services provide that men under parole, probation, suspended sentence, or conditional release from any term of confinement are unacceptable.

5. All services provide that any applicant who has been placed on probation, given a suspended sentence, or has had his sentence deferred, *contingent upon his enlistment,* shall be rejected.

6. For certain minor offenses, the decision to accept or reject may be lodged with the recruiting officer or the commanding officer of a recruiting station. For example, the Navy has an explicit category of "permissive rejections by

the Officer in Charge : any applicant who has been convicted of a felony, two or more misdemeanors (excluding traffic violations) or a series of youthful or juvenile offenses *may* be rejected by the Officer in Charge if investigation discloses that the applicant's overall rehabilitation has been unsatisfactory, leaving him morally unfit to associate with members of the naval service and, therefore, unacceptable for enlistment."

7. Some of the services make specific reference to *juvenile delinquency*.

a. In the Army *juvenile delinquents* are not considered separately from other delinquents. Thus "a registrant who has been convicted by a civil court, or who has a record of adjudication adverse to him by a juvenile court, for an offense not punishable by death or imprisonment for a term exceeding one year, may be approved" by waiver. Induction will not be denied solely on the basis of conviction or adjudication for such offenses. On the other hand, "in determining moral acceptability of registrants, the Department of the Army screens out individuals with serious offenses and ingrained delinquency behavior patterns."

b. The Navy states that "the fact of adjudication as a youthful offender or juvenile delinquent by local or state authorities, disposition by Federal juvenile authorities, arrest(s) or conviction(s) by civilian authorities for misdemeanors or felonies are not in themselves a bar to enlistment, if the applicant is ordinarily eligible." However, if the applicant admits such a record, or if there is reason to believe such a record exists, a more thorough investigation is to be carried out than is to be made for the ordinary applicant.

c. The Air Force similarly notes that "an adjudication that a person is a juvenile delinquent, youthful offender, wayward minor, or equivalent determination by a court having jurisdiction over juvenile cases is not in itself a bar to enlistment if the applicant is otherwise eligible." If there is a history of juvenile delinquency, a very thorough investigation is to be made and included in the request for waiver of the juvenile delinquency. "Waivers will not be granted for applicants who have, upon investigation, been found to have had frequent difficulties with law enforcement agencies, a history of antisocial behavior, sexual perversion, or questionable moral character which renders the person unfit to associate with members of the military service." Rejection is to be made on these grounds and not on the basis of juvenile delinquency.

d. The Marine Corps states more briefly that "the fact of adjudication as a youthful offender or juvenile delinquent by a state, or disposition by Federal juvenile authorities is not in itself a bar to enlistment if the applicant is otherwise eligible. An applicant is to be judged as to his fitness ... by his character at the time of his application for enlistment."

8. Each service has certain specifications different from those of other services.

a. The Army comments that "a civil court record combined with marginal mental and medical abilities predicts marginal functioning." Such persons are said to have difficulty adjusting to the demands of military service so that in addition to making only a marginal contribution they often become disciplinary problems. Thus such registrants are to be evaluated with unusual care, and additional information from the civilian community is to be sought.

b. The Navy places unusual emphasis upon the collection of information from the civilian community, and outlines procedures for conducting a home investigation for use in evaluating each applicant. The Navy also requires each applicant to complete a financial statement to preclude the enlistment of individuals with excessive financial obligations.

c. The Air Force is generally similar to the others. They specify certain details that are implied by the other services, such as that "persons who are under the influence of alcohol or drugs will not be processed for enlistment or re-enlistment."

d. The Marines specify a time period following release from confinement. Waivers may not be requested when "the applicant has been committed to a training school or corrective institution unless a minimum period of six months has elapsed since release from such an institution." Something similar is done by the Air Force, but not by the Army or Navy.

Related research studies

The current regulations outlined above have evolved over a period of years to meet a wide variety of specific problems, and they do contribute to the operation of the system. It is possible that research findings may contribute to improvement of these regulations, which grow and change as new information becomes available.

Certain selected studies that throw some light on the problem of the relation between preservice criminal behavior and subsequent military careers will be reviewed. There is a very extensive literature on juvenile delinquents that uses the fact of "adjudication" as an objective indicator of the presence of a problem. Most of these studies do not follow up on the adjudicated delinquents to find what happened to them later, but use adjudication as a terminal criterion with which other variables can be compared. As will be seen below, adjudication by itself is only one of various possible indices of delinquency that can be used in the prediction of later service adjustment.

The review of the literature will be limited to three studies, all directly relating to the military situation. None of these deals primarily with juvenile delinquents. They illustrate, however, the main kinds of research that have been done in this area.

In the first of these studies, Schneider and LaGrone worked backward from a sample of 500 general prisoners who had been sentenced to an army rehabilitation center.[3] (The term "general prisoner" refers to persons convicted by a general court martial, which is used only for the most serious military offenses.) They think that general prisoners who were sent to rehabilitation centers tended "to be the more chronic but less serious offenders among Army delinquents." Investigation showed that 35.4 percent of these men had not been arrested in civilian life prior to entering the Army, while 64.5 percent had been arrested at least once; of the latter, the average number of arrests was 4.2 per individual. It should be noted that these were not, in general, juvenile delinquents, but adult offenders. The World War II Army took in men ranging in age from 18 to at least 35, in a manner that was altogether different from anything that was done subsequently. It was later recognized by at least one of the authors that this study is incomplete in that it gives no information concerning the number of men who had been arrested prior to service, who got along without trouble, or had only minor difficulties.[4] The figures quoted thus do not give an accurate basis for deciding who should be accepted and who should be rejected on the basis of prior legal history, juvenile or adult.

A second study in this area is that of Joseph D. Lohman and his

[3] A. J. N. Schneider and C. W. LaGrone, "Delinquents in the Army," *American Journal of Psychiatry,* CII (1945), 82–91.
[4] LaGrone, personal communication.

associates in Illinois. They made an intensive follow-up study of a sample of convicted felons who were in service during World War II. These were adult rather than juvenile convictions. A published description of this in popularized form has been presented by Andre Fontaine.[5] Some 3,000 prisoners and former prisoners from Illinois entered service during World War II. They were selected by mobile units composed of psychiatrists, medical doctors, and an Army officer. The size of the total Illinois prisoner and former prisoner population from which these 3,000 men were selected is not known.

A random sample of 785 of these 3,000 men was selected for an intensive study of subsequent outcome. This included all available information from "prisons, police, the armed forces, Selective Service, the F.B.I. and the Veterans Administration." Each man in this special sample was also given an intensive postservice interview, "sometimes lasting as long as ten hours." Of these selected former prisoners, at least 87 percent obtained honorable discharges, while the remaining 13 percent presumably received dishonorable or other than honorable discharges. In that period the Army had not yet adopted the "general" discharge, but was largely limited to honorable discharges and "punitive" discharges. Thirteen percent is very high for punitive discharges, although it is only one out of eight in the sample. If the number of minor offenses, instances of unsatisfactory performance, and the like, was as high correspondingly, the number of somewhat unsatisfactory soldiers would be appreciably greater than one out of eight. On the other hand, many of these men undoubtedly did perform very creditably in service.

During World War II, the regulations concerning the induction of felons were relaxed at certain places and times, in response to the need for manpower. After the war, these regulations were tightened up again and in general a "waiver" of regulations forbidding entrance to those who have committed certain crimes is required from a headquarters above the recruiting officer. Under this waiver system the man's record is reviewed but he is not himself interviewed. "Lohman believes the waiver system ... should be abolished ... he would substitute a system whereby each man would be considered as an individual and his case treated on

[5] J. D. Lohman *et al.*, reported in A. Fontaine, "Are We Wasting 200,000 Soldiers?" *Saturday Evening Post,* CCVI (1953), 51–60.

its merits."[6] He thinks that a system of special boards could do a better job of evaluating individuals with criminal records than is done under the present military system.

In summary, Lohman and his associates dealt with a selected group of individuals with criminal records who seem to have been, in general, substantially beyond the juvenile delinquency age. Thus this study does not give a picture of results to be expected from the restricted admission of 17- and 18-year-old young men with serious histories of juvenile delinquency. On the other hand, the study does indicate the possibility of getting usable results from research in this area.

A more recent research project, "Prediction of Delinquency in Naval Recruits" has been reported by Gunderson and Ballard.[7] "For several years the Navy supported a research program concerned with the prediction and treatment of military delinquency in the hope of finding means to reduce the total disciplinary problem." A set of 474 items from the California Psychological Inventory and the Minnesota Multiphasic Personality Inventory was reduced to 119 items by an item analysis on samples of confined and nonconfined naval personnel and was called the Delinquency Scale. This was then administered to "all recruits entering the Naval Recruit Training Center, San Diego, over an 11-month period." Approximately 20,000 acceptable tests were obtained. Follow-up was made three years later, using all information then available. A sample of offenders was compared with a nonoffender control sample who had shown no disciplinary problems. A combined offender group of 745 individuals was constituted, using all individuals in the following categories: bad conduct discharge, current prison population, record of prison commitment, deserter status at the time of follow-up, unsuitable discharge (primarily for personality disorders), and unsuitable discharge (for inaptitude in training program).

Distributions of Delinquency Scale scores were compared for nonoffender and combined offender samples. With a cutting score of 40, 60 percent of the combined offenders would have been located as compared

[6] *Ibid.*
[7] E. K. E. Gunderson and K. B. Ballard, *Prediction of Delinquency in Naval Recruits,* Ninth Technical Report (revised), ONR Contract Nonr 1535(00), U.S. Naval Retraining Command, San Diego, California.

with 36 percent of the nonoffenders. With a cutting score of 44, 46 percent of the combined offenders would have been identified compared with 24 percent of the nonoffenders. The conclusion was reached that "such a small percentage (about 5 percent of the 20,000 recruits in this study) of the total population are discharged or confined for extreme non-conformity that it is probably impractical to attempt to screen potential offenders from among all recruits."

Since there is considered to be a higher concentration (about 10 percent) of potential serious disciplinary offenders among recruits who were seventeen years old at enlistment and had ten years or less of education, it was recommended that use of the Delinquency Scale be confined to this young and relatively poorly educated group. Its use was not recommended for older and better educated groups.

Adolescent maladjustment and service

The research reported here is part of a long-time project concerned with the relationships between childhood or adolescent maladjustment and personality problems and associated background factors, as described when they were occurring rather than retrospectively, and later adjustment as indicated by records of the military services and related agencies. The original samples employed were obtained in child guidance clinics. Information from these cases has been compared with psychiatric, personnel, and disciplinary information of the same individuals at the adult level.[8]

Following earlier work with child guidance samples, which included some delinquents along with many other types of problems, this work was extended to include samples consisting of juvenile delinquents to see what the experience was for groups of this kind in relation to military

[8] M. Roff, *Preservice Personality Problems and Subsequent Adjustment to Military Service : Gross Outcome in Relation to Military Service,* Report No. 55–138, School of Aviation Medicine, U.S. Air Force, 1956; "Relations Between Certain Preservice Factors and Psychoneurosis During Military Duty," *Armed Forces Medical Journal,* XI (1960), 152–160; "Childhood Social Interactions and Young Adult Psychosis," *Journal of Clinical Psychology,* XIX (1963), 152–157; M. Roff, W. Mink, and Grace Hinrichs, *Developmental Abnormal Psychology* (New York : Holt, Rinehart & Winston, 1966).

service.[9] The standards of acceptance of individuals with histories of conflicts with the law vary from one period to another, depending on whether the country is at war or at peace or somewhere in between these two conditions. The Schneider and LaGrone and the Lohman studies employed World War II samples, who entered service under regulations that reflected conditions prevailing at that time. The Gunderson and Ballard study employed a more recent population, and one that on the whole was more recent than that described here.

The samples used in the present research were born between January 1, 1928, and December 31, 1935. These dates were selected to include a group who would in general have been too young for World War II, but would have reached an age at which they normally would have completed military service when the criterion information was being obtained.

Experience on this project has indicated that there are many variations, both in populations and in administrative procedures, in different states and different parts of the country. Our juvenile delinquent sample was drawn from urban regions in Minnesota and in another state across the country from Minnesota. Work was first done in the other state (Sample 1), where in addition to the delinquent sample, a control group consisting of a random sample drawn from school files was employed to determine base rates for a randomly selected group. This state is among the poorest one-third of all states of the country in terms of the proportion of persons rejected from service because of low Armed Forces Qualifying scores. This is a simple index, but should indicate that the results reported here will not necessarily generalize to all other states.

Sample 2 was drawn from a metropolitan area in Minnesota, a state which consistently has a rejection rate for low aptitude that is about as small as any state in the country. In terms of this, and of other factors

[9] M. Roff, *The Service-Related Experience of a Sample of Juvenile Delinquents*, U.S. Army Medical Research and Development Command, Contract No. DA-49-007-MD-2015, Report No. 61-1, 1961; *The Service-Related Experience of a Sample of Juvenile Delinquents. II. A Replication on a Larger Sample in Another State*, U.S. Army Medical Research and Development Command, Contract No. DA-49-007-MD-2015, Report No. 63-2, 1963; *The Service-Related Experience of a Sample of Juvenile Delinquents. III. The Predictive Significance of Juvenile Confinement*, U.S. Army Medical Research and Development Command, Contract No. DA-49-007-MD-2015, Report No. 64-3, 1964.

that may be correlated with it, Minnesota is atypical, along with such states as Washington, Oregon, and Iowa.

Apart from the population differences of the two states, there was a difference in the method of selection of the delinquent cases. In Sample 1, only those cases were used that had a case file of at least five pages. After outcome information had been obtained, appropriate cases were microfilmed and sent to Minnesota for detailed analysis against the criterion data. This meant that a great many minor cases were not included at all, since we were interested only in those cases with enough content to permit analysis. Thus Sample 1 was made up of cases more serious than the total set of all youngsters who had had enough contact with the juvenile authorities to have a file.

On the other hand, for the Minnesota sample (Sample 2) the method of initial case-finding was changed to include all cases that had a file at all, so that we could see what happened to the large number of minor cases that had been excluded by taking only the more serious cases in Sample 1. It was considered more important to get information for these additional cases than to replicate exactly the procedure used with Sample 1. Since these cases are located where the project is based, it was not necessary to get the case reproductions done all at one time.

Both the population differences between the two states (as reflected in the aptitude scores mentioned above) and the method of case selection (with Sample 2 having its delinquents defined in broader terms to include more minor cases) would lead to the expectation that Sample 2 would yield a higher proportion of persons who would enter one of the services and perform satisfactorily there.

Rejection from service

An analysis of the outcome of former juvenile delinquents in the military services must take into consideration the fact that the inservice sample is a selected one, since there has been some rejection of the candidates who appear lowest on various dimensions. An outline has been presented above of some of the regulations concerning bad conduct in relation to entrance into the different services. Information will be presented here concerning the actual operation of rejection for moral or character reasons. One relevant question concerns the part played by juvenile and by adult offenses in the overall rejection procedure. Our data indicate the age at which offenses were committed and the age of confinement, if confinement occurred. Only those confinements were counted that were at least one month in length; overnight or even slightly longer detentions, as in a jail, were not counted as a confinement. Since our primary interest was in juvenile offenders, adult offenders are not divided as to confinement and nonconfinement. In general, the adult cases were confined. The same offense was much more likely to lead to confinement for adults than for juveniles.

Table 1 shows the proportion of individuals rejected for moral reasons in the two delinquent samples, with different combinations of preservice juvenile and adult offenses, and juvenile confinement or non-confinement.

The proportions of rejections for different patterns of offenses and

Table 1

OFFENSE AND CONFINEMENT DATA IN RELATION TO MORAL REJECTIONS OF THOSE WITH JUVENILE COURT RECORDS

Record of offenses and confinements (juvenile and adult)	Sample 1 ($N = 168$)		Sample 2 ($N = 97$)	
	N	percentage rejected	N	percentage rejected
Juvenile offense(s) with no record of juvenile confinement or of adult offense(s)	5	5.2%	11	6.5%
Juvenile confinement with no record of adult offense(s)	14	14.4	46	27.4
Juvenile confinement followed by adult offense(s)	56	57.7	68	40.5
Both juvenile and adult offense(s) with no record of juvenile confinement	22	22.7	43	25.6
Total		100.0%		100.0%

confinement are very similar in the two states. Less than 7 percent in each state were rejected because of juvenile offenses unaccompanied by either juvenile confinement or subsequent adult offenses. In general, a history of juvenile offenses without either confinement at that time or later adult offenses *was not* disqualifying. Whether or not any combination of juvenile offenses was followed by a disproportionate number of failures in service is a problem with which the present project is still concerned.

Between two-thirds and four-fifths of the moral rejections in the two samples had a record of adult offenses. The most common pattern in each state consisted of individuals with juvenile offenses that led to confinement, with subsequent adult offenses. These are individuals who started early and continued misbehavior as adults. (Since the initial samples consisted of former juvenile delinquents, individuals with adult offenses but no juvenile records would not, of course, appear in these samples.)

This picture can be supplemented by information obtained from the Minnesota cases only. When those rejected are examined to see what their exact status was at the time of their final classifications as IV-F, about half of those with a history of confinement were actually confined at the time they were rejected. Most of the remainder were on parole or probation or recently released from confinement, parole, or probation.

Rejection for moral reasons can be placed in context by comparing the proportions of rejections for all reasons for the three groups, as in Table 2.

The moral rejections in most cases occurred at the local board level so that individuals were not given induction examinations. Thus, the greater the number of moral rejections, the smaller the number of physical rejections would be for a group, since those rejected for moral reasons would not receive physical examinations. Thus, the physical rejections are relatively least frequent in Sample 1 and relatively most frequent in the control group. The proportion deferred because of dependents is smallest in Sample 1, the more serious delinquents. Even though the Minnesota sample consists of former delinquents, and thus might be expected to run somewhat lower in intellectual level than the total population of its area, it may be noted that rejections for substandard ability are relatively much less for this sample than for the control group from the other state; re-

Table 2

REASONS FOR REJECTION AND DEFERMENT FOR THE TWO DELINQUENT SAMPLES AND THE CONTROL GROUP

	Sample 1		Control		Sample 2	
	N	percentage rejected	N	percentage rejected	N	percentage rejected
Physical rejections	16	7.6%	83	32.9%	111	20.6%
Deferred, dependents	32	15.2	84	33.3	211	39.1
Substandard ability	30	14.2	24	9.5	15	2.8
Moral rejections	126	59.7	17	6.8	168	31.2
Miscellaneous other	7	3.3	44	17.5	34	6.3
Total	211	100.0%	252	100.0%	539	100.0%

jections for Sample 1, however, are higher than the control group. The category "miscellaneous other" includes individuals in the National Guard or one of the Reserves who saw no active duty; individuals deferred as students; several cases classified as 1-A who had not been called, and a scattering of others.

In Sample 1 and the control group there was no psychiatric screening. In Sample 2, there were ten psychiatric rejections for antisocial personality, which have been grouped with the moral rejections as essentially the same kind of case. There were a few rejections for psychoneurosis, psychosis, and the like, but these were not numerous enough to constitute a separate category; these have been placed with the physical rejections.

Outcome in service as indicated by service records

Outcome in service has been classified into four categories, which may be described as follows.

1. The noncommissioned or petty officer or officer group includes all those who had such status at the completion of their period of active duty, with honorable discharge. It does not include any who reached that level and were reduced. Individuals were not excluded from this outcome group for single minor disciplinary offenses. This represents the group

that achieved and held this level in one of the four services. They are also referred to as the "Promoted."

2. Recruit-Private-Private First Class (Rct-Pvt-Pfc) or equivalent includes cases who did not achieve noncommissioned status, but were not disciplinary problems. Some of these cases had rather brief terms of service; the small number who received medical discharges are almost exclusively in this group.

3. The minor disciplinary problems group includes those who had multiple disciplinary offenses that were not serious enough or numerous enough to result in a discharge. They had definitely more trouble than the average; whether or not they would have been accepted if their difficulties could have been predicted is uncertain.

4. The unsatisfactory group includes all those who received a discharge other than an honorable one, with a disciplinary component in the picture. A few additional cases are included here who had more than sixty days "bad time" (primarily Absence Without Leave [AWOL] and/or confinement) but still received an honorable discharge.

Outcomes in the four services for the two delinquent samples and the control group are shown in Table 3.

A graphic picture of the proportions promoted and unsatisfactory as given in Table 3 is shown in Figure 1, for the three groups and the four services. Sample 1 clearly has more unsatisfactory than promoted in all four branches of service, while the control group clearly has many more promoted than unsatisfactory. Sample 2 is much more like the control group from the other state than it is like Sample 1.

As mentioned above, the proportion of men rejected for military service because of low aptitude is a gross index of the number of "educationally disadvantaged" individuals in the different states. Minnesota, where our second sample comes from, averages as small a number of men rejected for low aptitude as any state in the country. The state from which Sample 1 was drawn is among the poorest one-third of all states on this index and its correlates. The two states consistently poorest in this respect are Mississippi and South Carolina. In these states there are occasional years in which as many as half of all men examined are rejected for military service because of low aptitude. When the same national norms are applied in Minnesota, there is a loss of around 2 or 3 percent.

Table 3

OUTCOMES IN THE FOUR SERVICES FOR THE TWO DELINQUENT SAMPLES AND CONTROL GROUP

	Army		Navy		Air Force		Marines		Total	
	N	percentage	N	percentage	N	percentage	N	percentage	N	percentage
SAMPLE 1										
Noncommissioned or petty officer or officer	30	21.0%	7	18.9%	11	28.2%	9	28.1%	57	22.7%
Rct-Pvt-Pfc or equivalent	19	13.3	8	21.6	4	10.3	9	28.1	40	15.9
Minor disciplinary problems	20	14.0	7	18.9	3	7.7	2	6.3	32	12.8
Unsatisfactory	74	51.7	15	40.6	21	53.8	12	37.5	122	48.6
Total	143	100.0%	37	100.0%	39	100.0%	32	100.0%	251	100.0%
CONTROL GROUP										
Noncommissioned or petty officer or officer	142	54.2%	77	52.0%	82	73.9%	26	56.5%	301	57.8%
Rct-Pvt-Pfc or equivalent	73	27.9	50	33.8	8	7.2	10	21.8	131	25.1
Minor disciplinary problems	11	4.2	9	6.1	3	2.7	3	6.5	23	4.4
Unsatisfactory	36	13.7	12	8.1	18	16.2	7	15.2	66	12.7
Total	262	100.0%	148	100.0%	111	100.0%	46	100.0%	521	100.0%

SAMPLE 2

Noncommissioned or petty officer or officer	298	44.6%	79	42.5%	134	59.3%	85	51.5%	596	47.8%
Rct-Pvt-Pfc or equivalent	229	34.2	49	26.3	19	8.4	32	19.4	329	26.4
Minor disciplinary problems	41	6.1	24	12.9	19	8.4	6	3.6	90	7.2
Unsatisfactory	101	15.1	34	18.3	54	23.9	42	25.5	231	18.6
Total	669	100.0%	186	100.0%	226	100.0%	165	100.0%	1,246	100.0%

Figure 1

PROPORTIONS PROMOTED AND UNSATISFACTORY IN THE THREE SAMPLES, FOR THE FOUR SERVICES

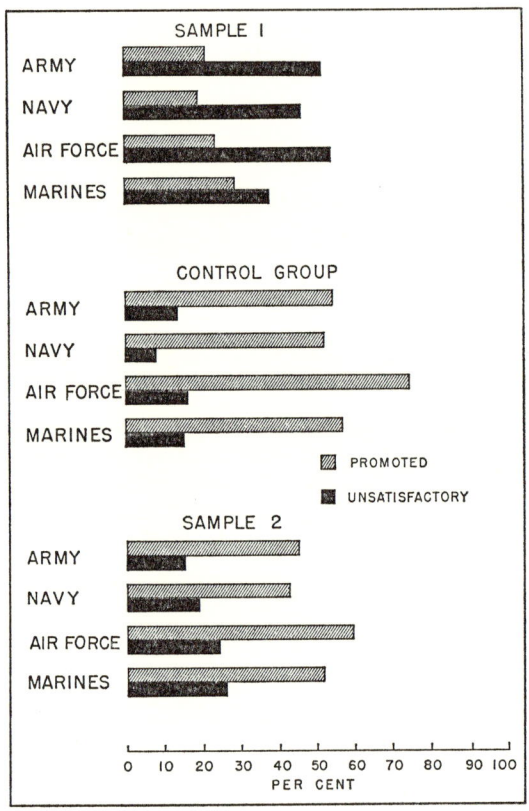

Apart from these population differences, there was also, as pointed out above, a difference in method of case selection. For Sample 1 only those cases were included that have case files of five pages or more. This restriction was made to insure a reasonable minimum of case information for use in the prediction of adult outcomes. When work was started with Sample 2, it was decided that it was important to get information on the minor delinquents who had been excluded by this minimum information requirement. We were not so much interested in showing that one state was or was not "better" than another, as in finding whether or not results obtained under one set of circumstances would also be obtained in a quite different setting. Because of differences in procedure, not only from state to state, but even from city to city, it is not possible to equate groups of delinquents exactly on degree of delinquency. What is called "auto theft" in one state may be called "using a car without permission" in another. The commonly used term "adjudicated" varies not only from state to state, but also from city to city, in the precise group of individuals included.

It is thus not at all unexpected that the delinquent Sample 2 should have a service outcome almost as good as the random sample of the entire population (the control group) from the same state as Sample 1. It would be expected, and earlier work in this project had demonstrated with an earlier sample, that a randomly selected control group for Minnesota would have outcomes somewhat better than those of a problem group. However, when the problem group is defined broadly, the differences would not be extreme.

There are no striking differences between the services in their experience with these different groups. The Air Force, with one exception, runs slightly higher than the other branches both in proportion promoted and proportion unsatisfactory, but the differences are not large.

It is clear that the differences in kinds of persons included in the samples were much more important in determining the results obtained than were the differences among the various services, either in regulations governing initial acceptability or in treatment while on active duty. Sample differences were more important than service differences.

Significance of age at time of enlistment or induction

For the Army, though not for the other services (in this period), it is possible to make a distinction between those who enlisted and those who were inducted (drafted). Those who enlisted were called Regular Army (RA), while those who were inducted were called Army of the United

States (AUS). It is recognized by some Army personnel officers that there is a substantially greater likelihood of difficulty with the young Regular Army personnel. Many delinquents join the Army as soon as (or even before) their age permits. In Sample 1, 96, or about two-thirds, enlisted, while 47 were drafted. Eighty-eight of the 96, or almost all who enlisted, were nineteen years of age or less; 65 percent of these were unsatisfactory. Forty of the 47 drafted were twenty years of age or more; only 20 percent were unsatisfactory.

On the other hand, the controls tended to wait until they were drafted at the age of twenty or more. Fifty-three of the 64 controls who enlisted did so at the age of nineteen or less. There were more unsatisfactory cases among these 53 young enlistees than among all those from the control group who enlisted at the age of twenty or more, or were inducted at any age (a total of 209). The Sample 2 delinquents show results that were similar to, but less pronounced than, those of Sample 1. Approximately 30 percent of the 245 who enlisted at the age of nineteen or less were unsatisfactory, as contrasted with 5 percent of the 267 who were drafted and the 37 who enlisted at the age of twenty or later.

Various factors may contribute to the proportion of unsatisfactory cases among the young enlistees. One significant factor is that those who entered at the age of twenty or later would tend to be those who had refrained from serious offenses in the years before that. The older group can be said to have been roughly screened by their own behavior while they were eighteen or nineteen years old.

It is not possible to make the same sort of distinctions between enlisting and inducted (drafted) men in the Air Force, the Navy, and the Marines, since all of their personnel enlisted, but it is possible to observe the relations between entrance age and outcome. In Sample 1, at least four-fifths of the former delinquents in service enlisted by the age of nineteen; about one-half of these were unsatisfactory. In Sample 2, also, at least four-fifths of those enlisting in these three services did so by the age of nineteen. The proportion of these who were unsatisfactory was about one in four, while only about one in ten who enlisted at the age of twenty or more was unsatisfactory.

The problem of unsatisfactory conduct is clearly most marked for the younger entrants. On the other hand, these younger persons are in some respects the most desirable recruits. Any attempt to screen out the bad conduct cases on the basis of age alone would be completely impractical, since it would exclude so many more successful men than unsatisfactory men. The basic research problem here is to develop ways of rejecting the maximum number of those who would be unsatisfactory, while rejecting the minimum number of those who get along all right.

Thus, age by itself is not usable as a screening procedure, but its part in the total picture should be recognized.

Prediction of outcome in relation to preservice juvenile confinement

There are many factors that may contribute to the prediction of good and poor outcome in service for delinquent samples. An approach could be made by way of type of offense, number of offenses, age at first offense, duration of contact with juvenile authorities, or a combination of these and other factors. A somewhat different method of approach is in terms of judgments based on both the offenses and the life situations of the offenders, made by the responsible authorities in dealing with each case.

Delinquency can be viewed in terms of degree and prevalence. The first stage is that of breaking a law without being observed; in terms of frequency, this would include practically everyone. A next step is being detected by a policeman and verbally corrected, perhaps without even being known by name to the officer involved. Beyond this is apprehension and more formal admonition, either by an arresting officer or at a juvenile department. A great many youngsters never reappear in the juvenile records after this. If there is further trouble, a youngster may be brought into juvenile court, become an adjudicated delinquent, and put under supervision or on probation. Again, many never proceed beyond this point. If there is further trouble, a decision may be reached to take the youngster out of an unsatisfactory home and neighborhood situation. In both the urban areas of this research, there was a county training school where boys could be sent until it was decided that they should be returned to the community. It is easily possible to get a count of these individuals, while it is not at all possible to get this for some of the informal contacts mentioned above.

As will be shown below, in the Minnesota sample about one-fifth of those from the county training school were later sent to the state training school. The state training school group is small in number as compared with the total group treated informally, but it is readily identifiable. A decision to send youngsters there is normally reached on the basis of assessments of their behavior, and the positive and negative factors in their life situations. Later, as they outgrow the juvenile age, a certain proportion of those sent to the state training school appear as adult offenders.

The values presented above for Sample 2 include all cases who had contact with the juvenile authorities formal enough to result in a file. Most, but not all, of these were "adjudicated delinquents." This is the total group for which service outcome was shown above in Table 3 and in Figure 1. The group so defined showed only 18.6 percent in the unsatisfactory category and 25.8 percent when the unsatisfactory and minor disciplinary categories are combined. It is desirable to attempt to separate out a subgroup of these who would show a larger proportion of unsatisfactory outcomes if this can be done in a practical way.

Where the cutting point should be on acceptance or rejection of individuals is a matter of policy that may be influenced by various factors, which change from time to time. If it were possible to reject one person who would be unsatisfactory in service at a cost of nine persons who would get along all right, this would almost certainly not be done. If it were possible to reject nine persons who would be unsatisfactory in service at a cost of one person who would get along all right, this would almost certainly be done. As a tentative guide in the present work, we have tried to see whether and how a group could be defined, in terms of preservice information, so that at least one-half would prove to be unsatisfactory in service. This is an arbitrary goal, but one which seems likely to give results that are of interest.

An exhaustive search was made in Minnesota at the local and the state training schools to ensure that we would have complete information on confinement in these institutions. Outcome in service was divided into the four categories described above : (1) promoted; (2) Rct-Pvt-Pfc or equivalent; (3) minor disciplinary problems; and (4) unsatisfactory.

Outcome in terms of these categories is shown in Table 4 for individuals with different histories of juvenile confinement in Minnesota. The first pair of columns gives the results for those confined in the local but not the state training school. The second pair of columns gives the results for the smaller number of cases who were sent to the state training school without having spent time in the local school. The third pair of columns gives the outcome for those sent to the state training school after being sent to the local training school. The fourth pair of columns gives the results for all those who had been sent as juveniles to either state or federal training school without regard for earlier confinement.

A graphic picture of the proportion promoted and unsatisfactory for the same confinement categories is shown in Figure 2. The group sent only to a local training school made the best showing in service. They had a somewhat larger number of promoted than unsatisfactory individuals. The group sent to the state training school following confinement in the local training school made the poorest showing. Sixty percent of these were unsatisfactory and only a few were promoted. The fourth category, sent

Figure 2

PROPORTIONS PROMOTED AND UNSATISFACTORY OF INDIVIDUALS WITH DIFFERENT HISTORIES OF JUVENILE CONFINEMENT, SAMPLE 2

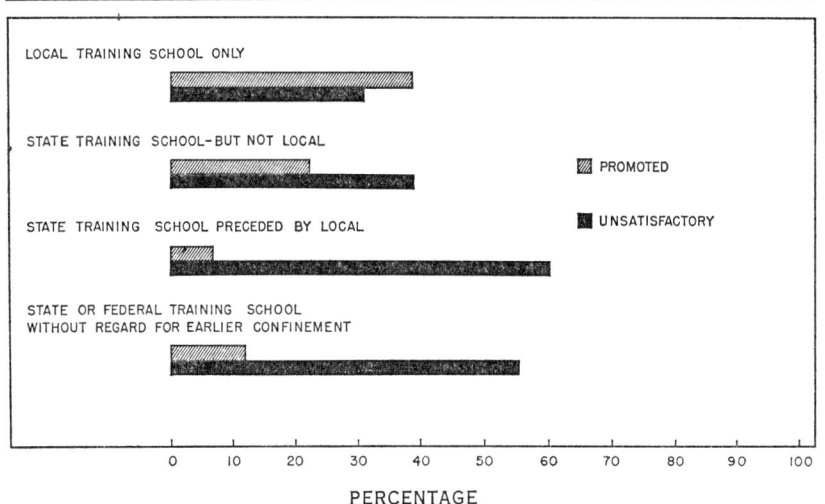

Table 4

OUTCOME IN SERVICE OF INDIVIDUALS WITH DIFFERENT HISTORIES OF JUVENILE CONFINEMENT

	Local training school only		State training school but not local		State training school preceded by local		State or federal training school without regard for earlier confinement	
	N	percentage	N	percentage	N	percentage	N	percentage
Noncommissioned or petty officer or officer	73	38.6%	4	22.2%	3	6.7%	8	11.9%
Rct-Pvt-Pfc or equivalent	37	19.6	5	27.8	11	24.4	16	23.9
Minor disciplinary problems	21	11.1	2	11.1	4	8.9	6	9.0
Unsatisfactory	58	30.7	7	38.9	27	60.0	37	55.2
Total	189	100.0%	18	100.0%	45	100.0%	67	100.0%

either to the state or federal training school, without regard for earlier confinement, is almost as poor as the third group.

For the Minnesota delinquent group as a whole, less than one out of five men fell in the category "unsatisfactory" in service. Within this larger group, it is possible to select out two overlapping groups defined in somewhat different ways, each with a proportion "unsatisfactory" exceeding one-half. Additionally, these individuals can be located easily and economically.

A partial cross-validation of the relationship between preservice juvenile confinement and outcome in service can be presented for the other state. The term "partial" is used because in addition to the differences in the total population of the two states, and the initial selection of more serious cases which has been described earlier, the complete case records for all cases were available here only for the first and the fourth categories. We did have some cases from the second and the third categories; these were primarily psychiatric cases who received honorable discharges.

For this sample there was also the possibility of confinement in either a local or a state training school. However, the relative number sent to the local school only was very much smaller than for the Minnesota sample. With all these differences in mind, a partial cross-validation shows that of the 20 individuals sent to the local but not to the state school, eleven, or 55 percent, were unsatisfactory. About twice as many, or 42 individuals, with or without earlier confinement, were sent to the state or federal training school. Of these, thirty, or 71 percent, were unsatisfactory while only three persons, or 7 percent, were promoted. If we had the complete record of all individuals from this sample who were included in the study, it would not increase the number of cases in the first category since we have information for all of these. It would not increase the *number* of cases in the fourth category, but would lower the *percentage* for the fourth category if we had all the cases with outcomes in category two and three. However, reference to Table 4 above indicates that the proportions in these two categories were relatively small for this group. Allowing for this difference in conditions, juvenile confinement, particularly at the state or federal level, still appears as unfavorable with respect to later military service.

Discussion

Although this book is primarily concerned with Selective Service and the draft, the results in service of former juvenile delinquents would be incomplete and misleading if only those inducted by Selective Service were considered. Large numbers entered the Army through enlistment rather than through the draft, and the Air Force, the Navy, and the Marines filled their manpower needs by enlistment. A follow-up based on drafted men alone would thus eliminate from consideration a majority of all former delinquents in service. The picture obtained would be not only partial, but also biased, since there is a marked tendency for former juvenile delinquents to enlist rather than to wait for the operation of the draft.[10] It is thus necessary to consider both inductions and enlistments to get an accurate picture of juvenile delinquency in relation to outcome in service.

We have been concerned only with histories of bad conduct, but bad conduct is a single variable in a multivariate situation. Army regulations for enlistment comment that a record of misbehavior combined with low mental level should be a special source of concern. This has not been checked in the present project, partly because many of those with the lowest mental level had been rejected for that reason alone. In general, a combination of predictor variables would be expected to improve on the effectiveness of the single variable, a history of delinquency, which is under consideration here.

The discussion of work by others indicated that it was known that many disciplinary offenders in the services had preservice records of bad conduct, but that it was not known how many with similar preservice records got along relatively well in service. Some answers to this problem have been presented here. It has been possible to define groups with minor preservice delinquency records, of whom only a minority of cases were unsatisfactory in service. It has also been possible to define groups with more serious records, of which more than half were unsatisfactory in service. Where the cutting level should be set is a matter of administrative decision, and can vary with circumstances. The purpose of research of

---

[10] Roff, *The Service-Related Experience of a Sample of Juvenile Delinquents*, 1961.

this kind, which is still in progress, is to permit the quoting of odds on various possible courses of action.

To find what proportion of the total sample entered service, it is essential to consider the rejections as well as those in service. It was noted that the proportions of rejections for different delinquency and confinement patterns were similar in the two samples. A careful consideration of the actual operation of the rejection process gives a picture of the results of application of the regulations governing acceptance and rejection of those with records of juvenile delinquency.

The samples used in this study were obtained in two separate parts of the country, with many differing characteristics. As explained above, the samples were drawn in somewhat different ways, so that Sample 1 consisted of more seriously delinquent individuals than Sample 2. These differences, both in sample and procedure, lend added force to similarities in results obtained in the two areas. They indicate that the results are not limited to a single part of the country or to a single way of dealing with juvenile delinquents.

Outcome in the four services was presented for the two delinquent samples and for a control group. The combination of difference in base populations and difference in method of selecting the delinquent groups produced a marked difference in service outcomes between these two samples. When the delinquent sample was defined broadly, as in Sample 2, the yield in service was not much different from that of the control group in the other state. This clearly indicates a need for an increasingly sharp definition of degree of delinquency, to permit an accurate evaluation of personal histories in the process of acceptance or rejection for service.

The work reported here is still in progress, and the approach by way of history of confinement is by no means a final solution to the entire problem. A closer approximation to a general solution will involve a multivariate approach using not only the information presented here, but also other variables such as age, type of offense, relevant test scores when available, and other variables of this nature. However, the present work has progressed to a point where practical, usable results have been obtained. It has been shown that in two quite different states, those who have progressed through the increasingly serious stages of delinquency, until they have been sent to a state training school, are more often unsatisfactory in service than not. As long as there are men available with a markedly more favorable prognosis for service (and any random sample from an entire state, who could pass the aptitude tests, would provide a better yield) it will contribute to the efficiency of any branch of the service if the more serious delinquents are rejected. The number of these is not great, but they can be identified at a relatively low cost in time and money. The use of samples obtained in two states in different parts of the country gives greater weight to these conclusions than they would have if the study were confined to one state alone.

The college students in the present study received their educations in a period before the current campus protest activities developed. It seems likely that most of those involved in illegal post-juvenile protest activities would not have earlier histories of juvenile delinquency, and at any rate the number of these would be very small in relation to the total college population. This *post-juvenile* delinquency at colleges is a different problem from the juvenile delinquency being studied in the present project. It seems likely that there would be no substantial change in the picture for 1968 samples corresponding to those reported here. This can only be answered definitely by additional follow-up studies.

The Negro and the draft

CHARLES C. MOSKOS, JR.

THE OPERATION of the Selective Service System has given rise to one of those Great Debates that periodically appear on the American public scene. At the same time that the draft has come under intensive scrutiny, the momentum of the civil rights movement shows signs of both stalling and fragmenting. For the persistent obstacles in the way of the ongoing quest of American Negroes for dignity and equality have led to new appraisals of the means and probabilities of attaining these goals. Thus, a special source of controversy in the draft debate has been the degree, nature, and consequences of Negro involvement in the armed forces.

The task before us is not only to examine the operation of the Selective Service System with regard to Negroes, but also to place this examination within the more general context of the Negro's position in the contemporary military establishment. More specifically, we will address ourselves to questions such as the following: What is the distribution and assignment of Negroes within the military? What is the rate and manner of Negro entrance into the armed forces? In what ways has the military become an avenue of Negro opportunity? What can be said about the equity of Negro participation in the military establishment?

Evidence is brought to bear on these and related questions wherever possible by utilizing available factual documentation. In addition to relevant Selective Service and Department of Defense data, the analysis relies on a 1964 survey conducted by the National Opinion Research Center (NORC). The NORC survey was based on a 10 percent sample of all officers and a 5 percent sample of all enlisted men on active duty at the time, and a national sample of civilian men, 16–34 years of age.[1]

Racial integration in the military

Some prefatory remarks concerning the present participation and involvement of Negroes in the military establishment are in order before turning to an examination of the mode and rate of Negro entrance into the armed services. For the man newly entering the armed forces, it is hard to conceive that the military was one of America's most segregated institutions less than two decades ago. The rapid racial integration of the armed services following President Truman's desegregation order in 1948 is an impressive achievement in directed social change.[2] Equally significant, there is universal agreement by military observers that the performance of integrated Negro servicemen contrasts sharply and favorably with that of all-Negro units in the segregated military. Today color barriers at the formal level are absent throughout the military community. Equal treatment regardless of race is official policy in such nonduty facilities as swimming pools, chapels, barber shops, post exchanges, movie theaters, snack bars, and dependents' housing as well as in the more strictly military endeavors involved in the assignment, promotion, and living conditions of members of the armed services. Moreover, white personnel are often

---

[1] The data collected during the 1964 Military Manpower Policy Study conducted by the National Opinion Research Center (NORC) were made available for secondary analysis by Peter H. Rossi. A detailed account of the sampling procedures used for this study is found in Ramon J. Rivera, *Sampling Procedures on The Military Manpower Surveys*, Military Manpower Survey Working Paper No. 3 (Chicago: National Opinion Research Center, University of Chicago, September, 1965). I am especially indebted to Albert D. Klassen, Jr., for his unstinting labors in preparing the NORC tabulations. I would like in this small way to acknowledge and sincerely thank him for his technical competence, conscientious assistance, and help in making sense out of the data. Additionally, Sidney Kronos gave valuable aid in preparing the tabular requests.

[2] An extended discussion of the Negro in the contemporary military establishment is Charles C. Moskos, Jr., "Racial Integration in the Armed Forces," *American Journal of Sociology*, LXXII (September, 1966), 132–148.

commanded by Negro superiors, a situation rarely obtaining in civilian life. Despite occasional deviations from stated policy at informal levels, military life is characterized by an interracial egalitarianism of a quantity and of a kind that is seldom found in the other major institutions of American society.

In their performance of military duties, whites and Negroes work together with little display of racial tension. This is not to say racial animosity is absent in the military. Racial incidents do occur, but these are reduced by the severe sanctions imposed by the military for such acts. Such confrontations are almost always off-duty, if not off-base. In no sense, however, is the military sitting on top of a racial volcano, a state of affairs contrasting with the frequent clashes between the races that were a feature of the military in the segregated era. Yet the fact remains that the general pattern of day-to-day relationships off the job is usually one of mutual racial exclusivism. On the whole, racial integration at informal as well as formal levels works best on-duty vis-à-vis off-duty, on-base vis-à-vis off-base, basic training and maneuvers vis-à-vis garrison, sea vis-à-vis shore duty, and combat vis-à-vis noncombat. In other words, the behavior of servicemen resembles the racial (and class) separatism of the larger American society, the more they are removed from the military environment. In brief, although the military has not become a panacea of racial relations, it, nevertheless, stands in sharp contrast to the racial discrimination so characteristic of civilian life.

As shown in Table 1, Negroes constituted 9.5 percent of the total

Table 1

NEGROES IN THE ARMED FORCES AND EACH SERVICE AS A PERCENTAGE OF TOTAL PERSONNEL, BY SELECTED YEARS

Year	Total Armed Forces	Army	Air Force	Navy	Marine Corps
1949	5.9%	8.6%	4.5%	4.0%	1.9%
1954	7.9	11.3	7.5	3.2	5.9
1962	8.2	11.1	7.8	4.7	7.0
1964	9.0	12.3	8.6	5.1	8.2
1965	9.5	12.9	9.3	5.2	8.3

SOURCE: Department of Defense.

armed forces in 1965, somewhat lower than the 11–12 percent Negro in the general American population. Also note, however, that the proportion of Negroes in the military has shown a consistent increase since 1949. Although the various military services are all similar in being integrated today, they differ in their proportion of Negroes. As given in Table 1, in 1965 Negroes made up 12.9 percent of the Army, 9.3 percent of the Air Force, 8.3 percent of the Marine Corps, and only 5.2 percent of the Navy.

There are also diverse patterns between the individual services as to the rank or grade distribution of Negroes. Looking at Table 2, we find

Table 2

NEGROES AS A PERCENTAGE OF TOTAL PERSONNEL IN EACH GRADE FOR EACH SERVICE, DEC. 31, 1965

Grade[a]	Army	Air Force	Navy	Marine Corps
OFFICERS				
07 Up (general)	0.0%	0.2%	0.0%	0.0%
06 (colonel)	0.2	0.2	0.0	0.0
05 (lt. colonel)	1.3	0.5	0.1	0.0
04 (major)	4.5	0.9	0.3	0.3
03 (captain)	5.2	2.0	0.5	0.3
02 (1st lieut.)	3.5	2.1	0.3	0.4
01 (2nd lieut.)	2.8	2.5	0.4	0.4
Total officers	3.6%	1.6%	0.3%	0.3%
ENLISTED MEN				
E9 (sgt. major)	3.7%	1.4%	1.3%	0.9%
E8 (master sgt.)	7.1	2.3	2.0	1.4
E7 (sgt. 1st. class)	9.8	3.4	3.0	2.7
E6 (staff sgt.)	15.5	5.6	5.0	5.3
E5 (sergeant)	18.4	11.0	6.5	11.9
E4 (corporal)	14.6	13.7	5.9	9.7
E3 (pvt. 1st. class)	14.9	10.0	6.6	8.6
E2 (private)	13.4	13.9	6.0	10.0
E1 (recruit)	10.1	10.4	4.4	8.4
Total enlisted men	13.9%	10.7%	5.8%	9.0%

[a] Army titles indicated in parentheses have equivalent pay grades in other armed services.
SOURCE : Department of Defense.

the ratio of Negro to white officers is roughly 1 to 26 in the Army, 1 to 60 in the Air Force, and 1 to 300 in the Navy and Marine Corps. Among enlisted men, Negroes are underrepresented in the top three enlisted ranks in the Army and the top four ranks in the other three services. We also find a disproportionate concentration of Negroes in the lower noncommissioned officer (NCO) ranks in all of the armed forces. This is especially so in the Army, where 18.4 percent of all sergeants are Negro. An assessment of these data reveals that the Army, followed in order by the Air Force, Marine Corps, and Navy, not only has the largest proportion of Negroes in its total personnel, but also the most equitable distribution of Negroes throughout its ranks.

Negro entrance into the military

An overriding finding concerning Negro participation in the armed forces is the consistently higher proportion of Negroes, compared to whites, who fail to meet the entrance requirements for military service. A look at the results of preinduction examinations given potential draftees over the past sixteen years shows Negro disqualification rates to be about twice that of whites. As reported in Table 3, for the time period 1950 through 1966, 63.4 percent of Negroes were disqualified compared to 35.4 percent of whites. Also, although the total rates of disqualification may vary by subperiods, the Negro-white disqualification ratio remains constant throughout the 16-year time span. Most important, the primary factor in the higher disqualification rates of Negroes is due to failures on the mental tests. That is, Negroes are four times more likely to be disqualified on mental grounds—a paramount indicator of socioeducational handicaps —than are whites. Indeed, with regard to failure for medical reasons only, white disqualification rates are greater than that of Negroes.

Even though the proportion of Negroes failing to meet the entrance standards required for military service is markedly higher than that of whites, the fact remains that Negroes are still more likely to be drafted than whites. The percentages of Negro draftees for the years 1961 through 1966 are given in Table 4. It can be seen that Negroes average about 15 percent of those drafted over this period, a figure higher than the 11–12 percent of Negroes in the eligible age groups. Inspection of Table 4 also reveals that Negro induction rates are inversely correlated with the total number of draft calls. That is, the proportion of Negroes drafted is highest during those years when draft calls are lowest. As will be discussed later, this holds true only if induction standards are not lowered. Put in another way, during times of high draft calls, with the resultant necessity of draw-

Table 3

PERCENTAGE DISTRIBUTION OF THE RESULTS OF PREINDUCTION EXAMINATIONS FOR MILITARY SERVICE, BY RACE AND SELECTED PERIODS

Results of examination	1950–1962	1963–1965	1966	Cumulative 1950–1966
WHITE				
Qualified	67.5%	56.9%	64.8%	64.6%
Disqualified	32.5%	43.1%	35.2%	35.4%
Administrative	1.2%	1.3%	1.2%	1.2%
Mental Tests	10.1	15.3	7.6	11.0
Medical Tests	18.8	24.8	25.3	21.1
Mental & Medical	2.4	1.7	1.1	2.1
Total	100.0%	100.0%	100.0%	100.0%
Number examined	5,771,812	2,196,374	1,436,415	9,404,601
NEGRO				
Qualified	40.0%	25.7%	42.5%	36.6%
Disqualified	60.0%	74.3%	57.5%	63.4%
Administrative	1.4%	1.2%	1.6%	1.4%
Mental Tests	44.4	58.6	39.2	47.4
Medical Tests	7.5	9.7	12.5	8.6
Mental & Medical	6.7	4.8	4.2	6.0
Total	100.0%	100.0%	100.0%	100.0%
Number examined	1,029,290	412,399	172,971	1,614,660

SOURCE: Bernard D. Karpinos, "Results of the Examinations of Youth for Military Service, 1966," *Supplement to Health of the Army* (Washington, D.C.: Medical Statistics Agency, Office of the Surgeon General, Department of the Army, March, 1967), pp. 14–15.

Table 4

TOTAL DRAFT CALLS AND NEGROES AS PERCENTAGE OF INDUCTIONS, FISCAL YEARS 1961–1966

Fiscal year	Total draft calls (in thousands)	Percentage of Negro inductions
1961	58.0	14.4%
1962	147.5	15.3
1963	70.0	18.5
1964	145.0	14.2
1965	102.6	16.3
1966	334.5	13.0
Jul.–Aug. 1966	68.4	12.5
Cumulative	926.0	14.8%

SOURCE: Department of Defense; and U.S. Congress, House Committee on Armed Services, *Review of the Administration and Operation of the Selective Service System,* 89th Congress, 2d sess. (Washington, D.C.: Government Printing Office, 1966), p. 10002.

ing deeper into the draft pool, the overproportionate induction of Negroes tends to decline—but not disappear.

The weight of evidence then—the disproportionate Negro induction rate coupled with the high Negro disqualification rate—strongly indicates the lower likelihood of Negroes obtaining draft deferments—deferments that are more available to whites and that often become *de facto* exemptions. While we may assert with some confidence that Negroes are less likely to receive draft deferments than whites, it must be stated, nevertheless, that there is no definitive data on deferment rates by race.[3] Given

---

[3] Supporting the statement that Negroes are much less likely to be deferred than whites is a Department of Defense finding, using the NORC data, that 30.2 percent of qualified Negroes were drafted, whereas only 18.8 percent of the qualified whites were. See National Advisory Commission on Selective Service, *In Pursuit of Equity: Who Serves When Not All Serve?* (Washington, D.C.: Government Printing Office, 1967), p. 22. However, Albert D. Klassen, Jr., reaches a different conclusion based on a cohort analysis of the NORC survey data. Klassen's study indicates that deferment rates vary only slightly by race. See his *Military Service in American Life Since World War II: An Overview* (Chicago: National Opinion Research Center, University of Chicago, 1966), pp. 35–36.

in Table 5 are gross deferment rates based on Selective Service information for 1966. We find that 10.4 percent of the total number classified are deferred for being college students. Without doubt, this is a deferment category greatly underrepresentative of Negroes. Likewise, the 1.4 percent deferred for occupational reasons, most of which are for technical and educational positions, would also be underrepresentative of Negroes. Concerning the largest group of deferments, however, the 19.6 percent deferred for dependency (i.e., support of family) reasons, one can only speculate as to the racial distribution in this category. But Selective Service data do reveal that of all the deferment groups, it is the dependency category that shows the most equitable spread across levels of formal

Table 5

CLASSIFICATION OF SELECTIVE SERVICE REGISTRANTS IN AGES OF MILITARY SERVICE LIABILITY, APRIL, 1966

Category[a]	Percentage
Available for Service	5.6%
Disqualified	26.6
Qualified only in national emergency	12.7%
Not qualified for any military service	13.9
Deferred	35.4
High school student	3.4
College student	10.4
Occupation	1.4
Dependency	19.6
Other	.6
In Service or Completed Service	32.4
Reserve or National Guard	6.6
Active duty	12.3
Veteran	13.5
Total	100.0%
Number classified	18,025,900

[a] Includes registrants from 18½ years up to age 26, as well as deferred registrants who had not entered military service in ages 26 up to age 35.

SOURCE: U.S. Congress, House Committee on Armed Services, *Review of the Administration and Operation of the Selective Service System,* 89th Congress, 2d sess. (Washington, D.C.: Government Printing Office, 1966), p. 10005.

Table 6

NEGROES IN EACH OF THE ARMED SERVICES AS A PERCENTAGE OF INITIAL ENLISTMENTS, FISCAL YEARS 1961–1966

Fiscal year	Army	Air Force	Navy	Marine Corps
1961	8.2%	9.5%	2.9%	5.9%
1962	9.0	8.6	4.1	6.5
1963	11.2	10.5	4.3	5.5
1964	12.2	9.1	5.0	8.7
1965	14.1	13.1	5.8	8.4
1966	11.2	8.0	3.4	8.6
1961–66 average	10.9%	9.8%	4.2%	7.2%

SOURCE : Department of Defense.

education. With regard to draft probabilities, it should also be noted that, barring total mobilization, membership in National Guard and Reserve units is in effect a deferment. And there is strong support for the assumption that Negroes are underrepresented in the 6.6 percent of the total number classified in this category.[4]

A more complete picture of Negro entrance rates into the military involves more than an assessment of disqualification, induction, and deferment rates. For excepting times of major war, voluntary enlistments account for approximately three-quarters of all incoming military personnel. Table 6 reports the Negro percentages of initial enlistments in each of the four armed services for the years 1961–1966. We find that it is the Army, besides its drawing upon the draft, that also has the highest Negro enlistment rate of any of the armed services. Taking the enlistment rates averaged over the six-year period, Negroes constituted 10.9 percent of Army initial enlistments, followed by 9.8 percent for the Air Force, 7.2 percent for the Marine Corps, and 4.2 percent for the Navy. As also shown in Table 6, there has been a sizable increase in Negro enlistments

---

[4] Indicative of Negro underrepresentation in the Reserve, the NORC Military Manpower Survey showed Reserve duty experience for 5.4 percent of those nonwhites qualified for military service, compared with 20.6 percent of the qualified whites (*In Pursuit of Equity,* p. 22). For documentation of racial barriers in the National Guard, see *Final Report: Military Personnel Stationed Overseas and Membership and Participation in the National Guard,* President's Committee on Equal Opportunity in the Armed Forces, November, 1964, pp. 12–22 (mimeographed).

Table 7
REASON FOR ENTERING MILITARY SERVICE FOR VOLUNTEERS, BY RACE

Reason	White	Negro
Personal	28.8%	28.7%
Patriotic	11.4	9.6
Draft-motivated	39.1	24.5
Self-advancement	20.7	37.2
Total	100.0%	100.0%
	N = 35,837	N = 4,120

SOURCE : NORC survey.

from 1961 to 1965 in all four of the armed services. The decline in Negro enlistment rates in 1966 can probably be explained by a consistent correlation between draft calls and voluntary enlistments. During those periods when draft calls are high, such as the year 1966, voluntary enlistments tend to increase. (Remember from Table 4 that the white percentage of inductees also increased in 1966.) This is an outcome of men seeking to increase their military options (i.e., choice of service and time of entrance) as the draft appears more imminent. This means that recruiting quotas can be met by more qualified applicants than usual, a selectivity factor that in turn means Negroes are less likely to be accepted for initial enlistments.

A better insight into the causes underlying volunteer initial enlistments can be gained by looking at the reasons mentioned for entering the armed forces. Based on responses elicited in the NORC survey, the motivations of volunteers were grouped into four categories : (1) *personal,* e.g., get away from home, mature, travel, excitement; (2) *patriotic,* e.g., serve one's country; (3) *draft-motivated,* e.g., choose time of service entry or branch of service; and (4) *self-advancement,* e.g., learn a trade, receive an education, military as a career. These reasons for entry among volunteers are reported by race in Table 7. There are only slight differences between whites and Negroes with regard to personal and patriotic reasons for service entry. The variation between the races is found almost entirely in their differing mentions of draft-motivated versus self-advancement reasons. Among white volunteers, 39.1 percent gave draft-motivated reasons compared to 24.5 percent of the Negroes. Conversely, only 20.7 percent of the white volunteers replied they entered the military for reasons of self-advancement compared with 37.2 percent of the Negroes who gave that reason. In other words, the draft serves as a major inducement for whites to volunteer, while the belief that self-advancement will be furthered through military service is much more typical of Negro volunteers.

Military requirements and Negro opportunities

A pervasive trend within the military establishment singled out by students of that institution is the long-term trend toward greater technical complexity and narrowing of civilian-military occupation skills.[5] An indicator, albeit a crude one, of this trend is the changing proportion of men assigned to combat arms. Given in Table 8, along with concomitant white-Negro distributions, are figures comparing the percentage of Army enlisted personnel in combat arms (e.g., infantry, armor, artillery) for the years 1945 and 1965. We find that the proportion of men in combat arms

Table 8

TOTAL NEGRO ARMY ENLISTED PERSONNEL AND WHITE AND NEGRO ENLISTED PERSONNEL IN COMBAT ARMS, 1945 AND 1965

Category	1945 [a]	1965
Negroes as percentage of total personnel	10.5%	13.9%
Percentage of total personnel in combat arms	44.5	22.9
Percentage of total white personnel in combat arms	48.2	21.5
Percentage of total Negro personnel in combat arms	12.1	30.6

[a] Excludes Army Air Corps.
SOURCE: Department of Defense.

[5] Morris Janowitz, with Roger Little, *Sociology and the Military Establishment* (New York: Russell Sage Foundation, 1965); Kurt Lang, "Technology and Career Management in the Military Establishment," in Morris Janowitz (ed.), *The New Military: Changing Patterns of Organization* (New York: Russell Sage Foundation, 1964), pp. 39–91; Charles H. Coates and Roland J. Pelligrin, *Military Sociology* (University Park, Md.: Social Science Press, 1965).

—that is, traditional military specialties—over the twenty-year period dropped from 44.5 percent to 22.9 percent. Also the percentage of white personnel in traditional military specialties approximates the total proportional decrease in the combat arms from 1945 to 1965.

For Negro soldiers, however, a different picture emerges. While the proportion of Negro enlisted men in the Army increased from 10.5 percent in 1945 to 13.9 percent in 1965, the likelihood of a Negro serving in a combat arm is two and a half times greater in 1965 than it was at the end of World War II. Further, when observations are made between military specialties *within* the combat arms, the Negro proportion is noticeably higher in line rather than staff assignments. In many airborne and Marine line companies, the number of Negroes is over half the unit strength. In other words, even though integration of the military has led to great improvement in the performance of Negro servicemen, the social and educational deprivations suffered by the Negro in American society can be mitigated but not eliminated by the racial egalitarianism existing within the armed forces. As reported in Table 9, in 1965 63.2 percent of all Negro draftees fell into the Army's lowest mental categories—those most likely to end up in combat units—compared with 23.2 percent of the white draftees. Similarly, among enlistees, Negroes were four times more likely to be found in the lowest mental levels than were their white counterparts.

A more detailed breakdown of the pattern of assignment by race in

Table 9

MENTAL GROUP CATEGORIES OF ARMY DRAFTEES AND ENLISTEES, BY RACE, 1965

Mental category	Draftees		Enlistees	
	White	Negro	White	Negro
Group I	5.3%	0.4%	6.5%	0.4%
Group II	28.0	5.3	36.7	8.3
Group III	42.8	31.1	50.1	63.4
Groups IV and V	23.9	63.2	6.7	27.9
Total	100.0%	100.0%	100.0%	100.0%

SOURCE: Department of Defense.

Table 10

PERCENTAGE DISTRIBUTION OF MILITARY OCCUPATIONS FOR ARMY ENLISTED MEN, BY MILITARY STATUS AND RACE

Category	Combat	Technical	Administrative	Service	Total	Number of cases
CAREER REGULARS						
White	19.9%	23.7%	24.9%	31.5%	100.0%	3,118
Negro	26.4	22.0	17.9	33.7	100.0	614
FIRST-TERM REGULARS						
White	22.9	26.6	20.0	30.5	100.0	6,965
Negro	33.2	25.0	14.0	27.8	100.0	1,183
DRAFTEES						
White	26.3	21.5	21.7	30.5	100.0	3,610
Negro	38.4	22.3	12.7	26.6	100.0	591

SOURCE: NORC survey.

the Army is given in Table 10. First, we must note that assignment to a combat arm, regardless of race, is most likely for draftees, followed by first-term regulars and, finally, career regulars. Yet, within each of these groupings, Negroes are more likely to be found in a combat arm than are whites. Negroes are underrepresented in administrative positions, and there are only small differences between the races with regard to their assignment in either technical or service positions. Looked at in another way, a Negro career regular is as likely to be in a combat unit as is a white draftee, but a Negro draftee is twice as likely to be in a combat unit than is a white career regular.

Whereas in World War II, low educational attainments kept most Negroes in support rather than combat units, these same educational handicaps operate in the middle 1960's to overconcentrate Negro soldiers in combat duty. The overconcentration of Negroes in combat arms, however, need not be interpreted as a decline in the "status" of the Negro in the integrated military. Actually there is evidence that higher prestige—but not envy—is accorded combat personnel by those in noncombat activities within the military. And taken within the historical context of the "right to fight," a slogan loudly echoed by Negro organizations with reference to the segregated military of World War II, the Negro's over-representation in the combat arms might be construed as a kind of ironic step forward.

Moreover, the military at the enlisted ranks has become a major avenue of career mobility for many Negro men.[6] As seen earlier in Table 2, in all four services, and especially in the Army, there is some over-representation of Negroes at the junior NCO levels. The disproportionate concentration of Negroes at these levels implies a higher than average re-enlistment rate as these grades are not normally attained until after a second enlistment. This assumption is supported by the data given in Table 11. We find that in 1964 for all four services the Negro re-enlistment rate was approximately twice that of white servicemen. Indeed, about half of all first-term Negro servicemen chose to remain in the armed forces for at least a second term. Data from the NORC survey also show that 50 percent of Negroes who were making a career of military life were initially draftees, as contrasted with 21.3 percent of the white career soldiers who also first entered the service through the draft.

The greater likelihood of Negroes to select a service career suggests that the military establishment is undergoing a significant change in its NCO core. Such an outcome would reflect not only the "pull" of the appeals offered by a racially integrated institution, but also the "push" generated by the plight of the Negro in the American economy. Indeed, there is rather conclusive evidence that the gap between Negro and white job opportunities in the civilian economy has actually increased rather than diminished over the past twenty years. At the minimum, it is very

Table 11

FIRST-TERM RE-ENLISTMENT RATES IN THE ARMED FORCES AND EACH SERVICE, BY RACE, 1964 (PERCENTAGES)

Race	Total Armed Forces	Army	Air Force	Navy	Marine Corps
White	21.6%	18.5%	27.4%	21.6%	12.9%
Negro	46.6	49.3	50.3	41.3	25.1

SOURCE: Department of Defense.

[6] The emphasis on academic education for officer careers effectively limits most Negro opportunity to the enlisted levels (Lang, *op. cit.,* 62).

The Negro and the draft

probable that as the present cohort of Negro junior NCO's attains seniority there will be a greater representation of Negroes in the advanced NCO grades. The expansion of the armed forces arising from the war in Vietnam and the resulting opening up of "rank" will accelerate this development.

That Negro servicemen have a more favorable view of military life than whites is reflected not only in their higher re-enlistment rates, but also in the survey data reported in Table 12. Whether broken down by branch

Table 12

PERCENTAGES OF ENLISTED PERSONNEL NOT LIKING MILITARY LIFE, BY RACE AND SELECTED GROUPINGS

Category	White	Negro
MILITARY BRANCH		
Army	51.4% (15,007)[a]	35.2% (2,641)
Air Force	36.1 (12,593)	27.0 (1,414)
Navy	44.2 (11,158)	29.6 (699)
Marine Corps	46.5 (3,262)	35.3 (300)
TOTAL MILITARY BY EDUCATION		
Less than high school	42.8% (8,431)	28.5% (1,084)
High school graduate	43.2 (24,027)	31.3 (2,985)
Some college or more	49.3 (9,562)	38.9 (985)
ARMY ENLISTED MEN BY MILITARY OCCUPATION		
Combat	49.5% (3,192)	36.1% (777)
Technical	52.9 (3,390)	35.6 (556)
Administrative	54.1 (2,976)	35.5 (352)
Service	52.5 (4,221)	33.0 (690)
VETERANS BY PRIOR MILITARY STATUS		
Volunteered	34.9% (1,293)	26.9% (78)
Drafted	52.4 (856)	25.3 (79)

[a] Number of cases on which percentages are based given in parentheses.
SOURCE : NORC survey.

of service, education, or military occupation, Negro servicemen consistently have a less negative view of life in the military. Thus, for example, 28.5 percent of Negro servicemen with less than a high school education dislike military life compared with 42.8 percent of white servicemen of the same educational level; among high school graduates, 31.3 percent of Negroes compared to 43.2 percent of whites do not like military life; and for those with at least some college, 38.9 percent of Negroes dislike service life compared to 49.3 percent of the whites. Perhaps most noteworthy is that Negro veterans, both those who were draftees as well as the volunteers, view military life as less onerous than white veterans. That military life is regarded in relatively benign terms by many Negro men speaks not only of the racial egalitarianism of the military, but, more profoundly, of the existing state of affairs for Negroes in American society at large.

Negro participation in the military : efficacy, equity, and morality

Views toward the relationship of the Negro American to the Selective Service System and/or the military establishment are beginning to coalesce into three more or less distinct concerns. One group sees the military system as an agency to improve Negro opportunity in American society. Then there are those who essentially seek to make Negro participation in the military more equitable. A quite different third viewpoint questions the basic legitimacy of Negro involvement in the armed forces. Each of these positions requires special comment.

The argument that the military system is a particularly effective way of reaching and rescuing large numbers of Negro youth (as well as, of course, many white youth) from the urban ghettoes and rural slums has some persuasion. Certainly, the Selective Service is the only screen through which virtually all male Americans—white and black—must pass. The existing Selective Service System, that is, can with alteration be used to identify those youth who would most benefit from education and even medical treatment. Once these youth have been so identified, remedial steps could take place within the military or some organizational arrangement modeled after the military system.

A variation on this scheme is the idea of "national service," a program that would entail a two-year obligation for every young person, even those not actually required for military duty. For those youth coming from the more privileged elements of our society, such national service would generally be along the lines of good works. For the youth of our depressed population, however, the period of national service would serve primarily as a time of acquiring occupational skills, formal education, and perhaps, most important, an exposure to something other than the life of the slum. Under the national service program, the training of these youths would be conducted under some kind of paramilitary organizational pattern.

While it is beyond the scope of this study to detail or trace out any possible benefits of military experience or quasimilitary educational programs for deprived youth, a provisional observation on this issue is warranted. Table 13 presents some evidence on the perceived value of service life on civilian job opportunities. By a variety of groupings, Negroes on active duty in every instance are more likely to state that their military training will be of "considerable use" in civilian employment than are their white counterparts. Most significant, perhaps, Negro veterans, those who were drafted as well as those who volunteered, are more than twice as likely to value their military training highly than are white veterans. Note, however, that favorable evaluation of one's military training for civilian employment is lowest among those in combat units—the very military occupations to which Negroes are most likely to be assigned.

Because of an announcement by Secretary of Defense McNamara in the summer of 1966, the issue of the utility of Selective Service and the military as agencies of identification and remedial treatment of deprived youth has become intertwined with the question of the equity of the draft. Starting in the fall of 1966 and extending through the summer of 1968, over 125,000 men from previously ineligible mental levels—those in the Selective Service Category I-Y—had been inducted or enlisted into the armed forces. About 40 percent of these entrants were Negro. Though couched in terms of the War on Poverty, drawing upon these men from the lower mental levels was in effect a way to increase the military manpower pool. Informed observers in the military agree that it is misleading to think these "I-Y's" will receive any special treatment or training. Rather they will be mixed in with the regular trainees and, in all probability, largely be assigned to combat units. Placed in a broader social context, the decision to lower the mental standards required for military entrance effectively eased the pressure for drafting college students. That is, with the increased demand for military manpower arising out of the Vietnam war, the draft pool could be extended in either of two directions: induct col-

Table 13

PERCENTAGES OF ENLISTED PERSONNEL BELIEVING THEIR MILITARY TRAINING WILL BE OF "CONSIDERABLE USE" IN CIVILIAN EMPLOYMENT, BY RACE AND SELECTED GROUPINGS

Category	White	Negro
ARMY ENLISTED MEN BY MILITARY OCCUPATION		
Combat	9.9% (3,087)[a]	11.3% (773)
Technical	32.9 (3,337)	42.4 (556)
Administrative	26.7 (2,942)	39.4 (348)
Service	36.0 (4,179)	41.1 (688)
ARMY ENLISTED MEN BY MILITARY STATUS		
Career regulars	47.5% (3,201)	49.2% (649)
First-term regulars	27.2 (7,594)	30.0 (1,315)
Draftees	10.2 (3,997)	17.1 (666)
DRAFTEES BY EDUCATION		
Less than high school	11.1% (1,000)	18.9% (190)
High school graduate	10.3 (1,771)	16.1 (311)
Some college or more	9.3 (1,224)	17.1 (164)
VETERANS BY PRIOR MILITARY STATUS		
Volunteered	11.4% (1,229)	29.9% (77)
Drafted	5.3 (826)	13.0 (77)

[a] Number of cases on which percentages are based given in parentheses.
SOURCE: NORC survey.

lege students—largely middle-class whites—or induct persons from the lower mental levels—overproportionately poor Negroes.

The 1966 decision to accept "I-Y's" into the armed services illustrates a consideration that is sometimes blurred in discussions of equitable participation in the military : the distinction between equity with regard to entrance into the military as opposed to equity in assignment within the military. The findings presented in this study show that Negroes are victims of inequity on both counts. That is, Negroes, even though markedly less qualified for military service on the grounds of mental examinations, are still overproportionately drafted. Moreover, once within the military system, Negroes are disproportionately concentrated in combat units—further testimony to the continuing consequences of Negro deprivation originating in the larger society. And it is to be expected that the newly incoming "I-Y's" will reinforce both of these sources of inequity.

An important feature of the entrance inequities facing Negroes is most alarmingly revealed by the make-up of many local draft boards. In the fall of 1966 a suit was brought into a Mississippi federal court seeking an injunction to prevent further induction of Negroes until Negroes are appointed to draft boards in proportion to their numbers in the population. Apparently, no Negro has ever been appointed to any local draft board or any appeal board in the entire state of Mississippi. Similar suits have been brought in other Deep South states. The extreme underrepresentation of Negroes on draft boards is also too frequently the case in local Selective Service units encompassing Negro areas in Northern urban cities. In fact, in December, 1966, Negroes constituted only 1.5 percent of all local draft board members in the entire country.[7]

Concerning inequities after placement within the armed services, the overconcentration of Negroes in combat units previously noted is all too obviously reflected in the casualty reports from Vietnam. As documented

---

[7] *In Pursuit of Equity*, p. 19. There were 23 states without a single Negro board member : Alabama, Alaska, Arkansas, Colorado, Hawaii, Idaho, Indiana, Iowa, Kansas, Louisiana, Maine, Minnesota, Mississippi, Montana, Nevada, New Jersey, New Mexico, North Dakota, Rhode Island, South Dakota, Utah, Vermont, and Wyoming. Of course, the question of Negro membership on local draft boards must be placed within the context of the proportional Negro population in the community.

in Table 14, among Army enlisted men Negroes are being killed at twice their proportion in the total American population.

The nature of Negro participation within the military establishment has also become inextricable from broader criticisms of America's current politico-military policies. Much attention has been given to a convergence of an important segment of the civil rights movement with the movement against the war in Vietnam. A Negro is barred from taking his seat in the Georgia legislature because he allegedly condones violations of the draft law. Civil rights organizers claim they find Negroes who do not want to fight "whitey's war." Rumors are heard of isolated incidents of Negro insubordination in the armed services. The Student Nonviolent Coordinating Committee and the Students for a Democratic Society, two leading organizations in the "New Left," have vehemently denounced American intervention in Vietnam. In a joint statement to the U.S. House Committee on the Armed Services, these two organizations assailed the draft with the words : "It is our belief that the draft injures our whole society, and we are in sympathy with and support of all young men who refuse to equate their responsibility to a free society with obligation to assist in military aggression. Those who work for a new society in this

Table 14

NEGROES AS PERCENTAGE OF MEN ASSIGNED TO VIETNAM [a] AND KILLED IN ACTION (K.I.A.),[b] BY OFFICERS AND ENLISTED MEN FOR EACH SERVICE

Service	Negroes in Vietnam	Officers K.I.A.	Enlisted men K.I.A.	Total K.I.A.
Army	14.8%	2.8%	22.1%	18.3%
Marine Corps	8.9	5.4	12.0	11.3
Navy	5.1	—	3.7	1.3
Air Force	8.3	—	—	—

[a] As of December 31, 1965. More recent Defense Department statistics, however, indicate a substantially lower—but still disproportionate—Negro casualty rate. For the year 1967, Negroes constituted 11.7 percent of Army personnel in Vietnam and accounted for 13.5 percent of all Army deaths caused by hostile action.
[b] 1961–1965 inclusive.
SOURCE : Department of Defense.

country should not be sent to destroy incipient social workers in other nations."[8]

Despite this chain of events, the major thrust of the civil rights drive has remained somewhat removed from those groups highly critical of this country's recent military policies. Indeed, the antiwar movement will likely aggravate an already existing cleavage between moderate and radical leaders—between those who accept versus those who reject the legitimacy of the American political and economic system—in the civil rights movement itself. The more pertinent question at this time appears to be not what are the implications of the civil rights movement for the military establishment, but what will be the effects of the Vietnam war on the civil rights movement itself. Although it would be premature to offer a definitive statement on any future interpenetrations between the civil rights and antiwar movements, a major turning away of Negroes per se from military commitment is viewed as highly doubtful. Most likely, and somewhat paradoxically, we will witness more vocal antiwar sentiment within certain civil rights organizations at the same time that the military is becoming an avenue of career opportunity for many Negro men.

Further, despite the demonstrable inequities for Negroes in the existing draft system, the fact remains that Selective Service even as it currently operates is seen in more favorable terms by Negroes than by whites. This anomalous circumstance is illustrated by the data in Table 15. We find for an assortment of groups, within and without the military, that Negro men consistently regard the draft as more equitable than whites.[9]

Looking first at civilians with no military experience, we see that while among white-collar workers Negroes are only slightly more likely to view the draft as very fair, among blue-collar workers 41.3 percent of Negroes, compared to 28.5 percent of whites, view the draft as very fair.

---

[8] *New Left Notes* (July 8, 1966), p. 1.

[9] Survey data for 1966 collected by Louis Harris show the same greater likelihood for Negroes to view the Selective Service as operating in an equitable manner : 63 percent of Negroes polled, compared with 48 percent of whites, said the draft was fair. Additionally, the same Harris poll reports that Negroes believe by better than two to one that the armed services offer Negroes a better chance to get ahead than does civilian life (Louis Harris and Associates, Inc., "Public Opinion and the Draft Poll," in J. A. Willenz (ed.), *Dialogue on the Draft* (Washington, D.C. : American Veterans' Committee, 1966), pp. 64–65.

Table 15

PERCENTAGE DISTRIBUTION OF ATTITUDES TOWARD THE DRAFT, BY SELECTED GROUPINGS AND RACE

Category	Very fair	Reasonably fair	Unfair	Total	Number of cases
CIVILIANS WITH NO MILITARY EXPERIENCE BY OCCUPATION					
White-collar					
White	22.7%	46.7%	30.6%	100.0%	(1,166)
Negro	23.1	53.8	23.1	100.0	(65)
Blue-collar					
White	28.5	50.0	21.5	100.0	(1,910)
Negro	41.3	43.1	15.6	100.0	(283)
ARMY ENLISTED MEN BY MILITARY STATUS					
Career regulars					
White	41.8%	31.8%	26.4%	100.0%	(2,442)
Negro	55.1	31.3	13.6	100.0	(521)
First-term regulars					
White	28.3	40.2	31.5	100.0	(6,518)
Negro	36.7	43.2	20.1	100.0	(1,074)
Draftees					
White	13.7	34.0	52.3	100.0	(3,681)
Negro	27.6	38.6	33.8	100.0	(577)

Among Army enlisted men, although the draft regardless of race is viewed as less fair by draftees compared to either career or first-term regulars, Negroes in all three enlisted categories are markedly more favorable in their views concerning the draft's equity. Looking at the draftees only, we find, regardless of race, higher education being associated with more negative attitudes toward the draft. But, again, Negroes at all educational levels think of the draft in more favorable terms than their white counterparts. Finally, with regard to civilians with military experience, both among the volunteers and the drafted, Negro veterans are much more favorably disposed toward the draft than whites. Indeed, only 3.0 percent of the Negro veterans who were drafted, compared to more than ten times that proportion among whites, said the Selective Service System was unfair. In fact, Negro veterans who were draftees were almost as likely to have a good opinion of the draft as were Negro veterans who were volunteers.

PERCENTAGE DISTRIBUTION OF ATTITUDES TOWARD THE DRAFT, BY SELECTED GROUPINGS AND RACE

Category	Very fair	Reasonably fair	Unfair	Total	Number of cases
DRAFTEES BY EDUCATION					
Less than high school					
White	24.2%	35.9%	39.9%	100.0%	(872)
Negro	42.6	33.5	23.9	100.0	(155)
High school graduate					
White	13.2	36.5	50.3	100.0	(1,624)
Negro	25.8	43.2	31.0	100.0	(271)
Some college or more					
White	6.6	29.2	64.2	100.0	(1,184)
Negro	15.3	35.3	49.4	100.0	(150)
VETERANS BY PRIOR MILITARY STATUS					
Volunteered					
White	36.1%	38.8%	25.1%	100.0%	(1,029)
Negro	50.0	36.5	13.5	100.0	(52)
Drafted					
White	26.8	41.4	31.8	100.0	(720)
Negro	48.5	48.5	3.0	100.0	(66)

SOURCE : NORC survey.

The implications of the findings presented in this study can be summed up somewhat as follows : Despite inequities suffered by Negroes both in being more likely to be drafted and once in the service being more likely to assignment in combat units, Negroes, nevertheless, are still much more likely than whites to have positive views toward the draft and military life. A tragic irony in our country is that many Negro youths by seeking to enter the armed forces are saying that it is even worth the risk of being killed in order to have a chance to learn a trade, to make it in a small way, to get away from a dead-end existence, and to join the only institution in this society that seems really to be racially integrated.

Is it not possible then to apply some sociological imagination to see how the positive aspects of the military organization can be taken advantage of while reducing its inequitable features? In this regard, the institution of a completely volunteer, but highly paid, military would in all likelihood augment the trend toward Negro retention in the military as well as the probability of Negroes being assigned combat duties. A lottery system of military induction, on the other hand, while realizing the goal of entrance equity, would not affect the overassignment of Negroes to combat units. Whatever method of selection is used—draft, highly paid volunteers, lottery—to bring men into the armed forces, Negroes, because of socioeducational handicaps, would continue to be much more likely than whites to end up in combat positions. Rather, the lessons of the military experience and Negro reactions to it seem to suggest something along the line of a comprehensive program of national service and remedial treatment. That such a program would involve a drastic reordering of the lives of many of our youth cannot be denied. That the present state of affairs is both practically and morally objectionable seems equally undeniable.

Military service and occupational mobility

IRVIN G. KATENBRINK, JR.

IN ITS REPORT of early 1964, the President's Task Force on Manpower Conservation found that one-third of all young men in the nation turning eighteen would be found unqualified if they were to be examined for induction into the armed forces. About half of this third would be disqualified for medical reasons while the remaining half could not meet the mental requirements. The report proposed a nationwide program to rehabilitate these young men.[1]

In August, 1964, the Department of Defense announced plans for a Special Training and Enlistment Program (STEP) to be conducted by the Army on a pilot basis to attempt rehabilitation of the unqualified third. The program was intended to reduce reliance on the draft by expanding the pool of qualified volunteers available for enlistment. Starting in November, 1964, 15,000 to 20,000 young men who had previously been disqualified for enlistment because of their failure to meet mental test standards or because of remediable physical defects were to undergo

---

[1] *One-Third of a Nation: A Report on Young Men Found Unqualified for Military Service* (Washington, D.C.: The President's Task Force on Manpower Conservation, January 1, 1964).

a six-to-twelve-month period of education and/or medical treatment. Those who satisfactorily completed the program would continue as Regular Army enlisted personnel for an additional two and one-half years. Because of the buildup of U.S. forces for the Vietnam war, the program was either postponed or canceled before it could be implemented.[2]

In spite of the delayed implementation of this particular program, the armed forces have contributed significantly to the education and training of a large segment of the male population.[3]

The purpose of this study is to determine whether short-term enlisted military service affects the occupational mobility of youth upon their return to the civilian community, and if so, to what extent. Because of time and fund restrictions, the study is limited in several respects; interpretation of the results should be made in light of the following:

1. The study is microscopic in nature, dealing with a single civilian community.
2. It concerns only returnees from U.S. Army service.
3. The individuals interviewed were not subject to military service during a period of full or partial mobilization.
4. The study is limited to male, white Americans.
5. For reasons to be explained below, individuals returning to the civilian community after a period of voluntary enlistment were not part of the survey.

Further, it should be noted that the study is not applicable to individuals who remain in the service as a career. While their Army educational and training experiences no doubt result in a general upgrading of their socio-economic standing, this particular result of active duty is beyond the scope of this study.

---

[2] Since this paper was written, many of the features of this program have been implemented as *Project 100,000* of the Department of Defense, by the acceptance for enlistment or induction of specific categories of men previously rejected for service. For the original issue see "Pilot Program for 60,000 Enlistees," *Army News Features,* Headquarters, U.S. Army Command, Information Unit, Washington, D.C., Release No. 37, August 14, 1964; *Army Times,* XXVI (August 18, 1965), 1; Hanson W. Baldwin, "Should We End the Draft?" *New York Times Magazine* (September 27, 1964), p. 118.

[3] *Manpower Report of the President* (Washington, D.C., March, 1965), p. 76.

Liability for military service

Congress has established liability of male youth for military service through the Universal Military Training and Service Act of 1951 and four-year extensions of the act in 1955, 1959, 1963, and 1967. One way an individual may discharge his obligation is through service in the Army and should he choose this route there are several options open to him.

1. *Enlistment.* An individual may enlist (volunteer) in the Army for a minimum period of three years of active duty. Over the past few years about half the men entering the active Army for the first time are enlistees. The advantages of this program are (*a*) the individual can usually select specialized training if he is qualified, (*b*) he is able to get his military obligation "behind him" rather than wait out the possibility of being drafted, and (*c*) his obligation upon discharge (should he not desire to re-enlist) is three years in the Reserves, all of which is in an inactive status, i.e., he is not required to attend weekly training meetings or summer active duty sessions. Regulations actually require a period of Active Reserve service but because Reserve units are at 100 percent strength there is no room for returning enlistees.

2. *Induction.* An individual may wait to be called to active duty by his local draft board, being subject to such action between the ages of 18½ and 26 years. Of course he may be exempted or deferred by the local board but if not, and if called, his period of active duty is two years followed by a similar period in the Active Reserves and two additional years in an inactive Reserve status. While in the Active Reserves he is required to attend 48 training meetings per year as well as 15 days of active duty each summer.

3. *Reserve programs.* An individual may enlist in one of the Army Reserve programs : ROTC, National Guard, or the Enlisted Reserves. The ROTC and National Guard programs will not be discussed in this paper except to point out that the obligations associated with the National Guard program are similar to those of the Enlisted Reserve program.

An individual volunteers for the Enlisted Reserves and if accepted serves six months of active duty followed by 5½ years in the Active Reserves; there is no period of inactive Reserve service under this program.

A description of the more important characteristics of each category follows :

Regular Army ("RA") enlistees are usually younger (average age in 1964 was 19.8) than draftees or Enlisted Reservists. They can enlist as early as age 17 with parental consent. Usually they are from slightly lower socioeconomic backgrounds and have completed less formal education than members of the two other categories. Many have either just finished high school or dropped out before graduation. As a result, many do not really know what they want to do in life.

Draftees ("US") tend to be the oldest. Average age of draftees in 1964 was 22.4 years.[4] They usually have more formal schooling than RA's; they want either to postpone active duty or to take their chances on being called by the draft board.

Enlisted Reservists' ("ER") average age is about 20 years. They neither want to serve three years as enlistees, nor risk two years active duty as draftees. A short active duty period (six months) with maximum Reserve service after returning to civilian life better fits into their plans.

Advantages associated with Army service

Through active duty participation, an individual may receive personal gains in the form of additional education and vocational training. Although not *all* soldiers are better for having served, *many* should be better as a result of opportunities that are never experienced by their civilian contemporaries. These opportunities for self-improvement are of two kinds: for technical training in Army schools, and for continuing or supplementing an academic program in off-duty programs.

Other studies have noted a greater degree of mobility for veterans (of World War II). Jackson and Crockett offered as one explanation the possible "effect of military service on many men in that such service perhaps broadens occupational aspirations" coupled with "post-war assistance in technical and academic training." [5] Duncan and Hodge also com-

[4] Bernard D. Karpinos, "Results of the Examination of Youths for Military Service, 1964," supplement to *Health of the Army* (Washington, D.C.: The Surgeon General), XX (May, 1965), 23.

[5] Elton F. Jackson and Harry J. Crockett, Jr., "Occupational Mobility in the United States: A Point Estimate and Trend Comparison," *American Sociological Review,* XXIX (February, 1964), 13.

ment on the mobility of samples differing in exposure to military service. They note that World War II veterans were more mobile than nonveterans but attribute the superiority to "the process of *selection* of members of the armed forces." [6] In the present study efforts were taken to control this selection factor by excluding all men classified as IV-F from the civilian sample.

The Army school system

Most young men entering the Army have had minimum civilian work experience, have only recently ended their planned formal schooling, and are not fully qualified for the varied specialized jobs in military organization. These men must be trained for periods ranging from eight weeks to more than one year before being placed in duty positions.

Since the active duty requirement of enlistees is three years, it is feasible for the Army to utilize up to a third of this time for specialized training. Most soldiers attending extended service school courses are thus enlistees. The Army regulation that establishes the length of active duty that must be served by a soldier following service school attendance is designed to insure the Army a fair return on its training investment. However, it also makes the draftee ineligible for long service school courses as he is on active duty a total of only twenty-four months. This does not mean that service school courses attended by draftees have *no* carry-over value to civilian life; only that there is a *lesser* degree of carry-over for draftees since fewer are selected to attend courses and those selected do not attend the more extended courses.

The Enlisted Reservist ("ER"), although on active duty for only six months, attends service school courses on an equal basis with draftees ("US"). After eight weeks of basic training (required of all categories), the ER is most likely to be sent to an eight-week service school course associated with the job to which he will be assigned when he returns to his Reserve unit. Like the draftee, the Enlisted Reservist does not attend the more "glamorous" courses like the twenty-two-week helicopter repair

[6] Otis D. Duncan and Robert W. Hodge, "Education and Occupational Mobility: A Regression Analysis," *American Journal of Sociology,* LXVIII (May, 1963), 643.

school or the forty-one-week course in maintenance of the NIKE fire control system.

The civilian carry-over value of service school courses is used as an inducement to prospective enlistees.[7] Two recruitment publications in particular are quite specific in informing the young prospect that the training he receives will be useful should he return to civilian life.[8] A 300-page guide to high school counselors, *Army Occupations and You,* outlines specific civilian jobs associated with each Army occupational area. In the other publication, *The Secret of Getting Ahead,* Henry Ford II, David Sarnoff of RCA, and I. W. Wilson of Alcoa are quoted as to their enthusiasm for hiring service-trained personnel upon their return to civilian life.

Credit for service school training

Aside from skill carry-over value, service school training also is accreditable to civilian education records. The Commission on Accreditation of Service Experience (CASE) of the American Council on Education was established in December, 1945, "as a direct need expressed by civilian education for a national agency to coordinate the evaluation of the many varied educational achievements of service personnel."[9]

One of the functions of the commission is the continuous evaluation "in terms of baccalaureate, terminal junior college, and high school credit of formal service school training conducted by the Armed Forces of the United States. These evaluations are reported to civilian educational institutions, upon their request, as a guide in determining the amount and type of credit to be granted."[10]

---

[7] *Army Personnel Letter,* Office of the Deputy Chief of Staff for Personnel, Headquarters, Department of the Army, No. 8–65 (August, 1965), p. 3.

[8] *U.S. Army Opportunities (Handbook for Counselors and Students)* (Hampton, Va. : U.S. Army Recruiting Command, 1966); *The Secret of Getting Ahead,* U.S. Army information pamphlet to high school students. The other services have similar publications : *The U.S. Air Force Occupational Handbook for Air Men* (1966–67); *United States Navy Enlistee Occupational Handbook* (1966).

[9] "Granting Credit for Service School Training," *The Bulletin,* Commission on Accreditation of Service Experiences of the American Council on Education, Washington, D.C., No. 8, 2nd ed. (January, 1959), p. iii.

[10] *Ibid.* Credit recommendations are made for those aspects of military training that have a counterpart in civilian education. The 1954 edition of *A Guide to the Eval-*

Educational opportunities in the Army

In addition to the opportunity for technical *training* through the Army School System, it is possible for the soldier to take advantage of the Army's General Educational Development (GED) Program.

The basic philosophy underlying the Army's General Educational Development (GED) Program is that an individual can improve himself through learning; that the process of learning does not stop with the completion of formal schooling at an early age, but on the contrary education is a lifelong process.[11]

This program, like the Army School System, although primarily designed to improve the quality of the career soldier, is open to all personnel on active duty. The minimum general educational development goal for Army enlisted personnel is the completion of high school or its equivalent and higher level studies as required.[12] During the period June 30, 1960, until December 31, 1963, the percentage of Army enlisted personnel who had graduated from high school increased from 62.3 to 75.4.[13]

Every installation or troop concentration having a troop strength of 750 or more is required to maintain at least one Army Education Center.[14] Personnel at smaller posts may travel to Centers at larger adjacent posts. Such Centers include space for administrative, clerical, and counseling offices; classroom instruction, registration, and testing activities; language, reading, and science laboratories; and shops for technical-voca-

---

uation of Educational Experiences in the Armed Forces outlines in detail the commission's recommendations for armed forces courses conducted from World War II to 1954. A copy of this guide was sent free to each high school and college in the United States in the fall of 1954. The commission's recommendations for courses conducted since 1954 are available to any school or college upon request. See Table 2 for information on the number of state departments of education that in fact grant such credit.

[11] *General Educational Development,* Army Regulation 621–5, Headquarters, Department of the Army (November, 1964), para. 2.

[12] *Ibid.,* para. 4a(3). For commissioned officers: at least a baccalaureate degree in subject areas of functional importance to the military profession with encouragement toward graduate study. For warrant officers: two years of college or its equivalent.

[13] *Sample Survey of Military Personnel,* SDB Report No. 114-60-SE, Department of the Army; *Selected Manpower Statistics,* prepared by the Directorate for Statistical Service, Office of the Secretary of Defense (April 11, 1966), p. 36.

[14] *General Educational Development,* para. 5a(1).

tional instruction. The regulation requires that each Center be headed by a "professional educator, normally a Department of Army civilian employee."[15] In 1965 there were 296 Centers in operation headed by 300 career civilian educators.[16] Basically, the head of each Center locally implements the program offered by the United States Armed Forces Institute (USAFI).

USAFI

The United States Armed Forces Institute (USAFI) began operations at Madison, Wisconsin, on April 1, 1942, under the designation "The Army Institute." [17] This agency came into being as a result of the efforts of the Joint Army-Navy Committee on Welfare and Recreation and the National Committee on Education and Defense (of the American Council on Education). The Army Institute initially provided educational opportunities only to enlisted personnel of the Army, but the services of the Institute were extended to enlisted members of the Navy, Marine Corps, and Coast Guard in September, 1942. In February, 1943, the name was changed to the United States Armed Forces Institute (USAFI). Commissioned personnel have been permitted to participate in the program since July, 1944. In 1946, Secretary of War Robert P. Patterson directed that USAFI be established as a peacetime educational activity.

USAFI operates throughout the world wherever members of the armed forces are stationed. In addition to the central USAFI at Madison, Wisconsin, there are five USAFI branches located in Frankfort, Germany; Tokyo, Japan; Fort Shafter, Hawaii; Anchorage, Alaska; and Fort Clayton, Canal Zone. The 296 Army Education Centers discussed above are active in administering the USAFI program at the local level in the Army. Of the 263,937 active enrollments with USAFI (as of May 1, 1964)

---

[15] *Ibid.*, para. 5a(2).

[16] *Army Times,* XXVI (September 29, 1965), 5.

[17] Information on USAFI history came from numerous sources : *Catalog of USAFI,* 12th ed., Department of Defense pamphlet 7–13 (1963); *USAFI General Information Bulletin,* undated; *USAFI Fact Sheet,* 3-page document furnished by USAFI, Madison, Wis.; Jeanne B. Eldridge, "The USAFI Testing Program," thesis for MA degree in political science, University of Wisconsin, 1961.

111,444 were Army personnel. This figure does not include individuals enrolled in spoken language courses. The average yearly enrollment since 1960 for all of the armed forces is 314,000; the total cumulative enrollment since the beginning of the USAFI program was 6,032,900 (as of June, 1964).[18] For data on a typical Army Education Center see Appendix 1.

Although the administration of USAFI is a responsibility of the Assistant Secretary of Defense for Manpower, it is essentially a civilian-type educational organization. The mission of USAFI is

> ... to provide common services and materials by which the Army, Navy, Air Force, Marine Corps, and Coast Guard may supplement, for members of their commands, educational opportunities in subjects normally taught in civilian academic institutions, in order that the individual may render efficient service in his present assignment, increase his capabilities for assuming greater responsibility, and satisfy his intellectual desires.[19]

More than 200 courses are directly available from USAFI in elementary, high school, college, and technical subjects. These courses may be pursued by either correspondence or the group-study method according to the student's preference (and availability of enough fellow soldiers interested in the same subject as well as a qualified instructor). Courses at the grammar school level *must* be conducted by the group-study method. These courses are conducted during both duty and nonduty periods, the soldier being excused from normal duties in order that he may attend.

In addition to the 200 courses offered directly by USAFI, more than 6,000 courses at the high school and college level are available through USAFI from the extension divisions of 43 leading colleges and universities.

An individual on active duty may apply for the 200 USAFI courses at an initial cost of five dollars; thereafter, he may take other USAFI courses at no further cost as long as he makes satisfactory progress in courses for which he has previously enrolled. He must complete a USAFI correspondence course within twelve months. The correspondence courses offered by the 43 civilian colleges and universities are available at reduced prices

---

[18] Enrollment data from personal correspondence with C. L. Munden, Director of USAFI, Madison, Wis.
[19] *Catalog of USAFI,* p. 5.

to military personnel, e.g., a two-semester-hour college-level sociology course, "War and Civilization," [20] is offered by the University of California (Berkeley) for $16.50, which covers the administrative cost of enrollment and price of textbooks and material. USAFI assumes the cost of the lesson service. The serviceman has 24 months to complete a course offered through this program.[21]

USAFI *testing* is provided without charge to soldiers on active duty and includes :

1. USAFI Subject Standardized Tests are designed for students desiring credit for the 200 courses offered by USAFI. These tests serve as end-of-course exams but the testee does not necessarily have to have been enrolled in the USAFI course; those who study independently of USAFI enrollment may receive credit.

2. General Educational Development (GED) Tests are designed to measure the general educational development of the soldier whether it was acquired through formal classes or through informal self-education and intellectual growth. The high-school-level GED Tests are intended for persons who have completed only a part of their high school work or who have never attended high school. The college-level GED Tests measure the extent to which the student has attained the equivalent of a college freshman-level education, which may have been obtained through survey courses or experience in the subject area covered by the tests. For a complete discussion of the GED testing program, see the American Council on Education's publication, *Conclusions and Recommendations on a Study of the General Educational Development Testing Program,* published in 1956. In 1965, 43,558 soldiers qualified for high school diplomas or equivalency certificates by passing the GED tests.

3. USAFI Achievement Tests aid in determining grade-level achievement of military personnel in grades 4–6 and 7–9. As of February 28, 1965, 28 percent of the enlisted strength of the Army had not completed at least twelve grades of education; an additional 1.9 percent had com-

---

[20] There are 190 other college-level sociology courses offered through the 43 colleges; there are 18 more offered at the high school level.

[21] For detailed information on the program offered by the 43 participating colleges, see *Catalog of USAFI* and *Correspondence Courses Offered by Colleges and Universities Through USAFI,* Department of Defense Pamphlet 7–12, revision of 1963.

pleted twelve grades but had not graduated from high school. Table 1 shows the breakdown of the 22.8 percent not completing a high school education.

Army regulations require that courses be provided in Army Education Centers for personnel (1) who have not completed the eighth grade, (2) who need review instruction on the adult level in English, social science, general science, or mathematics to meet certain minimum career obligations, (3) whose aptitude area scores are below those required for service school attendance, and (4) who are working toward a high school diploma or equivalent through high school GED tests. Commanders are permitted to authorize the use of duty time for such instruction "consistent with operational and training requirements." [22] My personal observation has been that commanders *always* excuse from duty those soldiers with less than an eighth grade education.

Results of USAFI Standardized and GED tests are sent to civilian high school and college authorities upon request; these officials may or may

Table 1

ARMY ENLISTED PERSONNEL NOT HAVING COMPLETED HIGH SCHOOL EDUCATION [a]

Last grade completed	Percentage of total enlisted strength
11	5.9%
10	6.6
9	4.9
8	3.8
Less than 8	1.6
	22.8%

[a] An additional 1.9 percent completed 12 grades of education but did not graduate from high school.

SOURCE: Department of Army Sample Survey of Military Personnel "Survey Estimate of Education Level of Male Enlisted Personnel by Grade and Component," 550 Report No. 52-65-E.

[22] *General Educational Development*, para. 10e(5).

not grant academic credit to the student. Results of USAFI Achievement Tests are for military purposes only and are not reported to schools or other civilian agencies; they are not kept on file of USAFI.

Civilian credit for USAFI courses

In addition to recommending credit for service school training, the Commission on Accreditation of Service Experiences also evaluates USAFI courses and tests and makes recommendations to school and college officials as to the amount of credit that should be granted for this aspect of the soldier's education. Table 2 summarizes the policies of the 50 state departments of education as well as those of the District of Columbia, Canal Zone, Guam, and Puerto Rico. It should be noted that 42 state departments of education also grant some credit toward education at the high school level for basic or recruit training, i.e., the first eight weeks of a soldier's Army experience.

Table 2

SUMMARY OF POLICIES FOR GRANTING HIGH SCHOOL CREDIT FOR SERVICE EDUCATIONAL EXPERIENCES

Type of educational experience	Number of departments of education		
	Recommending credit	Not recommending credit	Making no recommendations
USAFI courses	51	1	2
USAFI subject standardized tests	48	4	4
Cooperating college courses	50	2	2
Basic or recruit training	42	10	2
Formal service school training	48	4	2

SOURCE: Table 1, page 66, *The Bulletin* of the Commission on Accreditation of Service Experiences (American Council on Education). Number 5, eighth edition, January, 1963.

Table 3

SUMMARY OF POLICIES FOR ISSUANCE OF HIGH SCHOOL CERTIFICATES ON THE BASIS OF THE GED TESTS, 1963

Policy	Number of departments of education
Certificates issued *only* at state level	33
Certificates issued *only* at local level	10 [a]
Certificates issued by either	9
Departments recognizing GED tests	52
Departments not recognizing GED tests	2 [b]

[a] California, Indiana, Iowa, Michigan, Minnesota, Nevada, Oklahoma, Utah, Virginia, Washington.
[b] Delaware, Wisconsin.
SOURCE : Table 2, page 67, *The Bulletin* of the Commission on Accreditation of Service Experiences (American Council on Education). Number 5, eighth edition, January, 1963.

Table 3 summarizes the state policies relative to the issuance of high school certificates on the basis of successful completion of the GED tests. The Commission on Accreditation of Service Experiences recommends that the equivalency certificate be issued at the state department of education level rather than at the local high school level "in order that all citizens in the state will have [an] equal opportunity." Other educational opportunities for enlisted men exist in the form of attendance at civilian colleges either overseas or in the United States and either full time or after duty hours. These programs are not applicable to this study.

Method

To determine the influence of military service (in the Army) on civilian occupational mobility, a comparison was made of the intergenerational occupational mobility of two groups of white males in a city of 31,000 in southeastern New York State. One group (the experimental group) consisted of former service men who had returned to the civilian community and are referred to in this study as the "military sample." The second group (control) consisted of a comparable number of men who had not experienced any military service. This group is referred to as the "civilian sample."

THE MILITARY SAMPLE

Members of the only Army Reserve unit located in the survey city were selected as the experimental group. This unit was an engineer construction company. It consisted of all draftees returning to the civilian community after two years active duty, Enlisted Reservists, and a few former Regular Army members (now Reservists). The latter were all senior noncommissioned officers and may be considered to be "career" Reservists. Selection of the experimental group was based on the availability of individual service records (201 Files) of members of the unit. In short, these records contain all data pertaining to the soldier's background, active duty, and Reserve experiences. Any service school attendance or Army Education Center attendance is entered in each record.

THE CIVILIAN SAMPLE

It was originally planned to draw the nonmilitary sample from the Selective Service records located in the survey city. A request to review these records was denied by the Director of the Selective Service System.[23]

A second technique was somewhat more successful. After reviewing all 201 files in the Reserve unit, I was able to determine the age grades of the members of the experimental group as well as their educational background. I was able to determine when each man completed the eighth grade, for example. Permission was granted by the local Superintendent of Schools to extract information from the rosters of various past eighth-grade classes. By eliminating the names of female members of these classes as well as those of members of my military sample, I was left with a reasonably manageable list of names and addresses of *possible* members of the civilian sample.

The list of individuals for preliminary interviewing was made by the random selection of names from the modified rosters. If upon interview-

[23] Letter from General Lewis B. Hershey, April 1, 1964. The U.S. Department of Labor has had similar difficulties; see *New York Times,* June 19, 1964, p. 11.

ing I found an individual was Negro, I continued the interview but did not include the data in this study; the six Negro members of the Reserve unit were interviewed but not included in this report. Many of the remaining individuals had fulfilled their military obligation through other means—Navy, Air Force, Coast Guard, ROTC commissions, and the like. These individuals were not interviewed further.

I controlled the most important factors that underlie the occupational status structure—age, sex, race, ethnic background, and class. Ethnic background for the two groups was comparable (about 35 percent Italian, 25 percent German, and the remainder Anglo-Saxon and Middle European). All members of both samples were native American and in only fourteen cases (eight military, six civilian) were one or both parents other than native American. The religious composition of the two samples was also comparable (37 percent Protestant, 52 percent Roman Catholic, 4 percent Jewish, and 7 percent no preference, no religion). There were two individuals in the Reserve unit who refused interviewing and seven among the civilian sample.

Efforts to control class (origin) consisted mainly of noting the areas of the city from which the military sample came and balancing the proportion of the civilian sample to conform. Few if any of either sample could be classified according to W. Lloyd Warner's criteria as lower-lower class. Most of the youth in the survey city from such a background were unable to score sufficiently high on the AFQT to be acceptable for military service and I eliminated from the study those individuals (civilians) who were classified IV-F by the local draft board.

Occupational mobility measuring instrument

To measure an individual's childhood socioeconomic status as well as the extent of his occupational mobility, I utilized the occupation scale devised by Otis D. Duncan,[24] "A Socioeconomic Index for All Occupations." Dun-

---

[24] Otis D. Duncan, "A Socioeconomic Index for All Occupations," and "Properties and Characteristics of the Socioeconomic Index," in Albert J. Reiss, Jr., *Occupations and Social Status* (New York : The Free Press of Glencoe, 1961), pp. 109–161. See also Otis D. Duncan, "Occupational Components of Educational Differences in Income," *Journal of the American Statistical Association*, LVI (December, 1961), 783–784.

can's scale has been widely used since its development in the mid 1950's.[25] Two major features of this scale are : (1) A numerical socioeconomic index or score (SES) is available for all 270 occupations for which census data is available. Index values range from 0 to 96. (2) In addition to the socioeconomic index values, Duncan also grouped the 270 occupations into deciles that "are based on the distribution of the population not of the occupational titles." This means that the 63 occupations ranked in the 10th decile (highest ranked occupations) are performed by 10 percent of the population while decile number three, made up of an equal number of people, is applicable to only nine occupations.

Results

The individual records (201 files) of 126 individuals in the Reserve unit were reviewed. Fourteen were not suitable because major items were missing from the files of eight individuals and six sets of records belonged to Negro members of the unit who had been excluded from the sample in order to control the effects of race on occupational mobility.

Data for the military sample are based on the 106 usable sets of records. In some tables N will not always equal 106, as occasionally an individual record would be incomplete for a single entry or interview data conflicted with record data and I was unable to resolve the difference.

Table 4 depicts the age categories of the military and civilian samples : As will be noted later, 16 percent of the ER personnel had completed four years of college. Most tables in this study will show data for "ER with four years college" and "other ER." Only one US member had completed college and is included in the US sample.

The average age and distribution of ages of the civilian sample are very close to that of the military sample; this is to be expected in light of the method used to select the civilian sample.

---

[25] For example, Bruce K. Eckland, "Ability, Higher Education and Occupational Mobility," paper presented at the 1965 meeting of the American Sociological Association, Chicago, Ill.; Peter M. Blau, "The Flaw of Occupational Supply and Recruitment," *American Sociological Review,* XXX (August, 1965), 475–490; Otis D. Duncan and Robert W. Hodge, "Education and Occupational Mobility : A Regression Analysis," *American Journal of Sociology,* LXVIII (May, 1963), 629–644.

Table 4

AGES OF MILITARY AND CIVILIAN SAMPLES

Age as of July 1, 1965	ER with 4 yr. col. ($N = 9$)	Other ER ($N = 46$)	US ($N = 51$)	Total military sample ($N = 106$)	Civilian sample ($N = 82$)
21	0	1	0	1	0
22	0	5	1	6	1
23	0	3	2	10	9
24	2	7	2	11	7
25	2	7	3	12	8
26	1	5	10	16	12
27	0	5	17	22	17
28	4	4	10	18	14
29	0	3	3	6	9
30	0	0	1	1	1
31	0	1	2	3	4
32	0	0	0	0	1
Average age	26.2	25.0	26.8	26.0	26.6

The distance an individual had moved from his father's base status was related to age of respondent to a degree. The average socioeconomic index (SEI) change and decile change is shown below (Table 5) for both the military and civilian samples by age groups.

This table shows most young men dropping in status early in their occupational life. This would be expected in that one usually starts the occupational climb from the bottom of his particular field. The younger are at the bottom looking up, the older respondents have started to climb. At age 24, both samples had achieved an average position higher than that of their fathers; however, no definite pattern is evident.

From Table 5 there appears to be a slightly greater amount of mobility for the military sample.

The education level of the two samples and the method of satisfying the service obligation for the military sample is depicted in Table 6.

The civilian sample did not complete as much formal education as did the military sample, the major difference being at the high school

Table 5

AVERAGE SEI AND DECILE CHANGE FOR MILITARY AND CIVILIAN SAMPLES BY AGE [SEI AND DECILE CHANGE: RESPONDENT'S PRESENT OCCUPATION (JULY 1, 1965) SCORES MINUS FATHER'S OCCUPATION SCORES]

Respondents age as of July 1, 1965	Military sample		Civilian sample	
	SEI change	Decile change	SEI change	Decile change
21				
22	− 3.0	− 0.7	− 3.9	0.0
23	− 4.5	0.0	− 5.1	− 0.8
24	+ 15.8	+ 1.5	+ 12.8	+ 1.1
25	+ 6.7	+ 1.5	+ 5.0	+ 0.4
26	+ 23.5	+ 2.5	+ 19.1	+ 1.7
27	+ 7.4	+ 1.2	+ 17.7	+ 1.9
28	+ 39.6	+ 4.2	+ 10.9	+ 1.5
29	− 14.0	− 1.0	− 7.2	− 0.3
30			+ 14.3	+ 1.1
31	+ 22.5	+ 3.0	+ 12.8	+ 0.6
32			+ 12.0	+ 1.1
Average change	+ 12.6	+ 1.5	+ 9.4	+ 0.97

graduation level. Of the 25 civilians not completing high school, only one returned to local evening adult education classes and received an equivalency diploma. Three attended apprenticeship instruction in skilled crafts. Other than these four, no civilian participated in any form of educational or training experiences after their initial departure from formal schooling.

In the military sample the draftee group is overrepresented by men who did not finish or had only finished high school. Enlisted Reservists were three times as likely to have had college education as were draftees.

Relationship between intelligence and mobility

There were no available data that would allow an analysis of the relationship between intelligence and mobility for either sample; however, the "General Technical" (GT) scores were available for the military sample.

Table 6
EDUCATIONAL LEVEL[a]

Education completed	ER	Percentage ER	US	Percentage US	Total military	Percentage military	Civilian	Percentage civilian
4 years college	9	16.3%	1	1.9%	10	9.4%	6	7.3%
Some college	15	27.3	5	9.8	20	18.8	16	19.5
HS graduate	23	41.8	29	56.9	52	49.0	35	42.7
Less than HS graduate	8	14.5	16	31.4	24	22.7	25	30.5
Total	55	(99.9%)	51	(100.0%)	106	(99.9%)	82	(100.0%)

[a] For the military sample, data indicate education completed *prior to military service*. Civilian data based on years completed before a break of one year in school attendance.

Table 7

GT SCORES UPON ENTRY INTO SERVICE

Education level	ER	N	US	N	Total for military sample	N	Range of GT scores	Percentage of GTs less than 90
4 yrs. college	132	9	132	1	132	10	120–143	0%
Some college	127	15	122	5	126	20	100–140	0
HS grad	108	23	108	29	108	52	61–147	5
Less than high school	106	8	85	16	88	24	50–128	9
Average	118		102		110			

Table 8

FATHER'S SOCIOECONOMIC STATUS IN CIVILIAN AND MILITARY SAMPLES BY EDUCATION LEVEL OF RESPONDENTS

Education level	Average SES	SES range	Average decile	Decile range
MILITARY				
4 years college	36.6	14–90	7.3	3–10
Some college	32.1	15–50	6.3	2–9
HS graduate	35.6	9–76	6.2	2–10
Less than HS	14.0	7–19	3.0	1–4
Average	30.1		5.4	
CIVILIAN				
4 years college	37.1	12–92	7.1	2–10
Some college	34.2	11–75	6.3	2–10
HS graduate	33.3	6–80	5.8	1–10
Less than HS	14.9	4–21	3.1	1–5
Average	28.1		5.2	

While not directly correlated with other measures such as the "intelligence quotient," the GT score is to be interpreted as an equivalent index of general intelligence. It is a combination of separate tests of arithmetic reasoning, reading and vocabulary, and pattern analysis. A minimum score of 90 is required for attendance at most Army service schools. GT scores range from 40 to 160 with 100 representing the average.

Table 7 shows the average GT scores for the military sample in terms of educational level and service category (i.e., ER or US). As might be expected, GT scores varied directly with the educational level of the sample.

Using Duncan's scale I determined the childhood socioeconomic status of the civilian and military samples, using respondents' fathers' occupation at the time respondents were in the eighth grade as a base. Table 8 depicts the social origin of the samples in relation to the amount of education received by the respondents.

The relationship between father's status and service category (US or ER) is shown in Table 9.

Table 10 depicts the change in socioeconomic index scores and decile ratings for the military sample by service categories (US or ER).

Table 5 revealed that members of the military sample were slightly more mobile than their civilian contemporaries. While the difference is slight, it is clearly present. For the younger men, all of whom lost ground relative to the father, those in the military sample lost the least. The question still remains as to the reason for the differential, since in addition to the major difference between the samples, military or nonmilitary, there also existed a slight difference in educational attainment (see Table 5). Later discussion will show, however, that within the military sample, lack of extended formal schooling (prior to active duty) did not necessarily work against mobility.

Mobility within the military sample

Table 10 clearly shows a much greater degree of mobility for the draftees compared with the Enlisted Reservists. Yet earlier tables (6, 7, 8) showed the draftee to have come from a lower childhood socioeconomic level, to

Table 9

FATHER'S SOCIOECONOMIC STATUS BY LATER SERVICE CATEGORY (US OR ER) OF RESPONDENTS

Category	Childhood average SEI	Childhood SEI range	Childhood average decile	Childhood decile range
ER 4 year college	45.8	14–90	7.2	3–10
Other ER	40.8	9–76	7.1	2–10
Total ER	42.0	9–90	7.1	2–10
US	21.5	7–44	5.1	1–8

Table 10

CHANGES IN SOCIOECONOMIC STATUS BY SERVICE CATEGORY

	Socioeconomic index			Decile		
Service category	Childhood base	Position prior to active duty	Position July 1, 1965	Childhood base	Position prior to active duty	Position July 1, 1965
ER 4 year college	45.8	...[a]	70.0	7.2	...[a]	9.8
Other ER	40.8	31.3	43.6	7.1	6.1	7.6
Total ER	42.0	31.7	49.9	7.1	6.1	8.1
US	21.5	21.4	42.6	5.1	4.7	7.0

[a] Student at time, no score available.

have completed less formal education, and to have lower GT scores; the latter two probably resulting from the former.

Effect of service school attendance

Table 11 compares SES and decile changes for the two subcategories of the military sample as regards service school attendance.[26]

Both overall and within the ER and US categories, attendance at service schools did not seem to affect mobility; in fact, having *not* attended seems to be advantageous. This is not to minimize the effects of service school attendance on later civilian occupational mobility for, as

---

[26] Duncan, *op. cit.*, "A Socioeconomic Index for All Occupations," p. 129.

Table 11

RELATIONSHIP BETWEEN SOCIOECONOMIC INDEX / DECILE CHANGES AND SERVICE SCHOOL ATTENDANCE

Service category	Sent to service school			Not sent to service school		
	N	SES change	Decile change	N	SES change	Decile change
ER	39	+ 5.8	+ 0.9	16	+ 12.3	+ 1.5
US	32	+ 20.2	+ 2.4	19	+ 22.4	+ 2.4
Total	71	+ 12.3	+ 1.6	35	+ 17.8	+ 2.0

Table 12

REASONS GIVEN BY MILITARY SAMPLE FOR NOT HAVING ATTENDED ON OR OFF DUTY EDUCATION CLASSES

Substance of answer	N	Percentage	Composition
On active duty only 6 months—no time	42	39.6%	All ER
Military duties did not permit, too much field duty	24	22.7	20 US, 4 ER
Not interested in program	30	28.3	21 US, 9 ER
I did participate	10	9.4	All US
Totals	106	100.0%	

was pointed out earlier, the soldiers attending the extended service school courses are usually not the US or ER. For this study, however, service school attendance cannot be credited with the increased mobility of the military sample when compared with civilians, or the draftee when compared with the enlisted reservists.

Effects of army education program

Of the 106 members of the military sample only ten participated in any aspect of the education program of the Army. Table 12 depicts the answers given by those in the military sample to the question, "If you did not attend any education classes (on or off duty) while on active duty, why not?" (To a similar question civilian respondents indicated an even greater apathy to furthering their education. Ninety percent of the civilian sample were either "not interested" in adult education programs offered in the community or said they had not even considered participation. Only 9 percent indicated their job interfered with any desire to engage in further schooling. As pointed out earlier, only one man had taken any adult education courses.)

Note in Table 12 that all participants in the education program were draftees. That Enlisted Reservists did not participate (and the excuse given) is reasonable. Even though informed of educational opportunities during basic training, the ER was in no position to initiate such a program of study. Even though a man need be on active duty but 120 days to be eligible for USAFI courses, the ER was probably half way through his six months' active duty before he had much opportunity seriously to consider such an undertaking.

The extent of participation by the ten draftees is of interest. Of the ten participants, nine had failed to complete high school upon entering the service; in fact, two had no high school instruction at all. Seven of the top ten most popular USAFI courses are high-school-level courses, indicating that the major accomplishment of USAFI probably lies in the area of upgrading the education of the soldier with less than twelve grades of formal schooling—the Army's minimum goal for enlisted men.[27]

Table 13

TYPE PARTICIPATION IN ARMY EDUCATION PROGRAM	
Extent of participation	Number
Received 4th-grade-level instruction and equivalency certificate	1
Received 8th-grade-level instruction and equivalency certificate	1
Received high-school-level instruction and graduation equivalency	6
Started high-school-level instruction, did not complete testing	1
Attempted college-level GED equivalency testing, failed	1

[27] The ten USAFI courses with the largest enrollments (world-wide), in order of their popularity, are as follows:

Subject	Academic level	Subject	Academic level
Beginning Algebra I	High school	Review Arithmetic	High school
Practical English Usage I	High school	English Composition I	College
General Mathematics I	High school	American History I	High school
Ninth Grade English I	High school	General Science I	High school
Introduction to Electronics I	Technical	College Algebra	College

(Data from personal letter from C. L. Munden, Director of USAFI, Madison, Wis., June 26, 1964.)

How mobile were the ten USAFI participants? They gained an average of 33.5 SES points and raised themselves 4.5 deciles (compared with nonparticipating draftees, who gained 12.9 SES points and 1.3 deciles). The average gain for the six who completed the high school program while on active duty was 48.3 SES points and 6.0 deciles!

The interest in the education program (while on active duty) is related to the aspirations of the samples. To the question, "What do you think you will be doing five years from now?" replies were as depicted in Table 14. Of the civilian sample, the outlook was 52.3 percent seeing possible improvement and 47.7 percent seeing little or no change.

Social maturity

While much of the mobility differential in favor of the draftee may be attribute to on- or off-duty education participation, it should be noted that draftees *not* participating still gained 12.9 SES points and 1.3 deciles over their fathers. Table 10 revealed that the average change for the ER was 7.9 SES points and 1.0 decile. I attribute this difference to the third broad advantage available to a young man through active military service —social maturity. Miller and Form point out that management considers one of the functions of the schools that of inculcating "proper work attitudes" such as punctuality, regularity, and persistent application.[28] The disciplined way of life required of a soldier by the Army may serve to supplement or complement this function of secondary education. The

Table 14

RELATIONSHIP BETWEEN PARTICIPATION IN ARMY EDUCATION PROGRAM AND ASPIRATIONS OF OCCUPATIONAL IMPROVEMENT 5 YEARS FROM NOW

Reason for (not) participating in program	Percentage seeing improvement	Percentage seeing no improvement
Military duties did not permit ($N = 24$)	58.4%	41.6%
Not interested in program ($N = 30$)	30.0	70.0
Did participate	80.0	20.0

[28] William H. Form and Delbert C. Miller, *Industry, Labor and Community* (New York: Harper and Brothers, 1960), p. 257.

draftees in this study had less contact with formal education prior to active duty than did the Enlisted Reservist and they were exposed to the rigors of service life for a period four times as long.

Respondents in the military sample were asked whether their active duty was of any benefit to them. Fifty-seven (54 percent) felt that they gained nothing[29] while 49 (46 percent) saw some positive results of their service experiences. Of the 49, 15 felt that they got better jobs because of their active duty and 34 felt that their service experience helped them to perform their present job better.

Summary

A major inducement for enlistment, and a frequent justification for the drafting of men without occupational skills, consists of the prospect of opportunities for technical training in Army schools, or for completing or supplementing their preservice academic experience. An attempt was made to measure the effects of military service by comparing the improvement in socioeconomic status from that of the respondents' fathers, in a military and civilian sample. The military sample consisted of members of a Reserve unit, comprised of Enlisted Reservists and ex-draftees. The civilian sample was matched for age, ethnic origin, and other significant variables. All members of both samples were white. It was found that although draftees entering the service were lower in socioeconomic status than either their civilian age mates or Enlisted Reservists, they made significantly more progress in improving their socioeconomic status. The improvement was attributed to academic achievement in the service and social maturation.

Appendix : Army education center, Fort Carson, Colorado

PARTICIPATION IN ARMY EDUCATION PROGRAM FY 65 1 JULY 64–30 JUNE 65

Completed High School	1,587 Enlisted Men
Completed Two Years College	16 Officers

[29] Six of them had attended USAFI courses and had received equivalency certificates. Included in the 57 negative answers are those indicating "love of freedom because the Army took it all away," "met a girl," and the like.

Military service and occupational mobility

Completed College Degrees	20 Officers
	1 Warrant Officer
	2 Enlisted Men
Total	23
Passed Army Language Proficiency Test	66

ENROLLMENTS IN EDUCATION PROGRAM

College Enrollments with University of Colorado and Southern Colorado State College	424 Officers
	1,155 Enlisted Men
Total	1,579
MOS Related Enrollments:	
Clerk Typing	582
Electronics	83
Tuition Assistance	52
Foreign Languages (German, French, Russian, Spanish, Korean, Vietnamese)	1,094
Total	1,811
Preparatory Education Classes	812
Correspondence Courses	
High School Level	227
College Level	271
Total	498
Tests Administered	
High School GED	10,738
College GED	1,368
End of Course	1,496
Placement and Achievement	1,886
Total	15,488

Conclusion: implications for change

ROGER W. LITTLE

The National Advisory Commission on Selective Service in 1967 produced a report that set forth a program of reforming Selective Service. The main thrust of these recommendations was to improve the effectiveness of the administrative machinery of Selective Service by a more unified system and to increase the universality of the risks of service by eliminating various types of deferments. The specific recommendations of this report are compatible with—and in fact, built on—the type of institutional analysis presented in this volume. Organizational reform is central, as long as there is a need to rely on a Selective Service System. In fact, even if Selective Service is abolished, reform of the organization for voluntary recruitment and of policies of military manpower utilization will be even more required.

The findings of these papers point to at least three basic problem areas that stand above, so to speak, the numerous specific recommendations that will be debated for decades to come. First, there is the necessity for unifying and integrating the several programs and agencies involved in voluntary recruitment and Selective Service. Second, there is the problem of establishing a broader definition of eligibility for service, one that will permit maximum participation consistent with organizational effectiveness. Third, there is a requirement to establish a coordinated military manpower policy, embracing Reservists and volunteers as well as draftees. Basic to such a policy is a common definition of what constitutes fulfillment of the service obligation.

The evaluation of agencies for manpower procurement indicates the need for substantial changes in organization and direction of effort. Voluntary recruitment agencies perform an essential function by providing information in the local community as well as in obtaining long-term enlistees. However, their operations are isolated from the Selective Service System and Reserve recruitment activities. In the past, recruiters have tended to compete with Selective Service for the same limited segment of the manpower pool. However, recruiters have enlarged the universe of procurement by inducing unregistered youths and exempted or deferred categories of registrants to enlist. Although the number of such programs is small (such as for seventeen-year-old youths and college students for Officer Candidate Schools), their success is evidence of the potentially increased effectiveness of recruiting as a specialized form of manpower procurement.

The essays by Davis and Dolbeare and by Wamsley document the obsolescence of the procurement echelons of the Selective Service System: the local boards. The boards had the original objective of permitting the classification of registrants in categories of relative availability by older citizens with personal knowledge of the registrant and his community. On a national basis, the local board also had the effect of distributing the burden of service in the society on an equitable geographical basis. Problems are created by the indefinite tenure of board members, the ambiguity and diversity of criteria used in classification actions, and the fact that the boards are much less influential in the classification process than is asserted by the Selective Service System.

Our analysis suggests that the values of the local board system as an opportunity for community participation in military manpower procurement should be combined with the expertise and service identifications of the voluntary recruiters. The assumption that local communities would consider this consolidation repugnant is no longer tenable. The recruiting stations of the armed forces are viewed in a more positive perspective than when conscription was introduced during the Civil War. The operational consolidation of voluntary recruiters and local board activities would enhance the development of joint policies.

The second major issue discussed in this volume is pointed toward the need for a redefinition of the initial term of eligibility for service. The essay by Roff indicates that many youths with records as juvenile delinquents could be effectively utilized in the armed forces by a careful discrimination of the nature of the behavior as measured by the level at which the delinquent was confined. The essay by Moskos analyzes the overutilization of the Negro in military service, and the implications of his relatively higher rate of participation for American society. Finally, Katenbrink's study indicates the effects of military service on educational status and occupational mobility. These are three crucial areas of military manpower policy.

These essays indicate some underlying assumptions of military manpower policy that have remained untouched by the present draft controversy. For example, the escalation of entry requirements and the insistence on an inflexible term of service—policies within the discretion of the armed forces—tend to aggravate the problems of inequity in selection for service. Both tend to restrict the rate of voluntary participation in military organization and consequently shift the burden of discriminating among those who are eligible to serve.

One such assumption is that more rigid entry standards are necessary in order to satisfy the higher technological requirements of modern military organization. However, the assumption of the necessity for increased aptitudes for technical skills does not apply to *all* positions in the armed forces or even to a major fraction of them. It is plausible to assume that the requirements for training wheeled-vehicle mechanics, military police, medical aid men, and clerks, as well as basic infantrymen and seamen, have not changed as markedly as for the often mentioned but less frequently trained electronics technicians. More complex technology does not involve a corresponding increase in more highly trained personnel. Trends in industry suggest that job titles are often upgraded while the actual skill levels are reduced. This also occurs in military organization because operator skills are increasingly built into the design of complex weaponry. Requirements for operator skills are thus transferred to the repair and maintenance level. Even there, however, the designed complexity of weaponry is such that a defective component is more efficiently replaced than repaired, thus actually permitting a reduced skill level.

Spokesmen for military organization often reject proposals for changes in present initial term requirements for reasons other than individual or unit military effectiveness. An increased volume of recruits would expand the training mission that has traditionally held a lower priority than operational requirements. Training duties are thus less highly valued as an assignment in the career perspectives of professional officers.

The third and final issue with which we have been concerned is the necessity for establishing a coordinated military manpower policy. The need for such a policy is indicated by the fact that all three procurement agencies—voluntary, Reserve, and the draft—now operate with separate sets of entry requirements and contingencies in service. Thus the problem of equity is not entirely in the chances of service, but also in the mode of fulfilling the service obligation. One unfortunate consequence of the emphasis on the draft is that it has diverted attention from the larger issue of the inequities among the various ways in which service obligations may be fulfilled. The ultimate victims of this lack of coordination in military manpower policy are the youths who must bear the burden. For example, a draftee whose service includes a year in Vietnam remains obligated for an additional year of weekly drills in a Reserve unit, with age-mates whose active service was probably limited to six months of active duty training. Meanwhile, the three-year enlistee from their neighborhood is excused from all Reserve obligations, regardless of the sacrifice that his service might have involved. These inequities are clearly not related to the draft as a procurement method, but are the effects of a military manpower policy that is preoccupied with procurement and neglects the service experience itself and its sequel.

We would assert that more effort should be directed toward equalizing the conditions of service rather than the method of entry alone, by the development of a more equitable definition of what constitutes fulfillment of the service obligation. Under present arrangements, the draftee is doubly penalized, first by the method of his selection, and secondly by

Conclusion : implications for change

the requirement that he remain actively affiliated with the Reserves. On the other hand, the enlistee is doubly favored by the opportunity for specialized training, and thereafter by being excused from the Reserve affiliation. Even more fortunate, of course, are those who can so arrange their careers as to obtain deferments, and consequently serve only briefly or are missed completely.

The ultimate question that military manpower policy must answer in a democratic society is why *all* who are qualified cannot serve if indeed *some* must serve under the threat or fact of conscription. Substitute methods of selection that seek to eliminate the inequitable chances of service of recognizable segments of the society—and thus subdue their protest—may well create a new division more dangerous than the first : a distinction between a minority whose service entitles them to special claims on national values, and a majority who have not served at all. Innovations are required that will increase the fact and rate of participation as long as conscription is at all required. Our objective in these essays has been to promote the development of such a policy.

Bibliography

I. Manpower policy

BLUM, ALBERT A. *Drafted or Deferred: Practices Past and Present.* Ann Arbor : University of Michigan, Bureau of Industrial Relations, 1967.

CARMICHAEL, LEONARD, AND LEONARD C. MEAD (eds.). *The Selection of Military Manpower : A Symposium.* National Research Council Publication no. 209, National Academy of Sciences, Washington, D.C., 1951.

CARSON, J. J. "Making the Most of Man Power," *The New York Times Magazine* (May 13, 1951), p. 11.

CULLIGAN, ERNEST M. "Procurement of Man Power," *The Annals of the American Academy of Political and Social Science,* CCXX (March, 1942), 8–17.

FARNSWORTH, D. L. "The Eighteen-year-old : An Indistinct Portrait," *The New York Times Magazine* (March 4, 1951), p. 11.

GINZBERG, ELI. *Psychiatry and Military Manpower Policy : A Reappraisal of the Experience in World War II.* New York : Kings Crown Press, 1953.

KELLY, EVERETT L. "Manpower Utilization Under the Selective Service Act," *American Psychologist,* V (November, 1950), 641–642.

MURRAY, MERRILL G. "Civilian Aspects of Military Manpower Policy," *Academy of Political Science Proceedings,* XXIV (May, 1951), 371–382.

PATE, JAMES E. "Mobilizing Manpower," *Social Forces,* XXII (December, 1943), 154–162.

STRAUSZ-HUPE, ROBERT. "Mobilizing U.S. Man Power," *Current History,* L (August, 1940), 32–36.

U.S. DEPARTMENT OF THE ARMY, OFFICE OF THE ADJUTANT GENERAL. *Military Manpower Policy : A Bibliographic Survey.* Washington, D.C. : Government Printing Office, June, 1965.

U.S. DEPARTMENT OF LABOR, BUREAU OF STATISTICS. *Military Manpower Requirements and Supply 1954–1960.* Bulletin No. 1161. Washington, D.C. : Government Printing Office, March, 1964.

U.S. PRESIDENT'S TASK FORCE ON MANPOWER CONSERVATION. *One-Third of a Nation.* Washington, D.C. : Government Printing Office, January 1, 1964.

II. Conscription

A. MEN

BUSHLER, E. C. "Compulsory Military Service," *Annual Debaters Help Book,* Vol. 8. New York : Noble and Noble, 1941.

ESTY, JOHN C. JR. "Draft : Many Threatened, Few Chosen," *The New York Times Magazine* (October 20, 1963), p. 13.

EVERS, ALF. *Selective Service : A Guide to the Draft.* Philadelphia : Lippincott, 1957.

GRAHAM, DONALD, J. GOODMAN, AND K. R. JOHNSON. "Draft : Inequalities and Alternatives," *Atlantic,* CCXVII (February, 1966), 59–69.

GRAHAM, JOHN. *The Universal Military Obligation.* New York : Fund for the Republic, 1958.

JOHNSEN, JULIA E. (comp.). "Compulsory Military Training," *The Reference Shelf,* XIV, 6 (1941), 1–266.

JOHNSEN, JULIA E. (comp.). "Peacetime Conscription," *The Reference Shelf,* XVIII, 4 (1945), 1–327.

MAC CLOSKEY, MONRO. *You and the Draft.* New York : Richards Rosen, 1965.

NICKERSON, HOFFMAN. *Arms and Policy 1939–1944.* New York : Putman, 1945.

RAYMOND, JACK. "The Draft is Unfair," *New York Times Magazine* (January 2, 1966), p. 5.

STERN, FREDERICK MARTIN. *The Citizen Army : Key to Defense in the Atomic Age.* New York : Macmillan, 1957.

B. WOMEN

HORTON, M. H. M. "Drafting Women for the Armed Forces," *Journal of the American Association of University Women,* XLIV (April, 1951), 141–144.

STRATTON, DOROTHY C. "Our Great Unused Resource, Woman-power," *The New York Times Magazine* (October 1, 1950).

III. Universal military training

ANDERSON, PAUL RUSSELL (ed.). "Universal Military Training and National Security," *The Annals of the American Academy of Political and Social Science,* CCXLI (September, 1945), 1–168.

BOGARDUS, EMORY S. "Peacetime Conscription," *Sociology and Social Research,* XXIX (July, 1945), 472–478.

FITZPATRICK, EDWARD A. *Universal Military Training.* New York : McGraw Hill, 1945.

MARX, H. L., JR. (ed.). "Universal Conscription for Essential Service," *The Reference Shelf,* XXIII, 3 (1951), 1–178.

MC LAIN, R. S. "Men, Money, and Universal Military Training," *Army Information Digest,* II (June, 1947), 3–7.

NATIONAL SECURITY TRAINING COMMISSION. *Universal Military Training: Foundations of Enduring Strength.* First Report to the Congress by the National Security Training Commission. Washington, D.C. : Government Printing Office, 1951.

PHELPS, E. M. (ed.). "Universal Draft of Man-Space and Woman-Power," *University Debaters' Annual—1942–1943.* New York, 1942.

STAFFORD, R. H. *The Morality of Universal Military Conscription in Peacetime.* Washington, D.C. : Catholic University of America Press, 1952 (mimeographed).

SUMMERS, ROBERT E., AND HARRISON B. SUMMERS (comps.). "Universal Military Service," *The Reference Shelf,* XV, 2 (1941), 1–280.

U.S. PRESIDENT'S ADVISORY COMMISSION ON UNIVERSAL TRAINING. *Report: A Program for National Security.* Washington, D.C. : Government Printing Office, 1947.

IV. Public opinion

A. SURVEYS

CAHALAN, D., AND P. COLLETTE. *Career Preferences of Medical Students in the United States.* Report no. 60. Chicago : National Opinion Research Center, 1956.

CANTRIL, HADLEY. *Public Opinion, 1935–1946.* Princeton, N.J. : Princeton University Press, 1951, pp. 458–473.

CHILDS, E. DITCH. *Careers in the Military Service : A Review of the Literature.* Military Manpower Survey Working Paper no. 4. Chicago : National Opinion Research Center, May, 1966.

CRESPI, LEO P. "Attitudes Toward Conscientious Objectors and Some of their Psychological Correlates," *Journal of Psychology,* XVIII (July, 1944), 81–117.

CRESPI, LEO P. "Public Opinion Toward Conscientious Objectors : II; Measurement of National Approval-Disapproval," *Journal of Psychology,* XIX (April, 1945), 209–250.

CRESPI, LEO P. "Public Opinion Toward Conscientious Objectors : III; Intensity of Social Rejections in Stereotype and Attitudes," *Journal of Psychology,* XIX (April, 1945), 251–276.

CRESPI, LEO P. "Public Opinion Toward Conscientious Objectors : IV; Opinions on Significant Conscientious Objector Issues," *Journal of Psychology,* XIX (April, 1945), 277–310.

CRESPI, LEO P. "Public Opinion Toward Conscientious Objectors : V; National Tolerance, Wartime Trends and the Scapegoat Hypothesis," *Journal of Psychology,* XX (October, 1945), 321–346.

DEAR, R. E., AND L. R. TUCKER. *The Measurement of the Relative Appeal of Military Service Programs.* Princeton, N.J. : Educational Testing Service, 1961.

DUDYCHA, GEORGE J. "Attitudes Toward War," *Psychological Bulletin,* XXXIX (1942), 846–860.

LOPEZ, RAMON R. "A Study of Male High School Senior Attitudes Toward the Army and of the Relationship Between These Attitudes and Dominant Value Orientation." Unpublished doctoral dissertation, University of Chicago, 1961.

MISENAR, BURMAN J. "A Study of Defense Information and Orientation Programs in Selected Michigan High Schools." Unpublished doctoral dissertation, Michigan State University, 1961.

NATIONAL EDUCATION ASSOCIATION OF THE UNITED STATES, DIVISION OF RESEARCH. *Opinions of School Administrators and Teacher Leaders on Compulsory Military Training; Yes or No?* Washington, D.C. : National Education Association, 1945.

NATIONAL OPINION RESEARCH CENTER. *Compulsory Military Training in Peacetime?* Report no. 23. Denver : National Opinion Research Center, December, 1944.

NATIONAL OPINION RESEARCH CENTER. *Memo : Public Reaction to the Draft and Selective Service.* Study no. 119. Denver : National Opinion Research Center, 1943.

OPPENHEIM, KAREN. *The Military Plans and Experience of June, 1961 College Seniors.* Military Manpower Survey Working Paper No. 2. Chicago : National Opinion Research Center, 1965.

OPPENHEIM, KAREN. *Attitudes of Younger American Men Toward Selective Service.* Military Manpower Survey Working Paper No. 5. Chicago : National Opinion Research Center, 1966.

PUBLIC OPINION SURVEYS, INC. *Attitudes of Adult Civilians Toward the Military Service as a Career, Part 1; and Attitudes of 16 and 20 year old Males Toward the Military Service as a Career, Part II.* Washington, D.C. : Department of Defense, 1955.

"Quarter Polls," *Public Opinion Quarterly,* XIII (1949), 359; XIV (1950), 379-380, 810; XV (1951), 174, 392-393.

SUCHMAN, E. A., AND OTHERS. "Student Reaction to Impending Military Service," *American Sociological Review,* XVIII (June, 1953), 293-304.

TRESCOTT, PAUL. "54% in City Favor Year's Training if Peacetime Draft is Approved," *Evening Bulletin,* Philadelphia (July 17, 1945), p. G-3.

WILLIAMS, ROBIN M., AND OTHERS. "Reactions of College Students to Manpower Policies and the Military Service Prospect," *Educational Record,* XXXIV (April, 1953), 101-107.

WYANT, R., AND H. HERZOG. "Voting via the Senate Mailbag on the Issue of Conscription," *Public Opinion Quarterly,* V (Autumn, 1941), 359-382; V (Winter, 1941), 590-624.

B. OTHERS

DANHAM, ERNEST W. "*The New York Times* and Peacetime Conscription : An Interpretive Study of an Editorial Crusade." Unpublished master's thesis, University of Georgia, 1959.

HUZAR, ELIAS. "Prewar Conscription : Review of Public and Legislative Reactions," *Southwestern Social Science Quarterly,* XXIII (September, 1942), 112–120.

V. Selective Service studies

A. HISTORY AND BACKGROUND

ARMSTRONG, PAUL G. "Selective Service, Its History and Its Functions," *State Government,* XXIII (December, 1950), 267–270.

BAKER, NEWTON D. "On Executive Influence in Military Legislation," *The American Political Science Review,* L (September, 1956), 700–701.

FITZPATRICK, EDWARD A. *Conscription and America : A Study of Conscription in a Democracy.* Milwaukee : Richard Publishing Company, 1940.

HART, I. W. "Outline of Historical Background of Selective Service," *Army Almanac,* Washington, D.C. : Department of the Army, 1950.

KING, SPENCER BIDWELL, JR. *Selective Service in North Carolina in World War II.* Chapel Hill, N.C. : University of North Carolina Press, 1949.

KLEBER, VICTOR. *Selective Service in Illinois 1940–47.* Springfield, 1948. (No publisher listed.)

LEACH, JACK FRANKLIN. *Conscription in the United States : Historical Background.* Rutland, Vermont : C. E. Tuttle Publishing Co., 1952.

LEW, DANIEL HONG. "Selective Training and Service Act of 1940." Unpublished doctoral dissertation, Harvard University, 1942.

RANKIN, R. H. "A History of Selective Service," *Proceedings of the U.S. Naval Institute,* LXXVII (1951), 1073–1081.

SPENCER, SAMUEL R., JR. "Cornerstone of Defense : A History of the Selective Service and Training Act of 1940 from Inception to Enactment." Unpublished doctoral dissertation, Harvard University, 1951.

B. MEDICAL

BRITTEN, R. H., AND G. ST. J. PERROT. "Summary of Physical Findings on Men Drafted in the World War," *Public Health Reports,* LVI (January 10, 1941), 41–62.

Editorial, "Medical Survey Program of Selective Service," *Mental Hygiene,* XXVIII (April, 1944), 177–178.

Editorial Notes, "Medical Survey Plan," *Family,* XXIV (December, 1943), 314–315.

HEENSZEL, WILLIAM, AND E. T. TRACEY. "The Interpretation of Data Available on Selective Service Examination," *Connecticut Health Bulletin,* LXII (May, 1948), 128–134.

KARPINOS, BERNARD D. "Fitness of American Youth for Military Service," *The Milbank Memorial Fund Quarterly,* XXXVIII (July, 1960), 213–247.

KARPINOS, BERNARD D. "Induction Experience of 1945," *Bulletin of U.S. Army Medical Department,* VI (September, 1946), 263–275.

KARPINOS, BERNARD D. *Qualification of American Youth for Military Service.* Washington, D.C. : United States Department of the Army, Office of the Surgeon General, Medical Statistics Agency, 1962.

KARPINOS, BERNARD D. "Results of Examination of Youths for Military Service, 1963," *Supplement to Health of the Army.* Washington, D.C. : United States Department of the Army, Office of the Surgeon General, Medical Statistics Agency, April, 1965.

KARPINOS, BERNARD D. "Results of the Examination of Youths for Military Service, 1964," *Supplement to Health of the Army.* Washington, D.C. : United States Department of the Army, Office of the Surgeon General, Medical Statistics Agency, May, 1965.

KARPINOS, BERNARD D. "Review of the Results of the Examination of the 18-year-old Youths for Military Service," *Supplement to Health of the Army.* Washington, D.C. : United States Department of the Army, Office of the Surgeon General, Medical Statistics Agency, April, 1965.

KARPINOS, BERNARD D. "Results of the Examination of Youths for Military Service, 1965," *Supplement to Health of the Army.* Washington, D.C. : U.S. Department of the Army, Office of the Surgeon General, Medical Statistics Agency, May, 1965.

Notes and Comments, "Medical Survey Program for Selective Service," *Social Service Review,* XIX (March, 1945), 122–124.

ROWNTREE, LEONARD G., AND ALBERT N. BAGGS. "Health of Registrants and Rehabilitation of Rejectees," *The Annals of the American Academy of Political and Social Science,* CCXX (March, 1942), 81-88.

UNITED STATES DEPARTMENT OF THE ARMY. *Marginal Man and Military Service : A Review.* Washington, D.C. : Government Printing Office, 1965.

WALTON, GEORGE H. *The Wasted Generation.* Philadelphia : Chilton, 1965.

WOODWARD, LUTHER E. "Permanent Medical Survey," *Mental Hygiene,* XXX (April, 1946), 199-206.

C. LEGAL

American Journal of International Law, "Application of Selective Service Act to Canadian Nationals in the United States," XXXVI (July, 1942), 158-163.

BALDINGER, M. I. "The Constitutionality of Certain Phases of the Selective Service System." Unpublished thesis, School of Law, Georgetown University, 1941.

BULLOCK, J. R. "Judicial Review of Selective Service Board Classifications by Habeas Corpus," *George Washington Law Review,* X (May, 1942), 827-844.

CONNOR, JAMES THOMAS. "Due Process and the Selective Service System," *Virginia Law Review,* XXX (June, 1944), 435-461.

CORNELL, JULIEN. "Exemption from the Draft : A Study in Civil Liberties," *Yale Law Journal,* LVI (January, 1947), 258-275.

Current Notes, "Criminals and the Draft," *Journal of Criminal Law,* XXXI (January, 1941), 612-613.

DUGGAN, JOSEPH C. *Legislative and Statutory Development of the Federal Concept of Conscription for Military Service.* Washington, D.C. : Catholic University of America Press, 1946.

FITZHUGH, W. W., JR., AND C. C. HYDE. "Drafting of Neutral Aliens by the United States," *American Journal of International Law,* XXXVI (July, 1942), 369-382.

FREEMAN, HARROP A. "The Constitutionality of Peacetime Conscription," *Virginia Law Review,* XXXI (December, 1944), 40-82.

Harvard Law Review, "Mobilization for Defense : Conscription of Men Under the Burke-Wadsworth Act," LIV (December, 1940), 278-292.

HERSHEY, L. B., AND OTHERS. "Legal Aspects of the Selective Service Act," *Indiana Law Journal,* XVII (April, 1942), 271–299.

D. CONSCIENTIOUS OBJECTORS

BRYANT, MARKAM P. "Thirteen Thousand; The Civilian Public Service Program," *Antioch Review* (March, 1947), pp. 83–98.

Comment, "Constitutionality of Requiring Belief in a Supreme Being for Draft Exemption as a Conscientious Objector," *Columbia Law Review,* LXIV (May, 1964), 938–950.

CORNELL, JULIEN D. *Conscience and the State : Legal and Administrative Problems of Conscientious Objectors 1943–1944.* New York : John Day, 1944.

CORNELL, JULIEN D. *The Conscientious Objector and the Law.* New York : John Day, 1943.

EICHEL, SEYMOUR. "Dodging the Draft," *Liberation* (August, 1956), 7–9.

ELLIFF, NATHAN T. "Jehovah's Witnesses and the Selective Service Act," *Virginia Law Review,* XXXI (September, 1945), 811–834.

FRENCH, PAUL C. *We Won't Murder.* New York : Hastings House, 1940.

GINGERICH, MELVIN. *Service for Peace, A History of Mennonite Civilian Public Service.* Akron, Penn. : Mennonite Central Committee, 1949.

GOODMAN, WALTER. "They March to Different Drummers," *The New York Times Magazine* (June 26, 1965), p. 7.

HOPPOCK, ROBERT C. "How Do You Counsel A Conscientious Objector? Advice on the Subject for Both Counselee and Counselor," *Journal of College Placement,* XXI (December, 1960), 34–35.

KELLOGG, WALTER G. *The Conscientious Objector.* New York : Boni and Liveright, 1919.

KELLY, R. R., AND P. E. JOHNSON. "Emotional Traits in Pacifists," *Journal of Social Psychology,* XXVIII (November, 1948), 275–286.

MASCHTLE, LOWELL E., AND H. H. GERTH. "Conscientious Objectors as Mental Hospital Attendants," *Sociology and Social Research,* XXIX (September, 1944), 11–24.

MASELAND, W. A., AND OTHERS. "The Treatment of Conscientious Objectors Under the Selective Service Act of 1940," *American Political Science Review,* XXXVI (August, 1942), 697–701.

MAYOR, MILTON. "Rendered Unto Caesar," *Fellowship,* XXVIII (September 1, 1962), 11–16.

Notes, "Conscientious Objectors," *Minnesota Law Review,* XXXVI (December, 1951), 65–76.

PECK, JAMES. *We Would Not Kill.* New York : L. Stuart, 1958.

PETERSON, HORACE C., AND GILBERT C. FITE. *Opponents of War, 1917–1919.* Madison : University of Wisconsin Press, 1957.

RUSSELL, R. R. "Development of Conscientious Objection Recognition in the United States," *George Washington Law Review,* XX (March, 1952), 409–448.

SIBLEY, MULFORD, AND ADA WARD. *Conscientious Objectors in Prison, 1940–1945.* Pacifism and Government Series 5, No. 2. Pacific Research Bureau, October, 1948.

SIBLEY, MULFORD, AND PHILIP E. JACOB. *Conscription of Conscience : The American State and the Conscientious Objector.* Ithaca, New York : Cornell University Press, 1952.

STONE, HARLAN F. "The Conscientious Objector," *Columbia University Quarterly,* XXI (October, 1919), 253–272.

THOMAS, NORMAN M. *The Conscientious Objector in America.* New York : B. W. Huebsch, 1923.

WRIGHT, EDWARD NEEDLES. *Conscientious Objectors in the Civil War.* Philadelphia : University of Pennsylvania Press, 1931.

ZAHN, G. C. "The Catholic C. O. of World War II," *Catholic World,* CLXXIX (August, 1954), 340–346.

E. ECONOMIC ASPECTS

RENSHAW, EDWARD F. *An Inquiry into the Economics of Conscription.* Research Paper no. 5918. Office of Agricultural Economics, University of Chicago, 1959.

RENSHAW, EDWARD F. "The Economics of Conscription," *Southern Economics Journal,* XXVII (October, 1960), 11–117.

SMITH, GORMAN C. "Occupational Pay Differentials for Military Technicians." Unpublished doctoral dissertation, Columbia University, 1964.

F. NEGROES

GROVE, GENE. "The Army and the Negro," *The New York Times Magazine* (July 24, 1966), pp. 4–5.

LERNER, MAX. "Negroes and the Draft"; Reprint, *Common Ground*, VIII, 4 (1948), 95–97.

MOSKOS, CHARLES, JR. *Racial Integration in the Armed Forces.* Working Paper no. 26. Center for Social Organization Studies, University of Chicago, February, 1966.

G. STUDENTS

FELS, W. C. "Service Stripes and College Grades," *The New York Times Magazine* (May 27, 1951), p. 15.

LEVITES, M. "2-S, Too Smart to Fight? Report From University of Michigan," *The New York Times Magazine* (April 24, 1966), p. 27.

NATIONAL MANPOWER COUNCIL. *Student Deferment and National Manpower Policy.* New York : Columbia University Press, 1952.

TRYTTEN, M. H. *Student Deferment in Selective Service.* Minneapolis : University of Minnesota Press, 1952.

H. STATISTICAL

EDUCATIONAL TESTING SERVICE. *A Summary of Statistics on Selective Service College Qualification Test, December 13, 1951, April 24, 1952, May 22, 1952.* Princeton, N.J. : Educational Testing Service, 1953.

EDUCATIONAL TESTING SERVICE. *A Summary of Statistics on Selective Service College Qualification Test, May 26, 1951, June 16, 1951, June 30, 1951, July 12, 1951.* Princeton, N.J. : Educational Testing Service, 1952.

EDUCATIONAL TESTING SERVICE. *Statistical Studies of Selective Service Testing, 1951–1953.* Princeton, N.J. : Educational Testing Service, 1955.

EDWARDS, THOMAS I., AND L. P. HALLMAN. "Methods Used in Processing Data From the Physical Examination Reports of the Selective Service System," *American Statistical Association Journal*, XXXIX (June, 1944), 165–182.

MC GILL, KENNETH H. "Development and Operation of a Statistical Program of the Selective Service System," *American Sociological Review*, IX (October, 1944), 508–514.

MYERS, R. J. "Underenumeration in the Census as Indicated by Selective Service Data," *American Sociological Review,* XIII (June, 1948), 320–325.

PRICE, D. O. "Check on Underenumeration in the 1940 Census, Provided by the First Selective Service Registration," *American Sociological Review,* XII (February, 1947), 44–49.

SEBASTIAN, KIE KNEELAND. "A Statistical Analysis of Selective Service Rejection." Unpublished master's thesis, University of North Carolina, August, 1945.

I. LOCAL BOARDS

ALLEN, FREDERICK LEWIS. "Drafting This Army," *Harper's Magazine,* CLXXXV (July, 1942), 121–130.

CLARK, GEORGE R. "I'm on a Draft Board," *Harper's Magazine,* CLXXXII (April, 1941), 493–502.

COOK, FRED J. "The Draft Boards Escalate," *The New York Times Magazine* (September 12, 1965), 54–55.

COREY, H. "Three Anonymous Men on a Board," *Nation's Business,* XXX (December, 1942), 32.

Editorial, "And Speaking of Draft-Board Clerks," *Harper's Magazine,* CLXXXV (September, 1942), 402–403.

LEVINE, HAROLD. "Men Who Did It : Local Draft Boards," *Newsweek,* XXIX (March 31, 1947), 27–28.

LINDHEIM, B. "Draft Board Drama : Human Interest Stories," *The New York Times Magazine* (May 18, 1941), p. 14.

PECK, I. "Night at Local Draft Board no. 14," *The New York Times Magazine* (October 29, 1950), p. 15.

Saturday Evening Post, "Headaches of a Draft-Board Chairman," CCXV (January 23, 1943), 154.

STEWART, DONALD D. "Local Board : A Study of the Place of Volunteer Participation in a Bureaucratic Organization." Unpublished doctoral dissertation, Columbia University, 1950.

STEWART, DONALD D. "Place of Volunteer Participation in a Bureaucratic Organization (as illustrated by the Selective Service)," *Social Forces,* XXIX (March, 1951), 311–317.

U.S. News, "Why Draft Boards Resign," XXXV (July 24, 1953), 18–19.

J. APPEAL BOARDS

STEWART, DONALD D. "Selective Service Appeal Boards," *Southwestern Social Science Quarterly,* XXXI (June, 1950), 30–38.

K. SELECTIVE SERVICE AND SOCIETY

BASHFORD, E. C., AND H. L. ZUCKER. "Service to Selective Service Boards," *Family,* XXII (July, 1941), 157–161.

BEHNER, G. C., AND A. L. SCHORR. "Applying Short-Contact Skills to Interviewing Selectees; The Work of the Medical Field Agents," *Social Service Review,* XIX (March 19, 1945), 87–92.

BLUM, ALBERT A. "Sailor or Worker : A Manpower Dilemma During the Second World War," *Labor History,* VI (Fall, 1965), 232–243.

BLUM, ALBERT A. "Work or Fight : The Use of the Draft as a Manpower Sanction During the Second World War," *Industrial and Labor Relations Review,* XVI (April, 1963), 366–380.

FINDLEY, WARREN G. "Selective Service College Qualifying Test," *American Psychologist,* VI (May, 1951), 181–183.

HALPER, O. "Selective Service and the Case Worker," *Family,* XXIV (October, 1943), 214–221.

HEPPLE, LAWRENCE M. "Differential Selective Service Rejection Rates for the Rural Areas of Missouri," *Rural Sociology,* XII (1947), 388–394.

HEPPLE, LAWRENCE M. "Selective Service Rejectees in Missouri : An Ecological and Statistical Study." Unpublished doctoral dissertation, University of Missouri, 1946.

HYDE, R. W., AND L. V. KINGSLEY. "The Value of Social Service Information in the Examination of Selectees," *Family,* XXV (November, 1944), 266–271.

MCDERMOTT, ARTHUR V. "Problem of Dependency Deferments in Selective Service Administration," *Proceedings, National Conference on Social Work.* New York: Columbia University Press, 1945, 116–121.

Mental Hygiene, "Social Work in Selection for the Armed Forces; Symposium," XXVIII (October, 1944), 565–595.

MUDD, E. H., AND M. M. EVERTON. "Marriage Problems in Relation to Selective Service," *Family,* XXII (June, 1941), 129–130.

PARSONS, H. L. "Case Work Services to a Selective Service Board," *Family,* XXII (March, 1941), 26–28.

RAPPORT, VICTOR A. "Sociological Implications of Selective Service," *American Sociological Review,* VI (April, 1941), 225–229.

SMITH, MAPHEUS. "Differential Impact of Selective Service Inductions on Occupations in the United States," *American Sociological Review,* XI (October, 1946), 567–572.

STREET, A. J. "Hasty Marriage and the Draft," *Journal of Social Hygiene,* XXVII (May, 1948), 228–231.

WALTON, COL. GEORGE H. "Sole Source Procurement Through Selective Service," *Army,* XIV, 2 (1963), 32–34.

WOODWARD, L. E. "Social Case-Work in Relation to Selective Service and the Rejectee," *Mental Health,* XXVII (July, 1943), 370–389.

L. ADMINISTRATION AND POLICY

DRAPER, W. H. "Role of the States in Registration Under the Selective Service Law," *State Government,* XIII (October, 1940), 203.

DRURY, JOHN WILLIAM. "Universal Military Service : A Study of its Role in Supporting Requirements of National Security." Unpublished master's thesis, Ohio State University, 1950.

EDWARDS, WALKER STANLEY. "The Administration of Selective Service in the United States." Unpublished master's thesis, Stanford University, 1948.

GIEBEL, HOWARD A. "Procurement of Manpower for Armed Defense in a Bipolar World." Unpublished master's thesis, Columbia University, 1953.

HUZAR, ELIAS. "Selective Service Policy, 1940–1942," *Journal of Politics,* IV (May, 1942), 201–226.

M. OFFICIAL PUBLICATIONS

BAYROFF, A. G., AND OTHERS. *Screening Devices for Selective Service Registrants Who Fail AFQT 7+8.* Washington, D.C. : Army Personnel Research Office, 1963.

HERSHEY, LEWIS B. *Legal Aspects of Selective Service.* Washington, D.C. : Selective Service System, 1963.

U.S. Congressional Hearings, U.S. *Congressional Record.*

Bibliography

U.S. DEPARTMENT OF THE ARMY, OFFICE OF THE DEPUTY CHIEF OF STAFF FOR PERSONNEL. *Qualitative Distribution of Manpower*. Washington, D.C. : Government Printing Office, 1961.

U.S. DEPARTMENT OF DEFENSE. *Summary Tables, Sample Study of Military Service Experience Relative to Military Service and Ready Reserve Service Obligation for Men Born in Calendar Years 1934, 1935, 1936, 1937, and 1938*. Washington, D.C., 1962 (mimeographed).

U.S. SELECTIVE SERVICE SYSTEM.
Selective Service in Peacetime 1940–1941. First Report of the Director. Washington, D.C., 1942.
Selective Service in War Time 1941–1942. Second Report of the Director. Washington, D.C., 1943.
Selective Service as the Tide of the War Turns 1943–1944. Third Report of the Director. Washington, D.C., 1945.
Selective Service and Victory 1944–1945 with Supplement 1945–1946. Fourth Report of the Director. Washington, D.C., 1948.
Selective Service Under the 1948 Act June 24, 1948 to July 9, 1950. Report of the Director. Washington, D.C.; 1951; thereafter known as the *Annual Report of the Director*.

U.S. SELECTIVE SERVICE SYSTEM. *Selective Service,* I. Washington, D.C., January, 1941, and continuing.

U.S. SELECTIVE SERVICE SYSTEM. *Selective Service Regulation*. Washington, D.C., 1940; various editions since.

U.S. SELECTIVE SERVICE SYSTEM. *Backgrounds of Selective Service; A Historical Review of the Principle of Citizen Compulsion in the Raising of Armies*. Vol. 1, Special Monograph No. 1. Washington, D.C., 1945.

U.S. SELECTIVE SERVICE SYSTEM. *Backgrounds of Selective Service; Military Obligation : The American Tradition; A Compilation of the Enactments of Compulsion from the Earliest Settlements of the Original Thirteen Colonies in 1607 Through the Articles of Confederation 1789*. Vol. II. Special Monograph No. 1. Washington, D.C., 1947, pts. 1–14.

U.S. SELECTIVE SERVICE SYSTEM. *The Selective Service Act : Its Legislative History, Amendments, Appropriations, Cognates and Prior Instruments of Security*. Special Monograph No. 2. Washington, D.C., 1945, 4 vols.

U.S. SELECTIVE SERVICE SYSTEM. *Organization and Administration of the System*. Special Monograph No. 3. Washington, D.C., 1951, 2 vols.

U.S. SELECTIVE SERVICE SYSTEM. *Registration and Selective Service.* Special Monograph No. 4. Washington, D.C., 1950.

U.S. SELECTIVE SERVICE SYSTEM. *The Classification Process.* Special Monograph No. 5. Washington, D.C., 1950, 3 vols.

U.S. SELECTIVE SERVICE SYSTEM. *Industrial Deferment.* Special Monograph No. 6. Washington, D.C., 1947, 2 vols.

U.S. SELECTIVE SERVICE SYSTEM. *Agricultural Deferment.* Special Monograph No. 7. Washington, D.C., 1947.

U.S. SELECTIVE SERVICE SYSTEM. *Dependency Deferment.* Special Monograph No. 8. Washington, D.C., 1947.

U.S. SELECTIVE SERVICE SYSTEM. *Age in the Selective Service Process.* Special Monograph No. 9. Washington, D.C., 1946.

U.S. SELECTIVE SERVICE SYSTEM. *Special Groups.* Special Monograph No. 10. Washington, D.C., 1946.

U.S. SELECTIVE SERVICE SYSTEM. *Conscientious Objection.* Special Monograph No. 11. Washington, D.C., 1950, 2 vols.

U.S. SELECTIVE SERVICE SYSTEM. *Quotes, Calls and Inductions.* Special Monograph No. 12. Washington, D.C., 1948, 2 vols.

U.S. SELECTIVE SERVICE SYSTEM. *Reemployment and Selective Service.* Special Monograph No. 13. Washington, D.C., 1949, 2 vols.

U.S. SELECTIVE SERVICE SYSTEM. *Enforcement of the Selective Service Law.* Special Monograph No. 14. Washington, D.C., 1950.

U.S. SELECTIVE SERVICE SYSTEM. *Physical Examination of Selective Service Registrants.* Special Monograph No. 15. Washington, D.C., 1947, 3 vols.

U.S. SELECTIVE SERVICE SYSTEM. *Problems? Selective Service.* Special Monograph No. 16. Washington, D.C., 1952, 3 vols.

U.S. SELECTIVE SERVICE SYSTEM. *The Operation of Selective Service.* Special Monograph No. 17. Washington, D.C., 1955, 2 vols.

U.S. SELECTIVE SERVICE SYSTEM. *Report of the Director of Selective Service Records 1947–1948.* Washington, D.C., 1950.

VI. Reform

A. ISSUES

BALDWIN, HANSON W. "Should We End the Draft?" *The New York Times Magazine* (September 27, 1964), 20–21.

DENNIS, LLOYD D. "Draft Law Revision," *Editorial Research Report* (June 22, 1966), 441–461.

JANOWITZ, MORRIS. "American Democracy and Military Service," *Transaction*, IV, 4 (March, 1967), 5–11.

NATIONAL ADVISORY COMMISSION ON SELECTIVE SERVICE. *Who Serves When not All Serve?* Washington, D.C. : U.S. Government Printing Office, 1967.

B. ALTERNATIVES TO SELECTIVE SERVICE

EBERLY, DONALD J. (ed.). *A Profile of National Service.* New York : Overseas Educational Service, 1966.

FOOT, MICHAEL R. *Men in Uniform.* London : Praeger, 1961.

JANOWITZ, MORRIS. *The Logic of a National Service System.* Chicago : Center for Social Organization Studies, University of Chicago, 1966.

SANDERS, MARION K. "The Case for a National Service Corps," *The New York Times Magazine* (August 7, 1966), pp. 16–17.

VII. Bibliography

BOWER, ALY (ed.). "War Service," *Debate Handbook,* XXV, Midwest Debate Bureau (1951–1952), 17–27.

BUSHLER, E. C. "Compulsory Military Service," *Annual Debaters Help Book,* Vol. 8. New York : Noble and Noble, 1941.

CHANEY, FRANCIS (comp.). *Universal Military Training : A Selected and Annotated List of References.* With Supplement 1945. Washington, D.C. : Library of Congress, 1945.

DOTY, H. *Bibliography of Conscientious Objection to War : A Select List of 173 Titles, etc.* Philadelphia : Central Committee for Conscientious Objectors, 1954.

JOHNSEN, JULIA E. (comp.). "Compulsory Military Training," *The Reference Shelf,* XIV, 6 (1941), 1–266.

JOHNSEN, JULIA E. "Peacetime Conscription," *The Reference Shelf,* XVIII, 4 (1945), 297–327.

MARX, H. L., JR. "Universal Conscription for Essential Service," *The Reference Shelf,* XXIII, 3 (1951), 1–178.

PHELPS, E. M. (ed.). "Universal Draft of Man-Space and Woman-Power," *University Debaters' Annual 1942–1943*. New York : H. W. Wilson Co., 1942, pp. 117–157.

REEVE, JULIET, AND OTHERS (comps.). THEODORE PAULLIN (ed.). *Sourcebook on Peacetime Conscription*. Philadelphia : American Friends Service Committee, 1944.

SUMMERS, ROBERT E., AND HARRISON B. SUMMERS. "Universal Military Service," *The Reference Shelf,* XV, 2 (1941), 261–280.

ULMAN, RUTH (comp.). *University Debaters' Annual 1947–1948*. New York : H. W. Wilson Co., 1947, pp. 211–218.

ULMAN, RUTH (comp.). *University Debaters' Annual 1950–1951*. New York : H. W. Wilson Co., 1950, pp. 81–84.

U.S. DEPARTMENT OF THE ARMY, OFFICE OF THE ADJUTANT GENERAL. *Military Manpower Policy : A Bibliographic Survey*. Washington, D.C. : Government Printing Office, June, 1965.

Index

Adjudication, 13, 23, 116
Agger, Robert E., 61n.
Air Force, 26, 129, 130, 136, 142–143, 147, 177
   regulations concerning enlistment in, 111–115
Alford, Robert, 72n.
Almond, Gabriel, 64n., 65n., 94n.
American Council on Education, 168, 172
American Legion, 94, 107
American Revolution, 36
American Veterans Committee, 53n.
Anderson, Alan A., 27n.
Antioch College, 53n.
Appeal Board, 57
Armed Forces Examining and Entry Station, 13
Armed Forces Induction Not-Qualified Rates, 48–49
Armed Forces Institute, xvi
Armed Forces Moral Waiver Determination Board, 113
Armed Forces Qualification Test (AFQT), 17, 26–29
Army, xiii, 37, 41, 111, 116, 129–130, 136, 142–143, 147, 150–151, 152, 159, 164, 165, 170, 181
   regulations concerning enlistment in, 111–115

Army of the United States (AUS), 129–130, 184–185
Army School System, 167–175
   effects of, 184–187, 188
Association of American Universities, 44

Ballard, K. B., 118n.
Beale, Alan, 28n.
Bell, Wendell, 62n.
Bensman, Joseph, 70n.
Bias. *See* Social justice
Black Muslims, 100
Blau, Peter M., 178n.
Bloomberg, Warner, Jr., 72n.
Bounties, 37
Browning, Rufus P., 71n.
Bush, Vannevar, 44

Cadet Corps, 32
Career Days, 7
Careers, military, 25–29
"Channeling," 22, 86
Civil rights movement, 139, 158–159
Civil Service Register, 12
Civil War, 1, 32, 36–38, 83, 193
Civilian Advisory Panel on Military Manpower Procurement, 50–51
Clark, Greenville, 38
Classification. *See* Selective

Service classification
Classification Questionnaire, 13
Clerks, local board, 12–14, 89–93
Cline, Victor B., 28n.
Coast and Geodetic Survey, 14
Coast Guard, 170, 177
Coates, Charles H., 149n.
Cold War, 42
Commission on Accreditation of Service Experience (CASE), 168, 174–175
Conant, James H., 44
"Conant Plan," 44
Congress, 36, 38–39, 40, 41, 43, 52, 59, 107
Conscientious objectors, 13, 14, 74, 79, 80, 91, 100
Conscription. *See* Selective Service System
Continental Army, 36
Cost accounting in personnel programs, 26–29
Courtnay, Colonel Bentley, 54n.
Critical Skills List, 87
Crockett, Harry J., Jr., 167n.
Crowder, Enoch H., 38, 83

D'Antonio, William V., 61n.
Dailey, John T., 8n., 30
Decentralization, 6, 106
Deferments, 2, 11, 13, 21–23, 29, 51, 192
  attitude of local boards to, 73–81
  education as a basis for, 22–23, 33–34
  juvenile delinquency and, 111–115, 121–124
  Negroes and, 145–146
  occupational, 15, 16, 78, 96–97, 101
  student, xiv, 3, 15, 35, 39–40, 42, 43–47, 101
Delinquency. *See* Juvenile delinquency
Delinquency Scale, 118–119
Department of Defense, 8, 9, 10, 17, 32, 47, 50, 140, 163, 164n.
Department of Justice, 100
Dependency, 90, 91, 99–100
Desegregation, 140–143
Draft. *See* Selective Service System

Draft boards. *See* Local boards
Dubuisson, A. U., 28
Duncan, Otis D., 167n., 177n., 178n.
Dykstra, Dr. Clarence, 40–41

Eckland, Bruce K., 178n.
Economic Opportunity Act of 1964, 54n.
Education, xvi, 17, 20, 26, 33, 41, 164, 179, 187–188, 193
  in Army School System, 166–175, 184–187
  as basis for deferment, 43–47
  attitudes of local boards toward, 78–79
  inferiority of Negro, 143
Eisenhower, President Dwight D., 45–46
Eldridge, Jeanne B., 170n.
Enlisted Reserves (ER), 165–166, 167, 176, 181–182, 184–185, 186, 188
Enlistment, xvi, 5–9, 26–27, 28, 129, 136, 165, 192
  inadequacy of, 16–19
  length of service preferred in, 30
  Negro, 147–149
  regulations for, 111–115
Entry requirements, 25, 33, 110, 143, 193
Erickson, Eugene, 61n.
Exemptions, 37

Fararo, Thomas J., 72n.
Farmers, 74–75, 78
Federal Bureau of Investigation, 117
Fitzpatrick, E. A., 84
Flyer, Eli S., 26n.
Fontaine, Andre, 117
Ford, Henry, II, 168
Form, William H., 61n., 187n.
Fraudulent Enlistment Warning Sheet, 112
Freeman, Linton C., 72n.
French Revolution, 35

General Education Development (GED) Program, 169

Index

General Education Development
    (GED) Tests, 7, 172
Goldrich, Daniel, 61n.
Gordon, Mary Agnes, 26n.
Gunderson, E. K. E., 118n.

Hardship, 13, 15, 91
Harris, Louis, 5n., 159n.
Hausknecht, Murray, 64n.
Helme, William H., 27n.
Hershey, General Lewis B., 41, 42, 54,
    57, 81, 86, 95, 101, 106, 176n.
Hesseltine, William B., 37n.
High School ROTC, 5, 32
Hill, Richard J., 62n.
Hinrichs, Grace, 119n.
Hodge, Robert, 94n., 167n., 178n.
Holifield, Chet, 89
Hoult, Thomas F., 29n.
House Appropriations Committee, 81
House Armed Services Committee, 50
Hunter, Floyd, 61n.

Induction, 165
    schedule of priorities and, 11
Industrial Relations Research
    Association, 53n.
Information programs, 31
Institute for Research on Poverty, 54n.
Interest groups, 102

Jackson, Elton F., 166n.
Jacob, Herbert, 71n.
Janowitz, Morris, 149n.
Jehovah's Witnesses, 100
Joint Army and Navy Selective Service
    Committee, 40
Juvenile delinquency, 2, 109–138, 193
    outcome in service of, 124–129,
        131–135
    rejection from service and, 121–124
    research studies on, 115–119
    service regulations concerning, 111–
        115

Karpinos, Bernard D., 144n., 166n.
Klassen, Arthur D., Jr., 107n., 140n.,
    145n.

Klieger, W. A., 26n., 28
Koff, Stephen P., 72n.
Korean War, 21, 27, 42, 45, 107
Kronos, Sidney, 140n.

Labor unions, 102n.
LaGrone, C. W., 116n., 120
Lang, Kurt, 149n.
Local boards
    attitudes toward Selective Service of,
        73–81
    characteristics of members of, 59–73
    clerk's role in, 12–14, 89–93
    compared to voluntary recruiters, 6–9
    composition of, 11–16
    conscientious objectors and, 100
    decentralization and, 106
    decision-making in, 83–108
    deferments and, 23, 45, 99–103
    dependency and, 99–100
    members of, 6, 11–16, 53–82
    Negroes on, 157n.
    quota system and, 10–11
    recruitment to, 54–56
    students and, 101
    suggested reforms of, 192–193
    turnover on, 56–58
    in urban versus rural areas, 67–71
    et passim
Lockmiller, David A., 39n., 83n.
Lohman, Joseph D., 116, 117, 118, 120
Loomis, Charles P., 61n.
Lottery, xiii, xiv

Manpower procurement, xii, 11–34
    military viewpoint on, 25–29
    organizations for, 4–16
    policies of, 2–4
    reform in, 192–195
    social impact on, 16–25
    suggestions for changes in, 29–34
Marine Corps, 130, 136, 142–143, 147,
    150, 170
    regulations concerning enlistment in,
        111–115
Mayer, Albert J., 29n.
Media, 7, 75

Members, local board. *See* Local boards, members of
Mental groups, by service branch, 19
Middle-class values, 93–94, 103
Military, professional, 25–29
Military Selective Service Act of 1967, xi
Military service
 advantages associated with, 166–175
 liability for, 165–166
 and occupational mobility, 163–189
Miller, Delbert C., 61*n.*, 187*n.*
Mink, W., 119*n.*
Minority groups, xii, xv, 61, 64, 139–162
Mobility. *See* Occupational Mobility
Morison, Samuel Eliot, 37*n.*
Munden, C. L., 171*n.*
Murdock, Eugene C., 37*n.*

National Advisory Commission on Selective Service, 50, 52*n.*, 191
National Cadet Corps, 5
National Commission on Selective Service, 54
National Committee on Education and Defense, 170
National Defense Act of 1916, 38–39
National Guard, xiv, 10, 51, 75, 106, 124, 165
 Negroes in, 147
National Guard Association, 107
National Headquarters, 9, 10, 57, 75, 95, 105, 106
National Manpower Board, 51
National Opinion Research Center (NORC), 140
National Security Resources Board, 44
National Security Training Commission, 43
National service, xiii, 20
Navy, 7, 41, 118, 130, 136, 142–143, 147, 170, 177
 regulations concerning enlistment in, 111–115
Negroes, xv, 15, 66, 81, 88, 139–162, 177, 178, 193
 entrance into military of, 143–149
 integration of, in military, 140–143
 opportunities in military for, 149–162
New Left, 158
New York University, 53*n.*
Newsletter, 75
Neyman, Clinton A., Jr., 8*n.*, 30
NORC Military Manpower Survey, 147*n.*, 148
 See also National Opinion Research Center

Oates, General James, 37
Occupational mobility, 193
 intelligence and, 180–181
 military service and, 163–189
 service schools attended and, 184
Office of Selective Service Records, 41
Officer Candidate Schools, 192
Officer procurement, 2, 29
Organizational reform, 191–195

Palmer, Frederick, 38*n.*
Participation, barriers to, 73
Patterson, Robert P., 170
Peace Corps, xii
Pelligrin, Roland J., 149*n.*
Plag, John A., 26*n.*
"Plattsburg idea," 38
Post-juvenile delinquency, 138
President's Task Force on Manpower Conservation, 163
Project TALENT, 7, 27
Psychiatric disorders, 110
Public Health Service, 14

Quota system, 8, 10, 23, 111

Racial integration, 140–143
Recruiters, 6–9, 111
Re-enlistments, 17, 21
 and rates by race, 152
Regular Army (RA), 26, 129–130, 164, 166, 176
Reiss, Albert J., Jr., 177*n.*
Rejections, 47–50, 110, 137, 143
 juvenile delinquency and, 111–115, 121–124

Index 219

Reserve Forces Act of 1955, 45–46
Reserve Officer Training Corps (ROTC), 2, 6, 14, 44, 165, 177
Reserve Officers Association, 107
Reserve Specialist Training Corps (RSTC), 44
Reserves, xiv, xv, 6, 9, 17, 32–33, 35, 42, 44, 45–46, 51, 75, 90, 106, 124, 165–166, 176, 177, 178, 192, 194–195
  Negroes in, 147
  See also Enlisted reserves
Riots, 37, 83
Rivera, Ramon J., 140*n*.
Rivers, L. Mendel, 50
Roosevelt, President Franklin D., 40
Rossi, Peter H., 140*n*.
ROTC. *See* Reserve Officer Training Corps

Sarnoff, David, 168
Schlesinger, Joseph A., 71*n*.
Schneider, A. J. N., 116*n*., 120
School System, Army. *See* Army School System
Seidman, Dennis, 28*n*.
Selective Service Act of 1948, 42
Selective Service classifications, 14–15
  changes in, 90–91
Selective Service Law, The, 38
Selective Service Qualification Test, 46–47
Selective Service System
  attitudes toward, by race, 160–161
  changes suggested in, 31–34, 191–195
  classifications under, 14–15, 90–91
  compared to voluntary recruitment services, 5–9
  current controversy over, 50–51
  establishment of, 40–41
  historical background of, in U.S., 35–52
  juvenile delinquency and, 111–115
  liability for service under, 165–166
  local board members attitudes toward, 73–81
  Negroes and, 139–162
  priority categories under, 11
  profile of local board members of, 53–82
  quasi-military nature of, 9–10
  rejections under, 47–50
  student deferments under, 43–47
  universality principle and, 19–23 *et passim*
Selective Training and Service Act of 1940, 40
Selznick, Philip, 105
Shaycroft, Marion F., 8*n*., 30
"Six months program," 46
Social justice, xiv, 3, 22–23, 37, 79–80
  See also Negroes
Social maturity, 187–188
Society, impact of recruitment on, 23–24
State Headquarters, 9, 10, 11*n*., 54*n*., 55, 59, 73, 96, 98, 102, 105
State Scientific Advisory Board, 102
Stein, Maurice, 70*n*.
Stewart, Donald D., 53*n*.
Student Army Training Corps, 40
Student deferments. *See* Deferments, students
Student Nonviolent Coordinating Committee, 158
Students, 14, 23, 39–40, 42, 52, 74, 90, 101, 124, 138, 156–157
  attitudes of local boards toward, 78–79
  See also Deferments, student
Students for a Democratic Society, 158
Sunchine, Morris H., 72*n*.
Swanson, Bert E., 61*n*.

Teacher Corps, xii
Tenure, 12, 56–58
Testing, mass programs, 25–26
Thomas Committee, 44
Trainees, 28
Truman, President Harry S, 41, 43, 140
Trytten, M. H., 44*n*.
"Trytten Plan," 44–45

United States Armed Forces Institute

(USAFI), 170–175, 186–187
Universal Military Service and Training Act, 19
Universal Military Training Act of 1948, 41
Universal Military Training and Service Act of 1951, 43, 45, 46, 47, 48
  and extensions, 165
Universality, xii, 3, 19, 32–33, 95–96
University of Chicago, 53n.
University of Wisconsin, 54n.
Urbanization, 2, 69, 70, 80

Verba, Sidney, 64n., 65n.
Veterans, 60, 67, 79, 90, 94–95, 104
Veterans Administration, 117
Veterans' associations, 12, 67
Veterans of Foreign Wars, 107
Vidich, Arthur J., 70n.
Vietnam War, 47, 50, 52, 101, 104, 107, 111n., 156, 157, 158, 159, 164, 194
Vocational training, 20, 166–175, 188
Voluntary army, xii
Voluntary enlistment, 194
Voluntary recruitment, xiii, 1, 2, 5–9, 29
  criticisms of systems of, 8–9
  inadequacy of, 16–19
  motivational appeals of, 19–20, 192
  suggestions for changes in, 31–34
Volunteers in Service to America (VISTA), xii

War of 1812, 36
Willenz, June A., 5n.
Wilson, I. W., 168
Wilson, President Woodrow, 38, 39
Wood, General Leonard, 38
World War I, 37, 38–39, 60, 84
World War II, 20, 21, 42, 60, 88n., 110, 116, 117, 150, 152, 153, 166, 167
Wright, Charles R., 62n.